The Poet Resigns

Akron Series in Contemporary Poetics
Mary Biddinger and John Gallaher, Editors
Jay Robinson and Nick Sturm, Associate Editors

Editorial Board
Maxine Chernoff
Martha Collins
Kevin Prufer
Alissa Valles
G. C. Waldrep

Mary Biddinger, John Gallaher, eds., *The Monkey & the Wrench: Essays into Contemporary Poetics*
Robert Archambeau, *The Poet Resigns: Poetry in a Difficult World*

The Poet Resigns

Poetry in a Difficult World

Robert Archambeau

The University of Akron Press
Akron, Ohio

17   16   15   14   13   5   4   3   2   1

ISBN: 978-1-937378-41-7 (PAPER)

This book has been cataloged by the Library of Congress.

The paper used in this publication meets the minimum requirements of ANSI NISO z 39.48–1992 (Permanence of Paper). ∞

The Poet Resigns was designed and typeset by Amy Freels. The typeface, Mrs. Eaves, was designed by Zuzana Licko in 1996. The display type, Brandon Grotesque, was designed by Hannes von Döhren in 2009/10. *The Poet Resigns* was printed on sixty-pound natural and bound by BookMasters of Ashland, Ohio.

For Lila

Acknowledgments

During the years over which these essays were written I was gener- ously supported by Lake Forest College, by the Illinois Arts Council, and by the Swedish Academy, and I am grateful. I am grateful, too, to the many editors, conference panel chairs, and publishers who invited and welcomed the essays in this book: Boris Jardine of Cambridge University, Louis Armand of Charles University in Prague, Emily Mer- riman of San Francisco State, Adrian Grafe of the Sorbonne, Mary Biddinger of the University of Akron, Kelly Comfort of Georgia Tech, David Caplan of Ohio Wesleyan, John Gallaher of Northwest Missouri State, Miranda Hickman of McGill, Kevin Prufer of the University of Houston, Alan Golding of the University of Louisville, Don Bogen of the University of Cincinnati, John Matthias of Notre Dame, Jim Johnson of the University of Pittsburgh, John McIntyre of the University of Prince Edward Island, Joe Francis Doerr of St. Edward's University, Chris Hamilton-Emery of Salt Publishing, Aditi Machado of Washington University in St. Louis, Katy Evans-Bush of *Horizon Review*, and Don Share and Christian Wiman of *Poetry* magazine. Without them, most of what is collected here would not have come into being.

I have been fortunate in my editors, and I have also been fortunate in those with whom I converse about poetry: Mark Scroggins of Florida Atlantic University, Norman Finkelstein of Xavier University, Joseph Donahue of Duke, Michael Anania of the University of Illinois—Chicago, Stefan Holander of Finnmark University College, D. L. LeMahieu of Lake Forest College, and many others, including those who have offered comments on my blog. John Wilkinson of the University of Chicago, Keston Sutherland of the University of Sussex and Andrea Brady of Queen Mary—University of London clashed with me over one of these essays, and I wish to thank them for their passion and their arguments. I owe particular thanks to David Park of Lake Forest College for intro- ducing me to works in communications theory that have opened per- spectives on literature for me that would otherwise have remained hidden. I owe a great deal to Caitlin Meeter and Traci Villa, without whose support this project would have been far more stressful. Above all I must thank my wife Valerie and also our daughter, Lila—this book is for her.

A number of these essays have been published in books and journals, sometimes in slightly different form.

"The Discursive Situation of Poetry" appeared in *The Monkey and the Wrench: Essays into Contemporary Poetics*, ed. Mary Biddinger and John Gallaher. Akron: University of Akron Press, 2011.

"Poetry and Politics, or: Why are the Poets on the Left?" appeared in *Poetry* (November 2008).

"The Aesthetic Anxiety: Avant-Garde Poetics and the Idea of Politics" appeared in *Art and Life in Aestheticism*, ed. Kelly Comfort. New York: Palgrave MacMillan, 2008.

"Public Faces in Private Places: Notes on Cambridge Poetry" appeared in *Cambridge Literary Review* (September 2009).

"The State of the Art" appeared in *The Virginia Quarterly Review* (Spring 2012).

"Seeing the New Criticism Again" appeared in different form as a presentation at the Modernist Studies Association Conference, October 2006.

"The Death of the Critic" appeared in the book *Avant-Post*, ed. Louis Armand. Prague: Charles University Press, 2006.

"Marginality and Manifesto" appeared in *Poetry* (June 2009).

"A Portrait of Reginald Shepherd as Philoctetes" appeared in *Pleiades* (Spring 2008).

"True Wit, False Wit: Harryette Mullen in the Eighteenth Century" appeared in different form as a presentation at the Louisville Conference on Literature and Culture Since 1900 (February 2011).

"Emancipation of the Dissonance: The Poetry of C. S. Giscombe" appeared in *Cincinnati Review* (Summer 2010).

"In the Haze of Pondered Vision: Yvor Winters as Poet" appeared in *Notre Dame Review* (Summer 1999).

"The Protestant Ethic and the Spirit of Poetry" appeared in *Notre Dame Review* (Fall 2006).

"Power and the Poetics of Play" appeared in *The Salt Companion to John Matthias*, ed. Joe Francis Doerr. Cambridge: Salt, 2011.

"The Decadent of Moyvane" appeared in *Keltoi: A Journal of Celtic Studies* (Summer 2006).

"Laforgue / Bolaño: The Poet as Bohemian" appeared, in different form, in *Notre Dame Review* (Summer/Fall 2012).

"Oppen / Rimbaud: The Poet as Quitter" appeared, in much shorter form, in *Mimesis* (Winter 2009).

"Nothing in this Life" appeared in *Horizon Review* (Winter 2011).

Several essays began life on *Samizdat Blog*, generally in less developed form. These include: "Negative Legislators: Exhibiting the Post-Avant," "When Poets Dream of Power," "Can Poems Communicate?" "The Poet in the University: Charles Bernstein's Academic Anxiety," "Poetry / Not Poetry," "Neruda's Earth, Heidegger's Earth," "Remembering Robert Kroetsch," and "My Laureates."

Contents

Instead of an Introduction
Letter of Resignation

I've never thought about resigning from poetry myself, but perhaps that's because I haven't had to: looking back on the changes in the kinds of writing I've done, I see I've become less and less of a poet, and more and more of a critic. One needn't resign from a job when one has, for the most part, stopped showing up. When I first realized this, an inner dialogue broke out between my accusing superego and my ego, which stood like a guilty thing surprised. It was as if my superego had decided to play the part of Beckett's Estragon to my ego's defensive Vladimir:

> Estragon: Morpion!
> Vladimir: Sewer-rat!
> Estragon: Curate!
> Vladimir: Cretin!
> Estragon: (*with finality*) Crritic!
> Vladimir: Oh!
>   *He wilts, vanquished, and turns away.* (85)

When I'd recovered from this withering inner assault, I was left with a question: does writing less poetry, or no poetry at all, involve some kind of self-betrayal?

Not necessarily. George Oppen was poetry's great prodigal son, coming home to the art he'd left behind. And Rimbaud, in giving up poetry, was no traitor to himself: he was honest to his own rebellious trajectory—the very fact that his actions still scandalize so many *littérateurs* stands as testimony to this fact. I'm no George Oppen, still less am I any kind of Rimbaud. But, in looking back on what amounts to my *de facto* resignation from poetry, I think I can see it as honest, in its way, to my own trajectory.

If there's any kind of direction to the writing and thinking I've done since my student days, it has been guided by a compass aimed at the idea of the aesthetic, and behind that at the question of the meaning of the aesthetic in a world full of pain and troubles. One of the earliest poems I thought worth putting in my book *Laureates and Heretics*, "Pater and His Age," takes up the question. It doesn't have anything like an answer, though—just a worry:

> In coke fire, in kiln: accumulation.
> In furnace, in engine, in black iron machine.
> In loom-thrum, train clatter, in sulfur and mine shaft
> In ash from brick chimneys comes surplus, comes hoard.
>
> Percussion cap, cartridge, hard black hands of miners.
> Blasting of rock face, quick flash, hissing fuse;
> Engineer, steel wheel, white sparks from hard braking,
> Embankment, blue gas light, slum child, rank canal.
>
> Consumption in cough and in candelabra.
> Excess in the watch-chain's long droop to the fob,
> Use-value in square fingered hands warmed at ashcans
> Whose fires light tight tangled streets without names.
>
> And would I, too, flee the moralist's preaching
> To burn with the light of a hard, gem-like flame? (12)

I remember being proud of the pun on "consumption," which I now consider something of a groaner. And I was utterly oblivious to how the title already indicated an incipient literary critic at work: it sounds like the title of a book of dry scholarship more than a title for an unrhymed sonnet, doesn't it? But the concerns that animated me in the writing of this student poem some twenty years ago continue to animate me now:

the meaning of art and beauty and poetry in a world of power and pain and injustice.

Similar concerns animate a poem written about a decade later, "Poem for a War Poet, Poem for a War," which steals its refrain from a John Matthias poem, which in turn stole it from a poem in Serbian by Branko Miljković. Here's part one:

The lines inked on the map are railways and roads.
The lines on the road are refugees, and moving.
The lines inked on the page are a poem, your poem.
 While you are singing, who will carry your burden?

The lines on the page are a poem, words
that move toward the refugees, their tattered world
of hurt and proper names, their lost, their staggering.
 While you are singing, while you are singing.

The lines are helpless in this time of war. They survive,
if they are a poem, in valleys of saying, they survive
and reach for valleys where bodies cough, bleed, or stumble blind.

They survive while you are singing.
 While you are singing. (27)

The conclusion of the poem works variations on what's gone before:

The lines on the road are refugees,
Their paths are marked with ink, charted
on a General's table. Your lines are a poem.
 While you are singing, who will carry your burden?

A woman bends beneath her load, a young man stutters in his fear,
a guard at the valley's border lets them through,
or not. Your lines are a poem.
 Who will carry your burden? (27)

Again, there's nothing much by way of a conclusion, just a question. Indeed, if you'd asked me, back when I was writing either of these poems, just what it was that I was trying to get across, I'm pretty sure I'd have given you little more than a blank stare and a shrug. But something was eating at me, something about what art can and can't do—and turning

3

the line that Matthias had taken from Miljković over and over in my head was the closest I could come to formulating just what that something was.

The meaning of those little poems might have been obvious to others, but it wasn't to me, not for a long time. When I think of writing them, I think of what Jung said about a certain kind of art, which we might find "pregnant with meanings" that we can't quite pin down at once. The maker of this kind of art often can't speak about it very well, since for him the artwork is "the best possible expression for something unknown," or an "intimation of a meaning beyond the level of our present comprehension" (314–15). We might come back to such works later, when "our conscious development has reached a higher level" (315) and we can speak with comprehension of those things that came to us initially in forms other than discursive prose.

My slow turn from poetry to criticism has, I've come to see, been less a turning away from something than a continuation. That's what the poet John Peck assured me of, not long after my inner Estragon stood accusingly over my inner Vladimir. I wrote to him, wondering if I'd fallen away from poetry into something less important. Peck replied, saying: "rather than a falling-off, that kind of segue reflects a movement from a compact kind of symbolization to a more differentiated one."

I can see what Peck means: the questions I've been most compelled to pursue in critical writing come out of my poems: poetry and politics, poetry in relation to its social situation (and, in a different way, the relation of poetry to plain statement). If my critical writing has been harshest when I've examined the works of poets who want to see aesthetic commitment and a commitment to social justice as one and the same thing, it's because I dearly want that to be true but, like George Oppen, cannot convince myself of it.

Most of the essays collected here cluster loosely around a few themes, but this is not, to use Dwight MacDonald's phrase, a premeditated book "written in cold blood." Rather, these are the critical essays of a poet as he becomes a critic, written for a variety of journals and books. Some, too, started in the foul rag and bone shop that is my blog. Differences in format, tone, and rigor of argument stem from the differences in the origins of the essays. Such coherence as the collection may have is the coherence of a personality, not a plan.

Works Cited

Archambeau, Robert. *Home and Variations*. Cambridge: Salt, 2004. Print.
Beckett, Samuel. *Waiting for Godot: A Tragicomedy in Two Acts*. New York: Grove, 1982. Print.
Jung, Carl Gustav. "On the Relation of Analytic Psychology to Poetry." *The Portable Jung*. Ed. Joseph Campbell. Harmondsworth: Penguin, 1976. 301–22. Print.
Peck, John. Letter to Robert Archambeau. 24 March 2011.

Situations of Poetry

The Discursive Situation of Poetry

"Why *do* poets continue to write? Why keep playing if it's such a mug's game? Some, no doubt, simply fail to understand the situation."
—SVEN BIRKERTS

The important point to notice, though, is this:
    Each poet knew for whom he had to write,
Because their life was still the same as his.
    As long as art remains a parasite
    On any class of persons it's alright;
The only thing it must be is attendant,
The only thing it mustn't, independent.
—W. H. AUDEN

Statistics confirm what many have long suspected: poetry is being read by an ever-smaller slice of the American reading public. Poets and critics who have intuited this have blamed many things, but for the most part they have blamed the rise of MFA programs in creative writing. While they have made various recommendations on how to remedy the situation, these remedies are destined for failure or, at best, for very limited success, because the rise of MFA programs is merely a symptom of much larger and farther-reaching trends. These trends are unlikely to be reversed by the intervention of a few poets, critics, and arts administrators. I'm not sure this is a bad thing. Or, in any event, I'm not sure it is worse than what a reversal of the decline in readership would entail. Let me explain.

Decades of Complaint

While we don't have many instruments for measuring the place of poetry in American life, all our instruments agree: poetry has been dropping precipitously in popularity for some time. In 1992, the National Endowment for the Arts conducted a survey that concluded only 17.1% of those who read books had read any poetry in the previous year. A similar NEA survey published in 2002 found that the figure had declined to 12.1%. The NEA numbers for 2008 were grimmer still: only 8.3% of book readers had read any poetry in the survey period (Bain). The portion of readers who read any poetry at all has, it seems, been cut in half over sixteen years. Poetry boosters can't help but be distressed by the trend.

Poets and poetry lovers have somewhat less faith in statistics and rather more faith in intuition and personal observation than the population at large. They've intuited this state of affairs for more than two decades, beginning long before the statistical trend became clear in all its stark, numerical reality. As far back as 1983, Donald Hall sounded a warning note in his essay "Poetry and Ambition." Although he did not blame the rise of the graduate creative writing programs for the loss of connection with an audience, he did feel that MFA programs created a certain formal similarity among poems. The programs produced "McPoets," writing "McPoems" that were brief, interchangeable, and unambitious. His solution, delivered with tongue firmly in cheek, was to abolish MFA programs entirely. "What a ringing slogan for a new Cato," wrote Hall, "*Iowa delenda est!*" Five years later Joseph Epstein picked up Hall's standard, and carried it further. In the incendiary essay "Who Killed Poetry?" Epstein argued that the rise of writing programs led not only to diminishments of ambition and quality—it furthered the decline of poetry's audience. The popular audience for poetry may have shrunk by the 1950s, argued Epstein, but at least the poets of midcentury were revered, and engaged with the larger intellectual world. By the late 1980s, though, poetry existed in "a vacuum." And what was the nature of this vacuum? "I should say that it consists of this," wrote Epstein, "it is scarcely read." Indeed, he continues,

> Contemporary poetry is no longer a part of the regular intellectual diet.
> People of general intellectual interests who feel that they ought to read
> or at least know about works on modern society or recent history or
> novels that attempt to convey something about the way we live now, no
> longer feel the same compunction about contemporary poetry. . . . It
> begins to seem, in fact, a sideline activity, a little as chiropractic or
> acupuncture is to mainstream medicine—odd, strange, but with a small
> cult of followers who swear by it. (n.p.)

The principle culprit in the sidelining of poetry was, for Epstein, the
credentialing and employment of poets in graduate writing programs.
"Whereas one tended to think of the modern poet as an artist," argued
Epstein, "one tends to think of the contemporary poet as a professional," and, "like a true professional, he is insulated within the world
of his fellow-professionals." The poet, instead of responding to the
audience-driven world of the book market, responds only to his peers,
with the effect that the audience simply melts away.

Après Epstein, *le déluge*. The 1990s saw a phalanx of poets and critics
complaining about the decline of poetry's audience, and linking this
decline to the rise of MFA programs. Dana Gioia fired the loudest shot
in *Can Poetry Matter?* (published as an article in *The Atlantic* in 1991, republished in book form a year later). "American poetry now belongs to a
subculture," said Gioia, "no longer part of the mainstream of intellectual life, it has become the specialized occupation of a relatively small
and isolated group" (1). While he allows that they have done so "unwit-
tingly," it is "the explosion of academic writing programs" that is to
blame for this sad state of affairs, as far as Gioia is concerned (2). Gioia
was by no means alone in this opinion. Vernon Shetley's 1993 study *After
the Death of Poetry: Poet and Audience in Contemporary America* tells us that poetry
has "lost the attention not merely of common readers but of intellectuals" (3)—and that creative writing programs have contributed to this loss
by cultivating "a disturbing complacency" and by "narrowing of the
scope" of poetry (19). Bruce Bawer introduces his 1995 book of criticism
Prophets and Professors by lamenting the professionalizing of poetry. He
tells us that "those who read poetry—which, in our society, basically
means poets" shy away from being too critical of the art, since "they

conside[r] poetry so ailing and marginal a genre that criticism was . . . like kicking an invalid" (8). In the same year, Thomas Disch claimed in *The Castle of Indolence* that "for most readers . . . contemporary poetry might as well not exist." The reason, he says, is

> . . . that the workshops, which have a monopoly on the training of poets, encourage indolence, incompetence, smugness, and—most perniciously—that sense of victimization and special entitlement that poets now come to share with other artists who depend on government or institutional patronage to sustain their art, pay their salaries, and provide for their vacations. (5)

Blaming writing programs for the isolation of poetry extended beyond the fairly conservative literary preserves inhabited by the likes of Bawer, Disch, and Epstein. Charles Bernstein's 1995 essay "Warning—Poetry Area: Publics Under Construction," argues "it is bad for poetry, and for poets, to be nourished so disproportionately" by universities, adding that "the sort of poetry I care for has its natural habitat in the streets and offices and malls."

By 1999, the chorus had grown so loud that Christopher Beach claimed we were "discussing the death of poetry to death" (19). Not that this stopped anyone. In 2006, Poetry Foundation President John Barr caused a stir with "American Poetry in the New Century," an article in *Poetry* magazine in which he noted poetry's "striking absence from the public dialogues of our day," as a sign that we have a reading public "in whose mind poetry is missing and unmissed." The problem, he asserts, stems from the writing programs. These produce poets who "write for one another," producing "a poetry that is neither robust, resonant, nor . . . entertaining." It cannot exist without "academic subsidies" and fails in the market, unable to sell in "commercial quantities." While Barr surveys the terrain from the heights of the Poetry Foundation offices in Chicago, more recently the poet Daniel Nester has come to similar conclusions (albeit without the invocation of the values of the marketplace) from the depths of New York's poetry scene. Nester has characterized that scene as the product of the writing programs. Looking around at poetry events, he says he'd see university cliques such as the "Group of People Who Went to Iowa" and those starting "Teaching Jobs Out

West." The scene was isolated from a larger engagement with society, with "a lack of connection to the reader" and readings attended only by "other aspiring poets" (Nester 2009). "It's an unsustainable system," he said when asked by an interviewer about his article. "Even the most niche of niche art forms has an audience. Not so with contemporary poetry" (Nester 2010).

As even this brief and incomplete survey of writers makes clear, American poets have noted the decline of the audience for poetry, and found it troubling. But when decriers of the decline make MFA programs their whipping boy they misunderstand the role such programs play in the distancing of poet from audience. In fact, poetry's decline of popularity predates the rise of writing programs, and such programs are properly seen as the latest episode in of a larger and long-enduring drama, a drama that began in the nineteenth century.

Bohemia Misunderstood

Both Dana Gioia and Joseph Epstein contrast the contemporary situation with what they imagine to be better times for poets: for Gioia, the golden age took place in the 1940s, while for Epstein it took place a decade later.

What strikes one most immediately about Gioia's imagined halcyon days for poetry is the strange combination of market-driven values and the idea of bohemia. The whole apparatus of poetry in the 1940s was, in Gioia's view, based on meeting consumer demand. In the 1940s, says Gioia, poets wrote with the idea of reaching a general readership, and "a poem that didn't command the reader's attention wasn't considered much of a poem." Editors of poetry journals looked to the market when determining their choices, picking not poems that met their own particular aesthetic standards, but choosing "verse that they felt would appeal to their particular audiences" (7). The problem since the professionalization of poetry has, for Gioia, been that "a poetry industry has been created to serve the interests of the producers and not the consumers" (10). Even critical judgment was bent to this end, as "the reviewers of fifty years ago knew that their primary loyalty must lie not with their fellow poets . . . but with the reader" (16). Such conditions continued only so long as poets remained outside of an organized profession, and a preponderance of them "centered their lives in urban bohemias" (12).

Gioia's idea of a market-driven bohemia is, to put it mildly, singular. One can find nothing like it in the annals of the sociology of bohemian life and art. The standard view is that bohemia emerges in response to the marginalization of artists, poets, and other creative producers. Cesar Graña's classic study *Bohemian vs. Bourgeois*, for example, finds the origin of bohemia in the economic dislocations following the destruction of the aristocracy in the French Revolution. These dislocations led to a migration into urban centers of a "large marginal population" of educated people formerly connected to, or dependent on, the aristocracy. Here they worked in opposition to, or at best on the fringes of, the market-driven world of the bourgeoisie (39). Albert Parry argues in *Garrets and Pretenders* that bohemia can only exist when there is an overproduction of certain kinds of skills and talents in relation to market demand for those skills. Pierre Bourdieu has famously defined the world of artistic production, especially as it involves poetry or occurs under bohemian conditions, as "the economic world reversed" (29). "The literary or artistic field," says Bourdieu, "is at all times the site of a struggle between the two principles of hierarchization: the heteronomous principle, favorable to those who dominate the field economically (e.g. 'bourgeois art') and the autonomous principle (e.g. 'art for art's sake')" (41). The heteronomous principle—that art should serve a force outside itself, such as the market—is certainly the force Gioia saw at work prior to the rise of writing programs. But the heteronomous principle is not the dominant force at work in the poetic and bohemian worlds. In such conditions, says Bourdieu, "the economy of practices is based, as in a generalized game of 'loser wins,' on a systematic inversion of all ordinary economies" including that of the market, because "it excludes the pursuit of profit and does not guarantee any sort of correspondence between investments and monetary gains" (39).

Validation for the poet, under bohemian conditions, cannot come in any great measure from the support of the market. Indeed, as Parry and Graña point out, bohemia comes into existence because there is too much literary and artistic talent for the market to absorb. In the absence of market support, poets do not seek to command the attention of a large readership for a sense of their worth. Rather, they start to seek validation from one another, and from a literary community separate from the broad, commercially profitable marketplace of readers. As the sociologist Ephraim Mizruchi puts it, the establishment of bohemia depends upon conditions where "status opportunities contract or organizations fail to expand in time to absorb" artistic producers (39). Under such conditions, artistic producers such as poets work "to establish and monitor what they alone determine to be the highest standards of artistic output" (15). That is, artistic producers in bohemia start to set their own standards for what counts as good or meaningful work.

Gioia's notion that bohemia represented a market-driven world for poets is deeply at odds with the sociological consensus. In point of fact, bohemia represented a stage in literary development quite close to that which we have come to see in the (admittedly less colorful) world of MFA professionalization: in both cases, poetic value is determined by a community of poets and critics, not by a market. One could follow Mizruchi and argue that the development of writing programs is little more than a matter of organizations finally expanding to absorb the artistic producers they could not absorb during the time of literary bohemia. The absorption involved little change in the notion of the validating principle of poetry. In both conditions it remained a matter of autonomy, or poets deciding for themselves what was of value, and ignoring the market forces Gioia imagines were dominant in what he takes to have been happier times.

Like Gioia, Joseph Epstein laments the failure of contemporary poetry to be governed by market forces. "Sometimes it seems as if there isn't a poem written in this nation," he writes, "that isn't subsidized or underwritten by a grant either from a foundation or the government or a teaching salary or a fellowship of one kind or another." Unlike Gioia, he is too aware of the conditions and values of the pre-professionalized literary era he valorizes to claim that this was an era in which poets were broadly popular. Praising the modernists writing in the 1950s, Epstein tells us:

They published their work in magazines read only by hundreds; their names were not known by most members of the educated classes; their following, such as it was, had a cultish character. But beyond this nothing else seems comparable [to the world of the writing programs]. Propelling the modernist poets was a vision, and among some of them a program—a belief that the nature of life had changed fundamentally and that artists now had to change accordingly. . . . New, too, was their attitude toward the reader, whom they, perhaps first among any writers in history, chose in a radical way to disregard. They weren't out to *épater*. If what they wrote was uncompromisingly difficult, they did not see this as their problem. They wrote as they wrote. . . . Somehow, through the quality of their writing, the authority of the sacrifices they made for their art, the aura of adult seriousness conveyed in both work and life, the modernist poets won through. (n.p.)

The "somehow" is, one fears, a little desperate. Epstein dearly wants the poetry of the 1950s to have been central to the general culture of the time, but he is too well-informed and intellectually honest to omit mention of the evidence to the contrary. Unfortunately, he is not able to prevent himself from simply dismissing it with a wave of the hand.

Should we wish to provide evidence for the centrality of poetry to national culture in the 1950s, filling in the virtually blank space where Epstein gives us a vague "somehow" and an even vaguer "won through," we would be a bit hard up. The only truly dramatic piece of evidence, one oft-cited by critics and journalists, would be T. S. Eliot's appearance before several thousand people in Minnesota. This event, prominently misrepresented as a poetry reading in a baseball stadium in Peter Ackroyd's biography of Eliot, was in fact a lecture held in the rather smaller confines of a university basketball arena. Few records of the event are available, but those we have tend to deflate any sense that the event represented anything like a massive popular interest in poetry in the 1950s. Consider the testimony of Theresa Enroth, an audience member for Eliot's lecture, writing to the *New York Times* in 1995 to disabuse readers of some inaccuracies in the paper's representation of the event:

When Eliot appeared at the University of Minnesota in 1956, his performance had no similarity to what is generally meant by "poetry reading." He read his essay called "The Frontiers of Criticism." That the poet drew a big crowd probably had something to do with his having received the 1948 Nobel Prize in Literature. For a great many readers at that time, his voice defined the disillusionment and angst of the midcentury. In addition, Eliot's poetry and criticism were central to the study of poetry in many college English departments where the New Criticism held dominion. The department lions at the University of Minnesota included, successively, Robert Penn Warren and Allen Tate. (Their friend John Crowe Ransom gave a poetry reading there—to a small crowd in the auditorium of the science museum.) (n.p.)

The cultural capital of the Nobel Prize, the novelty of the presence of a Nobel Laureate in a provincial city in the 1950s, and the incipient academicizing of poetry all seem to have played a role in the size of the audience, and the event was both atypical and unrepeatable, as the modesty of Ransom's audience shows. The notion that Eliot attracted an audience disillusioned with the dominant values of the times also argues against the idea that poetry was connected to the central values of our society in the 1950s.

When, then, was poetry popular, and in sympathy with the values of a broad public? When and where was it viable in terms of the values of the market? Epstein actually does give an example of such a time and place, before getting bogged down in nostalgia for the poetry of his own youth in the '50s. "The crowds in London once stood on their toes to see Tennyson pass;" writes Epstein, "today a figure like Tennyson probably would not write poetry and might not even read it. Poetry has been shifted—has shifted itself?—off center stage." To understand our own discursive condition, we need to contrast it not with the 1940s or '50s, but with the mid-Victorian period, when much poetry truly did have popular appeal, market viability, and a deep affinity with the values of the reading public. Only by such a contrast can we understand the forces that got us from there to here.

Empire of the Man of Letters

What were the conditions capable of producing a crowd standing on tiptoe to see the poet Tennyson? The discursive situation of poetry—that is, the conditions of writing, publishing, and reception of the mid-

Victorian period (roughly 1830 to 1870) differed sharply from those of our own time. Firstly, the verse published in journals appeared not in little magazines devoted solely, or even primarily, to poetry, but in more general journals, featuring poetry alongside essays, reviews, and reports of a kind we might not consider literary. This sort of publication, of course, is part of Barr, Gioia, and Epstein's imagined world of the modern poet before the professionalization of poetry. But what is important is not just the medium of publication (the general interest journal), but the way poetry was read when it appeared in those publications. Much more so than at any point in the twentieth century, poetry in the mid-Victorian period was read for reasons similar to the reasons the public read nonfiction prose. Indeed, the poet was not generally considered to be a writer categorically different from other kinds of writers: the poet was a subset of a much broader group, 'the men of letters,' a category now extinct. Historian T. W. Heyck describes the nature of the beast:

> By "men of letters," or "literary men" the Victorians meant more than producers of literature as such. Towards the end of the century, it is true, 'men of letters' was beginning to take on the sense of its most common twentieth-century definition—a quaint, second-rate writer in *belles lettres*. But throughout most of the century, 'men of letters' was a broader and more respectable sobriquet, including a wide variety of writers—poets, novelists, biographers, historians, social critics, philosophers and political economists. It was applied to writers of imaginative literature like Dickens, Thackeray, and Tennyson, to critics and social thinkers like Carlyle, Ruskin, and Arnold; and to political philosophers like Mill, G. H. Lewes, and John Morley. (24)

In our own world, the very existence of the professional journal called *Poets & Writers* asserts the deep division between poets and their relatively close cousins, fiction writers. We simply do not class poets with historians, social critics, and writers of political economy, as the mid-Victorians did. We see poets as different from such writers, and we read them for different reasons than we read writers on economics. For the mid-Victorian, though, poets fit neatly into the broader category of the men of letters. Like others in the category, the poet wrote for the market, had work appear in general interest magazines and, most importantly, was read for the same reasons Ruskin, Thackeray, or Mill were read: for moral guidance.

The great majority of mid-Victorian readers came from the rising middle class that, in 1851, constituted some 20% of the population (Cole 57). This class, growing into unprecedented political and social dominance in a rapidly changing and industrializing society, understandably felt dislocated. "As members of a relatively new social order," writes Heyck, "the middle class lacked the traditions and connections that might satisfy some of their needs, and they turned instead to publications for instruction and guidance." This need for guidance created a market for a certain kind of moralizing literature, and may even be credited with having "called into being the man of letters as a social type" (28). It was also responsible for raising the poet, as man of letters, to an unprecedented status and popularity. It is not for nothing that Carlyle titled two of his more famous lectures "The Hero as Man of Letters," and "The Hero as Poet." It speaks volumes about his audience's expectations, too, that they so heartily embraced Carlyle's claim that what England most needed was "a Prophet or Poet to teach us" (*On Heroes, Hero-Worship, and the Heroic in History* 8). To get a full sense of how closely the poet was associated with other kinds of writers, and how thoroughly didactic the role of the poet was in this high noon of the man of letters, we need look no further than the title of Alexander H. Japp's 1865 book *Three Great Teachers Of Our Own Time: Carlyle, Tennyson, and Ruskin*, although we might also do well to read a little of his text, especially his claim that he anticipates his readership as, in large measure, consisting of lovers of Tennyson "searching eagerly for truth, honestly inquiring what the great poet or rhythmic teacher of the age really means, and what his chief aims and ends are" (89). It's a notion of the poet entirely alien to our own. One can hardly imagine one of John Ashbery's readers calling him a "rhythmic teacher of the age" without tongue placed firmly in cheek.

Why, we should ask, would the middle class readership trust in poets to act as their moral teachers? To a great extent, this was because men of letters, including poets, were drawn from, and remained a part of, the same social class as the reading public, and as such they articulated that class' own views, anxieties, and values. Before the rise of mass literacy, the reading public had a tremendous social homogeneity—so much so that opinion in the public sphere of published writing was generally considered to be coterminous with the opinion of the middle class (Briggs 56–57). As Noel Annan has exhaustively documented, the men of letters came overwhelmingly from this class—and, indeed, the leading intellectual families of England frequently intermarried with the leading political and intellectual families of the dominant middle class. The men of letters were also in frequent face-to-face social contact with the leaders of the emerging political establishment. A partial list of the men of letters who rubbed shoulders with this establishment as members of the Athenaeum Club would include Matthew Arnold, Robert Browning, Edward Bulwer-Lytton, Thomas Carlyle, Arthur Hugh Clough, Charles Dickens, Thomas Hardy, Thomas Babington Macauley, John Ruskin, Robert Louis Stevenson, William Makepeace Thackeray, Anthony Trollope, and many more. This was not an alienated group of intellectuals. Indeed, the self-interest of the men of letters was, before the migration of writers and thinkers into bohemia or academe, identical to the interest of the market-dependent middle class as a whole. While we have come to expect our poets to be in some (often vague) way oppositional to, or critical of, the dominant values of the middle class and the market in which that class makes its living, this was not the case in the mid-Victorian period. The man of letters spoke for, not against, the values of the broad reading public, a fact that lay behind the success of his works in the marketplace. As one Victorian reader, J. H. Froude, put it, when he and his peers read the poems of Tennyson "they became part of our minds, the expression, in exquisite language, of the feelings which were working in ourselves" (Cruse 187).

It is not the case, of course, that the Victorian poet, as man of letters, was limited to simple cheerleading for the expanding and expansionist middle class, with its ideals of patriotism, imperialism, deferred gratification, and duty—although a reader of "The Charge of the Light Brigade" may well be forgiven for thinking so. As the historian Stefan Collini has argued, the man of letters was at times expected to raise his voice in favor of mitigating the bad behavior of the dominant class. Such criticism did not, however, extend to criticizing the nature of the social and economic system itself: it was generally a matter of emphasizing the need of living up to one's personal ideals, and acting altruistically within the confines of the existing system (62–66). The moral guidance expected of the man of letters was not revolutionary or even particularly oppositional: it was largely a matter of exhorting the reader to be a kinder version of the type of person he or she already was. One might think here of the critic Alan Sinfield's observation that Tennyson saw the poet's role as "recalling his society to its best self," not reforming it (176). Or one might think of Dickens' staggeringly popular "A Christmas Carol," in which Ebenezer Scrooge never becomes a socialist: he merely becomes a more sensitive bourgeois.

Such were the discursive conditions under which the man of letters rose to prominence and established his imperium of letters. And here, in the mid-Victorian period rather than in the 1940s or 1950s, are the conditions for which writers like Gioia, Epstein, and Barr yearn: conditions in which poets are read widely, are taken seriously by the broad reading public, succeed in the marketplace, and are in conversation with other intellectuals. Though Barr and company don't know it, what they've really done is to mount a Victorian critique of contemporary poetry or, more properly, a Victorian critique of the discursive conditions of contemporary poetry (in fact, complaints such as theirs about poetic precocity and specialization had already begun to emerge at the end of the nineteenth century, perhaps most prominently in the writings of Frederic Harrison). What people like Barr, Gioia, and Epstein really yearn for is a return to the era when the poet functioned as a man of letters. Such an era was by no means the natural state of poetry, since there can be no such state. It was, instead, like our current situation, in that it was quite contingent on temporary circumstances. It was a brief zenith of popularity, in which the poet was no longer writing for a tiny audience while living on the patronage of the court or the church. The poet was not yet a bohemian, free but off in the margins of society; nor was the poet yet a professional, writing primarily for other professionals. How did the sun set on the poet's brief but ample empire? How, that is, did we get from there to here?

Twilight of the Man of Letters

A study of greater length than the present essay would, of course, be necessary to present anything like a full picture of the transformation of the world of the poet as man of letters into the world of the poet as creative writing professor. Two main forces can, nevertheless, be isolated here: changes in the nature of the reading public, and changes regarding the kind of the thinking that was considered useful in guiding the public. Both kinds of changes conspired to put an end to the relationship the poet had to the audience in the mid-Victorian period.

During the mid-Victorian apex of the man of letters, the poet tended to share a general outlook on the world with his readership. As members of the same class as their public (and, like that public, dependent on the forces of the market for their living) most poets shared an ideology with them. But this situation was dependent upon the small size and social exclusivity of the reading public. From the 1840s to 1900, literacy rates rose with unprecedented speed, and by 1900 illiteracy had been all but eliminated in England and Wales, with more than 97% of men and 96% of women in possession of at least basic reading skills (see Altick 188–213). One cannot decry such a development, but it did, in tandem with the rising financial wellbeing of the working classes, have the unfortunate effect of making the kind of publishing that had supported the poets and men of letters less profitable. Many of the newly literate lacked sufficient education to read or take an interest in the kind of work that had flourished during the noontime of the man of letters, and publishers found that the best return on their investments came from the publication of the kind of writing elite readers dismissed as the "penny-dreadful" novel, many of which sold in the range of 60,000 copies, a figure almost no book of poetry could match. Poetry, which had for a time been a viable market commodity, began its long retreat to the realm of subsidized publishing.

Even among the more elite sort of readers, the affinity with poets and other men of letters began to fade. The rising middle class had turned to men of letters for guidance at a time when they were not yet confident in their status, and had not yet developed traditions and norms of conduct to sustain their sense of status. But as the nineteenth century wore on the old landed classes increasingly intermarried with the bour-geoisie, forming a newly confident class that developed an ethos of self-interest, utilitarianism, and conspicuous material consumption—an ethos that represented a rejection of the moralizing of the men of letters (Heyck 198). Not only had poetry become less viable in the expanded book market: it had become less interesting to the class that once turned to it for guidance. The bourgeoisie, no longer lacking confidence about its utilitarian and materialist tendencies, broke with the poets. They were decreasingly in need of buying what the mid-Victorian poets were selling.

Reinforcing this turn away from the poet as moralist were revolutions in the realm of knowledge. While the public had once looked on the man of letters as a source of truth, the growth of science and of all forms of quantifiable knowledge reduced the status of the poet. Few among the mid-Victorian men of letters saw this, although Carlyle did, writing prophetically as early as 1829 that the sciences were "engrossing every day more respect and attention" and that soon the public would assume that "what cannot be investigated and understood mechanically, cannot be investigated and understood at all" ("Signs of the Times"). The situ-ation had become much clearer for writers working in the later decades of the century, though. Social reformer Beatrice Webb, for example, looked back on the later Victorian years and asked:

> Who will deny that the men of science were the leading British intel-lectuals of the period? That it was they who stood out as men of genius with international reputations; that it was they who were the self-confident militants of the period; that it was they who were routing the theologians, confounding the mystics, imposing their theories on the philosophers, their inventions on the capitalists, and their discoveries on medical men; whilst they were at the same time snubbing the artists, ignoring the poets . . . (126–27)

Even that greatest of the men of letters, Matthew Arnold, wondered if the time for his kind was passing, writing in 1882 "the question is raised whether, to meet the needs of modern life, the predominance ought not now to pass from letters to science" (Arnold). Perhaps most telling about the decline of the status of poetry as a guide to truth and morals are the comments of the ever-pessimistic Thomas Hardy who, after courting public scandal in his prose works, wrote in 1897:

> Perhaps I can express more fully in verse ideas and emotions which run counter to the inert crystallized opinion—hard as rock—which the vast body of men have vested interests in supporting. . . . If Galileo had said in verse that the world moved, the Inquisition might have left him alone. (284–85)

Of course Hardy was wrong about the Inquisition: heresy in verse or prose amounted to the same thing in Galileo's time. But the point Hardy makes about his own time is clear. Poetry was no longer considered a guide to life by the broad reading public, so controversial claims made in poetry lost their capacity to provoke much response.

The rise of science as a source of truth was, to a large degree, the product of the professionalization of science. Early in the nineteenth century science was conducted either on an amateur basis, or as an adjunct to profit-oriented industrial research. Over the course of the century it took on something approaching its modern form as a profession, something autonomous, removed from the immediate concerns of industry and the market. It entered the university and, in the process, changed the ancient academic institutions, remaking them along the lines of professionalized research and autonomous fields of study. This, too, had an effect on poetry, taking it closer to the world of the poetry professional. Literature entered the university and became a professional field of study. Literary academics did not write for the market, nor did they share in the market-based form of life of the middle class at large, so their experiences and values were not, by and large, in accord with those of the business-based middle class. They shied away from both moralism and the idea of utility. Walter Pater, for example, ensconced in Oxford, wrote in favor of literature as an opportunity for nothing more than intensity of experience. For this he was pilloried by the bourgeois press. One anonymous critic, writing for *Blackwood's*, saw Pater as belonging to "a class removed from ordinary mankind by that ultra-culture and academical contemplation of the world as a place chiefly occupied by other beings equally cultured and refined," a group that "forms an inner circle of illuminati in almost every university" (604). Clearly the Paterian idea of literature did not please the middle class readership. It did, however, inspire Oscar Wilde and an entire generation of poets in the aesthetic movement. Many of these figures, driven from the marketplace by developments in mass literacy and publishing, escaped into bohemia, where the idea of poetry for itself, or at any rate for other poets, took root in fertile ground.

Professionalized literary studies and bohemianized poetry were close cousins, both products of broad shifts in economics and culture that took poetry and the broad reading public in different directions. The wonder isn't that poetry writing became a professionalized academic career, then: the real wonder is that it took so long, since by the end of the nineteenth century the man of letters had become all but extinct and his role had, in the words of T. W. Heyck, "altered from cultural leadership to one of isolated practice of an art—from a concept of a cultured minority integrated with the whole of society to one of a minority culture" (190).

Bleeding Poets with Leeches

For the world of the men of letters to have endured, so too would the conditions that existed before the rise of mass literacy, before the rise of science, before the establishment of middle-class self-confidence, and before the conversion of academe from a training center for clergy to a modern center of professional knowledge. It is by no means clear that return to such conditions would be worth the price, even if it were possible to destroy working-class literacy, intimidate the middle class with aristocratic arrogance, discredit science, and disestablish the universities except for the departments of classics and theology. No one advocates such draconian actions, though, perhaps because most critics who yearn for the discursive situation native to the mid-Victorian period imagine that discursive situation to have occurred later, in the 1940s and '50s. What, in the absence of a return to mid-Victorian conditions, do they offer to remedy what they consider the benighted current condition of poetry? Would their remedies, if put into effect, produce results? The remedies can be broken into two broad categories: market-based solutions and cultural paternalism. Neither, when looked at in the context of available evidence, would appreciably change the conditions of contemporary poetry. Decades of complaint have, it turns out, given us remedies about as efficacious as the bleeding of poets with leeches.

Thomas Disch advocates the most extreme form of market solution. Seeing the writing programs as a form of subsidization for an otherwise unviable poetic commodity, Disch calls for "the disestablishment of poetry workshops as an academic institution" (14), although how the removal of such programs, with so many vested interests, would be accomplished is left unsaid. The question of whether the solution would work in bringing poetry back to a broad audience is also left unaddressed. Given that the public, for complex historical reasons, no longer demands poetry as it did in the mid-Victorian period, one rather doubts that a mere ending of subsidy would return poetry to prominence. Given, too, the changes in the size and composition of the reading public since the mid-Victorian period, one does not see a return of poetry to viability as a marketable commodity. In the end, what Disch offers is less a plan than a statement of resentment for subsidized writing, made, it is worth noting, by a man who makes his living as a science fiction writer— that is, as a writer who needs to succeed in the marketplace. His solution is less a solution *per se* than it is a version of the private sector's resentment of the very existence of the public sector.

John Barr is less extreme in his views, but like Disch he sees the market as the solution to poetry's lack of prominence. He sees poetry as deeply subsidized, saying that poets "are sustained by a system of fellowships, grants, and other subsidies that absolve recipients of the responsibility to write books that a reader who is not a specialist might enjoy, might even buy." He does not call for changes in the audience, saying "the responsibilities of the public to poetry are nil." His primary suggestion is to change the product to make it more appealing to the consuming public. Significantly, what he advocates is a return to large-scale poetry of "moral urgency" that can "instruct through pleasing." That is, he wants a poetry of moral guidance, of the kind that appealed to the mid-Victorian reader. What he does not apprehend is that the conditions that made a broad reading public yearn for such a poetry no longer apply.[1] Of course Barr is a product of the market-oriented world, having spent much of his career working with such energy trading companies as Dynegy and Enron, so it is perhaps unsurprising to see a certain market fundamentalism on his part ("the human mind," Barr claims, "is a marketplace"). But the particular market-based reforms he proposes for poetry don't take full account of the nature of the current potential market for poetry.

Dana Gioia, whose career has involved both high-ranking corporate positions and, more recently, public sector administration, offers a mixed-bag of market-based and public sector solutions to the problem of poetry's lack of popularity. Much of what he suggests are versions of cross-marketing, of putting poetry in front of readers who don't seek it out on their own. Poetry readings, he suggests, should "mix poetry with the other arts, especially music," a strategy intended to draw fans of other arts into proximity of poets and poems (22). Poets should, too, "recapture the attention of the broader intellectual community by writing for nonspecialist publications" (23). Assuming editors would comply, this would also put poetry in front of audiences who don't generally seek it out, potentially converting these readers into a large fan base for poetry.

Gioia combines these market-based ideas with a kind of cultural paternalism, a paternalism he shares with another nonprofit sector employee, Charles Bernstein. Both suggest using public radio to put poetry in front of millions of potential poetry readers (Gioia 23, Ber-

---

1. Indeed, Barr's own long, morally uplifting book of poetry, *Grace*, published by a non-academic press, hovers somewhat below the abysmal position of my own, amoral, non-uplifting book of poems—written largely during a professor's summers, therefore subsidized—in online sales rankings. At the time of writing, my book *Home and Variations* was the 2,262,913th most popular book on Amazon, while Barr's was the 2,641,383rd most popular. Both books have been out for some years, and neither Barr nor I seem to be succeeding in the marketplace, with or without subsidy, with or without moral uplift. It is with some small and illegitimate pleasure that I notice used copies of his book sell for one cent in the marketplace, a mere $1/_{79}$th the price of a used copy of *Home and Variations*. In this one limited sense my subsidized amorality has, it seems, a stronger market than Barr's attempt at a market-based moralism.

nstein). This isn't a matter of responding to public demand, as the putting of poetry on commercial radio would have to be. Instead, it is in the long tradition of paternalism in public media, which assumes that (to quote the first General Director of BBC radio, Sir John Reith) "an active faith that a supply of good things will create a demand for them" and assumes, too, that we who know what those good things are should not wait "for the demand to express itself" (see Barnouw 247–48).

The problem with both cross-marketing and the Reithian use of the public media is that believing either would do much to change the rate of poetry reading flies in the face of the data collected by the National Opinion Research Center. According to the 2006 N.O.R.C. report *Poetry in America*, even people who "read and like the poetry that they find in unexpected places" say "it doesn't inspire them to seek out more poetry" (iv). While John Barr, who headed the organization that commissioned the study, is technically right in saying the study indicates that when people find poems in public transportation and general interest magazines, they will often "read it when they see it" (or, in the case of radio, listen when they hear it), but this statement blithely elides the survey's finding that "incidental exposure seems to reinforce existing poetry behaviors" (69) of reading or not-reading verse, and that such exposure has no effect on influencing people's "intent to read poetry in the future" (71). It is as if people saw advertisements, but were not influenced by them. This can hardly be considered a successful strategy for increasing poetry's readership. One wonders how John Barr, whose foundation spent more than $700,000 on the report, could omit mention of such a pessimistic finding, although perhaps the answer is in the question itself.

Underdevelopment and the Last Professors

Short of a return to the social conditions of the mid-Victorian era, can there be a return to a discursive situation in which poetry matters to a broad public? One hopes not. When we consider the evidence, we find that, historically, the conditions under which poetry becomes widely popular are not conditions we should seek out. In addition to the singular mid-Victorian situation, we find poetry to be prominent in another kind of situation. Sadly, though, this is a situation of socio-political disenfranchisement. The great scholar of Irish literature Declan Kiberd explains:

> A writer in a free state works with the easy assurance that literature is but one of the social institutions to project the values which the nation admires, others being the law, the government, the army, and so on. A writer in a colony knows that these values can be fully embodied only in the written word: hence the daunting seriousness with which literature is taken by subject peoples. This almost prophetic role of the artist is often linked to 'underdeveloped' societies. (118)

In colonies, and among people oppressed by their governments and unable to find expression in the institutional life of their countries, poetry takes on a great social importance. But just as we would not wish to return to mid-Victorian levels of literacy and social development just to see the rise of a new Tennyson, we would not wish to fall victim to colonization just to have our own Celtic Revival. Those of us who live with discursive conditions that keep poetry unpopular may count ourselves lucky.

None of this is to say that the present professionalized conditions will continue. Just as the poet as man of letters depended on specific historical contingencies, so too is the idea of the poet as a professional working in relative autonomy from the market. The oversupply of academically credentialed poets points toward a shifting of the center of gravity away from academe. Moreover, academe itself is facing increasing pressure to respond to the forces of the market. In Britain, this includes new government guidelines for departments to demonstrate the market utility of their activities. In the United States the situation remains milder, but, as Frank Donoghue argues in *The Last Professors: The Corporate University and the Fate of the Humanities*, the encroachment of market values on the previously semi-autonomous academic system is well under way, and is probably irreversible. Critics who long for changes in the relation of poets to the public and the market may take comfort in knowing that some sort of change is surely underway, although it will occur with or without any of the efforts at publicity and cross-marketing those critics may make.

Works Cited

Ackroyd, Peter. *T. S. Eliot: A Life*. New York: Simon and Schuster, 1985. Print.

Altick, Richard. *The English Common Reader: A Social History of the Mass Reading Public, 1800–1900*. 2nd ed. Columbus: Ohio State University Press, 1998. Print.

Annan, Noel. "The Intellectual Aristocracy." *Studies in Social History*. Ed. J. H. Plumb. London: Longmans, 1955. 241–87. Print.

Anonymous. *Blackwood's*, Nov. 1873. "New Books": 604. Print.

Arnold, Matthew. "Literature and Science." Ian Lancashire, n.d. Web. 1 July 2011.

Bain, Marc. "The End of Verse?" *Newsweek*. Newsweek, 25 Mar. 2009. Web. 1 July 2011.

Barnouw, Erik. *A Tower in Babel: A History of Broadcasting in the United States*. Vol. 1. New York: Oxford University Press, 1966. Print.

Barr, John. "American Poetry in the New Century." *Poetry*. The Poetry Foundation, n.d. Web. 1 July 2011.

Bawer, Bruce. *Prophets and Professors*. Brownsville, Oregon: Storyline, 1995. Print.

Beach, Christopher. *Poetic Culture: Contemporary American Poetry Between Community and Institution*. Evanston: Northwestern UP, 1999. Print.

Bernstein, Charles. "Warning—Poetry Area: Publics Under Construction." *Electronic Poetry Center*. Electronic Poetry Center, n.d. Web. 1 July 2011.

Bourdieu, Pierre. *The Field of Cultural Production*. Ed. Randal Johnson. New York: Columbia University Press, 1999. Print.

Briggs, Asa. "The Language of Class in Early Nineteenth-Century England." *Essays in Labor History*. Ed. Asa Briggs and John Saville. London, MacMillan, 1960. 43–73. Print.

Carlyle, Thomas. *On Heroes, Hero-Worship, and the Heroic in History*. New York: Wiley, 1861. Print.

Carlyle, Thomas. "Signs of the Times." *The Victorian Web*. The Victorian Web, n.d. Web. 2 July 2011.

Cole, G. D. H. *Studies in Class Structure*. London: Routledge, 2003. Print.

Collini, Stefan. *Public Moralists: Political Thought and Intellectual Life in Britain 1850 1930*. Oxford: Oxford University Press, 1991. Print.

Cruse, Amy. *Victorians and Their Books*. London: Allen, 1962. Print.

Disch, Thomas. *The Castle of Indolence*. New York: Picador, 1995. Print.

Donoghue, Frank. *The Last Professors: The Corporate University and the Fate of the Humanities*. New York: Fordham University Press, 2008. Print.

Enroth, Theresa. Letter. *The New York Times* 23 Apr. 1995: 735. Print.

Epstein, Joseph. "Who Killed Poetry?" *Commentary*. Commentary Magazine, Aug. 1988. Web. 1 July 2011.

Graña, Cesar. *Bohemian vs. Bourgeois: French Society and the French Man of Letters in the Nineteenth Century*. New York: Basic Books, 1964. Print.

Hall, Donald. "Poetry and Ambition." *Poets.org*. The Academy of American Poets, n.d. Web. 2 July 2011.

Hardy, Thomas. *The Life of Thomas Hardy*. London: Macmillan, 1962. Print.

Harrison, Frederic. *Autobiographic Memoirs*. Vol. 1. London: MacMillan, 1911. Print.

Heyck, T. W. *The Transformation of Intellectual Life in Victorian England*. Chicago: Lyceum, 1982. Print.

Hildreth, Elizabeth. "An Interview with Daniel Nester." *Bookslut*. Bookslut, Jan. 2010. Web. 1 Mar. 2010.

Japp, Alexander H. *Three Great Teachers Of Our Own Time: Carlyle, Tennyson And Ruskin*. London: Smith, Elder And Co., 1865. Print.

Mizruchi, Ephraim. "Bohemia as a Means of Social Regulation." *On Bohemia: The Code of the Self-Exiled*. Ed. Cesar and Marigay Graña. Edison, New Jersey: Transaction, 1990. 1–41. Print.

Nester, Daniel. "Goodbye to All Them." *The Morning News*. The Morning News, 23 Sept. 2009. Web. 12 June 2010.

Parry, Albert. *Garrets and Pretenders*. New York: Dover, 1960. Print.

Schwartz, Lisa K., Lisbeth Goble, Ned English and Robert F. Bailey. *Poetry in America: Review of the Findings*. Chicago: National Opinion Research Center, 2006. Print.

Shetley, Vernon. *After the Death of Poetry: Poet and Audience in Contemporary America*. Durham: Duke UP, 1993. Print.

Sinfield, Alan. *Alfred Tennyson*. Oxford: Blackwell, 1986. Print.

Webb, Beatrice. *My Apprenticeship*. London: Longmans, Green, 1926. Print.

Poetry and Politics, or:
Why are the Poets on the Left?

We don't spend much time wondering what poetry has to do with neuroscience or television writing or college basketball, yet these are important areas of American life that involve assertions about truth, form, morality, and the nature of culture—all subjects regularly claimed as poetry's turf. Yet the connection between poetry and politics interests us in ways that the arguably more obvious connection between poetry and linguistics does not. Why?
—DAVID ORR

Why are we so endlessly fascinated with the connection between poetry and politics? We keep asking about how poetry relates to the political. And when we ask about poetry and politics in the United States, we find ourselves asking another question, too: why are the poets on the political left? Lucia Perillo found herself pondering this second question after a conference call with other contributors to the Poetry Foundation's Harriet blog, when "some kind of anti-Bush or anti-war entendre that was uttered by someone produced among us a knowing chuckle." One imagines the chuckle to have been of the same order as a stockbroker's chuckle over tax-and-spend liberals: it probably had more to do with political solidarity than with wit.

I have a hypothesis about poets and politics, though the hypothesis isn't really mine, not at the root. It's an adaptation of a passage in my dusty copy of Marx's *Contribution to the Critique of Political Economy*. In the preface to that work Marx claimed "it is not the consciousness of men that determines their being, but, on the contrary, their social being that determines their consciousness" (11). Poets are no more an exception to this rule than stockbrokers. And the social being of poets in contemporary America contributes to their widespread sense—a sense not generally shared by politicians—that poetry and politics are intertwined. It influences, too, their prevalent leftishness. Both phenomena can be explained by the position poets tend to inhabit in American society.

*

What poets and politicians have in common, says Orr, is "a totalizing vision" of things—a sense that the problems they address aren't merely matters of self-interest, but of more general concern. This, I'm sure, is entirely true. But *why* is it true of poets? It used to be a matter of national representativeness. The poet's sense of somehow representing a community larger than the self was, in the nineteenth century, often a matter of literature's link with nationalism. Longfellow's yearning for an American epic provides one example; Walt Whitman's creation of a representative American self provides another. But, despite a few striking exceptions like Robert Pinsky's *An Explanation of America* (written, as Pinsky has said, with Whitman in mind), most American poets no longer think of themselves as representatives of the nation. In fact, most poets who see themselves as representative of a group are either postcolonials or members of other historically or currently oppressed groups. But the sense of a connection between poetry and politics extends beyond poets with a strong connection to identity politics. Why?

We can get at something like an answer via the thinking of Alvin Gouldner, one of America's greatest writers on the sociology of intellectuals. In his brisk little study *The Future of Intellectuals and the Rise of the New Class*, Gouldner points out that intellectuals, particularly humanistic intellectuals like poets, revel in their semi-autonomous situation vis-a-vis market forces, forces that would dictate that they pursue their own material self-interest. This isn't to say that poets are angelic creatures devoid of self-interest. It's merely to note that the field of poetry is somewhat insulated from market forces, if for no other reason than that the material rewards are so small—and the self-image poets cultivate reflects this. By and large, poets don't tend to think of themselves as motivated primarily by material self-interest.

What Gouldner says about teachers is apposite here, in part because so many poets teach, and in part because both poets and teachers tend to define themselves with reference to their cultural, rather than their material, capital. "As teachers," Gouldner writes, "intellectuals come to be defined, and to define themselves, as responsible for and 'representative' of society as a *whole*" (3). This is a very different way of thinking than that of, say, the typical owner of a small business, who is out, in most of his activities, to advance his own enterprise, and to represent his self-interest. If he doesn't do this, after all, no one else will. This doesn't mean that his activities don't benefit society as a whole—as Adam Smith said in *The Wealth of Nations*, such a person "generally . . . neither intends to promote the public interest, nor knows how much he is promoting it" (400). But unlike teachers and humanistic intellectuals, such people are unlikely to think of what they do as, first and foremost, a matter of general social advancement. Poets, like Gouldner's teachers, are often semi-insulated from market forces, working in universities or the public sector, and when they are in business many poets keep their business-selves and poetry-selves in separate compartments, as did Wallace Stevens and T. S. Eliot. So they don't generally think in terms of immediate self-interest, but in terms of a large, social interest: this is what lies behind what David Orr calls their "totalizing visions."

*

What about the overwhelmingly left-leaning nature of the "totalizing visions" of poets in America? Lucia Perillo comes close to the source of this leftism when she speculates that "it may be that poets are aligned with the left because they tend to share the concerns of the poor, or at least the not-rich, having only moderate incomes and job stability." There is certainly a sense in which poets, and humanistic intellectuals generally, stand outside the zone of power in America. The situation is a bit more complicated than that, though. Poets are, after all, generally people with a lot of resources—but those resources are more cultural than economic. This is the case even when poets do well economically. A poet who is a full professor in an English department, for example, makes a solidly upper-middle-class salary, and has the kind of job security you don't find in many fields anymore. While she's comfortably bourgeois in economic terms, though, her real status comes from her cultural resources: in that realm, she's an aristocrat. It's this emphasis on cultural capital that gives poets a somewhat unusual position in society. They have status, but not the kind of status you need to really stand at the helm of power. As Pierre Bourdieu tells us, in *The Field of Cultural Production*, such people

> ...are neither dominant, plain and simple, nor are they dominated (as they want to believe at certain points in their history). Rather, they occupy a dominated position in the dominant class. They are the owners of a dominated form of power.... This structurally contradictory position is absolutely crucial for understanding the positions taken by writers and artists, notably struggles in the social world. (164)

The odd position in which poets find themselves explains, for example, both their critical attitude toward business leaders (whom they tend to resent from below), and their often-sentimental identification with the disempowered (with whom they identify by virtue of experiencing themselves as outside of true power). None of which is to say that their political beliefs are wrong or inauthentic, merely that poets aren't exempt from having their views conditioned by their social position. If political views weren't influenced by factors like social position—if, that is, social being didn't determine consciousness—it'd be a hell of a coincidence to have a phalanx of Harriet bloggers chuckling in agreement at the same political comment.

One imagines the leftward lean of the poets will only increase, in part because of the migration of the poets into the groves of academe, and in part because of the growing exclusion of so many poets from those groves. The poet-as-professor trends left, for the reasons described by Bourdieu: she's in the dominated part of the dominant class. But with the overproduction of MFA and PhD-bearing poets relative to the market for their skills in tenure-track academe, we're likely to see an even greater trend to the left among the poets. Back in the late 1970s Alvin Gouldner noted that "we have now entered a period in which there may be more educated manpower than demand for it" (67). Consequently, the educated feel pressure to accept work of a sort other than that for which they'd trained, ending up with increased job dissatisfaction and an attendant growth in alienation, which often manifests as a more radicalized politics.

*

One of the great things about David Orr is the way he doesn't shy away from embarrassing questions, and the question that most embarrasses poets when the topic of poetry and politics comes up is that of efficacy. Can a poem have a political influence, and if not, then what, exactly, is the political (as opposed to the aesthetic) *point* of the thing? "Should we draw a firm line, and say that a political poem has to have some actual poetic effect?" Orr asks, along with a related question, "should it attempt to persuade us in the way most 'normal' political speech does?"

Some poets have written with the idea that the poem certainly should attempt to persuade in the manner of normal political speech. One thinks of Shelley's "Song to the Men of England," or, in America, of Vachel Lindsay's "Abraham Lincoln Walks at Midnight," or of Allen Ginsberg on the right day. Others write in a less overtly rhetorical way, and act on their political convictions the way any concerned citizen would, volunteering during elections, writing letters to the editor, signing petitions and the occasional contribution check, and maybe hitting the streets for a demonstration. Still others—mostly in the experimental camp—consider their kind of poetry political by virtue of its very eschewal of the normal language of persuasion. A non-communicative, non-commodifiable poem is, after all, a kind of declaration of autonomy from the world of power. One may wonder just what good it does, if any, for the wretched of the earth, but the intention is plainly one of defiance.

Perhaps the most interesting way poets respond to the tension between their desire for political influence and the seeming inability of their poetry—that "dominated form of power" of which they are the owners— to have a political effect is to dramatize the contradiction. Consider "Unpleasant Letter," a poem from John Matthias' sojourn in England in the 1970s. It begins with found text lineated as poetry—the text in question being a court summons Matthias received for a bicycling offence. Apparently he'd been riding a bike that

did not
Carry (a) one bright lamp which showed

White light to the front
And (b) one bright lamp which showed

Red light to the rear
Visible from a reasonable distance

Contrary to Section 74
Of the Road Traffic Act, 1972.

And what did this offense, depicted in the language of law and bureaucracy—in, that is, the language of power—warrant? A summons to court. "You," declares the unpleasant letter to its unfortunate recipient,

Are summoned to appear on 23.5.77
At the hour of 10 a.m.

Before the Magistrates' Court sitting
At the Court House, Guildhall . . .

The second of the poem's two parts gives Matthias' response, in which the language of power is answered not in its own terms, but with a language signaling (through incantation and exaggerated bardic grandiosity) its status as poetry. "O ancient magistrates and ancient guilds / Of Cambridge," it reads,

O reason and reasonable distance
O information that's laid

O hours of deepest darkness O lights
Both white & red which flash

Toward the future and signal
The past and the passing: O vision O visions

I was illuminated all over all tingling
Fluorescent & flashing in

> Every direction at once: I had read
> For a day in your citadels O Marlowe O Newton
>
> O John Maynard Keynes

Here Matthias asserts poetic authority against legal authority, and invokes cultural capital ("O Marlowe O Newton...") against political power. At the end of this incantation, he reverses the power-relation implied by the court summons, and demands the presence of the court officials at his own secret rituals and rites:

> With my bicycle chain and both of my pedals
> With my deer's antler and medals
>
> Where I wait with my middle-American vowels
> Where I summon you all
>
> To the stone-age shaft where I hide & abide
> With the ghosts
>
> Of hairy Fenmen: Constable, magistrate, prefect,
> Bursar, provost, torturer, cook...
>
> I summon you all: all of you: to appear! (174)

The action, here, is all in the punning on "summons" as both a matter of being served with a legal notice, and a matter of demonic conjuring. Matthias proposes the archaic, shamanistic form of symbolic power wielded by the poet as a negation of the court's legal power. In a sense, the poet wins, at least in the realm of symbol and language: he summons the constables and magistrates into his poem, and this is where we find them. Then again, the poet loses in the realm of law, where his form of power truly is the dominated one: Matthias assures me he dutifully went to Guildhall and paid his fine.

Works Cited

Bourdieu, Pierre. *The Field of Cultural Production*. Ed. Randal Johnson. New York: Columbia University Press, 1999. Print.

Gouldner, Alvin. *The Future of Intellectuals and the Rise of the New Class*. Oxford: Oxford University Press, 1982. Print.

Marx, Karl. *Contribution to the Critique of Political Economy*. Trans. N. I. Stone. Chicago: Kerr, 1904. Print.

Matthias, John. *Northern Summer*. Athens, Ohio: Ohio University Press / Swallow Press, 1984. Print.

Perillo, Lucia. "Why are Poets Aligned with the Left?" *Harriet*. The Poetry Foundation, n.d. Web. 11 July 2011.

Orr, David. "The Politics of Poetry." *Poetry*. The Poetry Foundation, n.d. Web. 21 July 2011.

Smith, Adam. *The Wealth of Nations*. Vol. 1. London: Dent, 1957. Print.

The Aesthetic Anxiety
Avant-Garde Poetics and the Idea of Politics

I f you are personally acquainted with any significant number of poets, you will perhaps not be surprised to find that the thesis of this essay is as follows: poets want to have their cake and eat it too. The particulars of the argument, though, go beyond the intuitive and the obvious, or so I hope. What I want to say is this: since the nineteenth century, poets have faced a dilemma. On the one hand, many poets have felt the allure of the radical freedoms of an entirely autonomous art, an art not in the heteronomous service of any religious function, ideological formation, moral system, any cause, or any institution—an art that exists for art's sake alone. On the other hand, poets have faced the anxieties that such autonomy seems, inevitably, to create: fears of losing their readerships, their social roles, and their political utility. Many poets of the twentieth century, especially those affiliated with avant-garde movements, have been haunted by such anxieties, and have sought to assuage them by claiming that a commitment to aesthetic autonomy can, in and of itself, be a form of political action. Such an identification does not bridge the chasm between a belief in autonomous art and a belief in the kind of heteronomous art that serves a cause. Rather, it denies the existence of such a gap, and asserts that the disinterested pursuit of art for its own sake is also, by its very nature, politically efficacious.

Positions of this kind are by their nature fraught with contradictions, and raise many a question. Can withdrawal from political engagement be anything other than quietism? What are the politics of audience, when the art speaks neither to the disempowered classes nor to a significant element of the power elite? Can a political art still be autonomous, or does it bend its craft to a political end? Indeed, the attempt to work through such questions has been the driving force behind many an avant-garde polemic. Despite the difficulty of maintaining the identity of aesthetic autonomy and political utility, though, this dream of the poets has endured for the better part of a century.

Two groups of poets who attempt to identify aesthetic autonomy with the political—the surrealists and the language poets—are of particular interest because of the different forms of politics to which they link autonomous aesthetics. Starting in the 1920s, the surrealists, under the general guidance of André Breton, sought a link between the radical imaginative freedom of their movement and the project of Communist revolution. Later, beginning in the 1970s, the American language poets sought to identify aesthetic freedom with a kind of negative politics—a politics of critique and resistance, rather than one conducted with a specific revolutionary utopia in mind. Whatever the form of politics, though, the enduring nature of the poet's anxiety about reconciling aesthetic autonomy and political efficacy indicates that we may have reached a point in the history of poetics in which what I am calling the aesthetic anxiety (that is, the anxiety about the apparent political and social inutility of autonomous art) isn't so much a passing crisis as it is a lasting condition of poetic production. Whether the solution to this anxiety proposed by the avant-garde poets can survive is, of course, another question, and one to which the answer, increasingly, seems to be "no."

To understand the aesthetic anxiety, we need to look briefly at certain conditions of the creation of aestheticism, which was born of a rejection of utility. Aestheticism, at least in part, grew out of the alienation of those committed to imaginative expression from the powerful classes. The alienation was palpable enough for the Goncourt brothers to note that the social world of the writer had become "curious when you compare it to the society life of *littérateurs* of the eighteenth century, from Diderot to Marmontel; today's bourgeois scarcely seeks out a man of letters except when he is inclined to play the role of mysterious creature, buffoon, or guide to the outside world" (Cassagne 342). Animosity ran in both directions between bourgeois and *littérateur*, but the fundamental conditions for this situation lay in the newly powerful bourgeoisie's rejection of literary means of expression. As Pierre Bourdieu has argued, to understand "the horror the figure of the bourgeois sometimes inspired" for literary people "we need to have some idea of the impact of the emergence of industrialists and businessmen of colossal fortunes. . . . [T]hey were self-made men, uncultured parvenus ready to make both the power of money and a vision of the world profoundly hostile to intellectual things triumph within the whole society" (48). The artistic and literary tastes of the bourgeoisie created a market dominated by heteronomous principles of aesthetics, an environment in which art and literature were to be judged not as art and literature *per se*, but as expressions of bourgeois religious, moral, and economic systems. The producer of imaginative works unwilling to reconcile himself to such systems was driven toward a self-authorizing position, in which artistic activity was made legitimate on the basis of artistic values alone. We sense this revulsion from the bourgeois world when Flaubert writes, in a letter of 1871, that everything in the bourgeois order is "false": ". . . all this falseness . . . was applied especially in the manner of judging. They extolled an actress not as an actress, but as a good mother of a family. They asked art to be moral, philosophy to be clear, vice to be decent, and science to be within range of the people" (200). The rejection of the bourgeois order here involves turning one's back on the powerful, who see everything in terms of utility and morality.

Aestheticism, of course, is not the only response to growing bourgeois hegemony in the nineteenth century. While realism and naturalism, with their strong social commitments and occasionally careless artistry, are often seen as antithetical to aestheticism, there is another sense in which they are aestheticism's counterparts. The followers of Hugo and Zola share with the practitioners of art for art's sake an opposition to the bourgeoisie, its art and its institutions (Bourdieu 75). Baudelairian rejection of moralisms of all stripes notwithstanding, it is remarkable how often one finds, among those associated with aestheticism, a sense of anxiety about the lack of the realists' strong social engagement. There is a certain buried envy, among aesthetes, for the clear social purpose of a different kind of art. Indeed, those drawn to the aesthete's rejection of bourgeois hegemony often show signs of anxiety about their mode of rejection. Algernon Charles Swinburne, Arthur Symons, and W. B. Yeats all provide examples of these anxieties.

The literary trajectory of Algernon Charles Swinburne has often been described as a matter of rapid acceleration in the direction of aestheticism, followed by a sudden reversal with a turn toward writing in the service of politics. While this is not entirely untrue of the broadest outlines of Swinburne's career, it would be more accurate to say that Swinburne constantly vacillates between aestheticism's autonomous art and a heteronomous writing in the service of politics. While his early period is dominated by aestheticism, it is haunted by the specter of the political.

Having been introduced to ideas of *l'art pour l'art* after meeting Dante Gabriel Rossetti while at Oxford in 1857, Swinburne tried to embrace the principles of his mentor and, through him, of the work of Baudelaire and his school in France. His enthusiastic 1857 review of Baudelaire's *Flowers of Evil* (suppressed and republished in slightly different form in 1862) was meant to be his declaration of aestheticist principles, a proud waving of the banner of autonomous art. The essay certainly begins with an unambiguous declaration of the autonomy of art. "A poet's business," says Swinburne,

> is presumably to write good verses, and by no means to redeem the age and remold society. No other form of art is so pestered with this impotent appetite for meddling in quite extraneous matters; but the mass of readers seem actually to think that a poem is the better for containing a moral lesson or assisting in a tangible and material good work. The courage and sense of a man who at such a time ventures to profess and act on the conviction that the art of poetry has absolutely nothing to do with didactic matter at all, are proof enough of the wise and serious manner in which he is likely to handle the materials of his art. (*Works* XX, 432)

"Here is an aesthete rampant," the reader may well declare. By the end
of the review Swinburne is already hedging his bets. Responding to
unnamed critics who have, he says, accused Baudelaire of immorality,
Swinburne backs away from the idea that art need not serve morality,
and tells us that, despite appearances, "there is not one poem of the
Fleurs du Mal which has not a distinct and vivid background of morality
to it." While "the moral side of the book is not thrust forward in the
foolish and repulsive manner of a half-taught artist," Swinburne assures
us that "those who will look for them may find moralities in plenty
behind every poem of M. Baudelaire's" (*Works* XX, 436). When the review
was brought to Baudelaire's attention, he wrote to the young English-
man, denying that he was a covert moralist: the tempering of art's
autonomy was, it seems, more present in the mind of the anxious
reviewer than in the poems under review (Lang 88).

Swinburne's commitment to autonomous aesthetics wavered time
and again, and his correspondence reveals the reason. Explaining, in a
letter of 1866, why he had stopped writing poetry for much of 1861 to
work for the cause of Italian liberation, Swinburne claims "it is nice to
have something to love and believe in" and "it was only Gabriel [D. G.
Rossetti] and his followers in art (*l'art pour l'art*) who for a time frightened
me from speaking out" (Lang 195). Autonomous art seemed devoid of
the kind of meaningful causes to be found in political action and engaged
writing. That this letter was written the same year that saw Swinburne's
Poems and Ballads—widely considered "his *Flowers of Evil*" (Cassidy 49)—only
underlines the ambivalent nature of Swinburne's aestheticism, fraught
continually with anxieties about art's potential for moral and political
commitments.

Perhaps the most fascinating passage in Swinburne's prose, for our
purposes, comes in his study *William Blake* (published in 1868 but written
by 1866). Here, his vacillation with regard to autonomous art momentarily leads him to a position very like that adopted by the avant-garde
poets of the twentieth century: the identification of autonomous artistic praxis with moral or political efficacy. "The contingent result of
having good art about you and living in a time of noble writing," Swinburne writes, "is this":

...that the spirit and mind of men then living will receive on some points a certain exaltation and insight caught from the influence of such colors of verse or painting; will become for one thing incapable of tolerating bad work...which of course implies and draws with it many other advantages of a sort you may call moral or spiritual. But if the artist does his work with an eye to such results or for the sake of bringing about such improvements, he will too probably fail even of them. Art for art's sake first of all, and afterwards we may suppose all the rest shall be added to her (or if not she need hardly be overmuch concerned); but from the man who falls to artistic work with a moral purpose shall be taken away even that which he has...(XVI, 137–38)

Here, a commitment to autonomy is essential to any true artist, but that commitment will, without the conscious intention of the artist, lead to the "moral or spiritual" improvement of the world. The heteronomous writer, committing his pen to causes, will by contrast inevitably go awry. The position isn't so much argued as it is asserted, and like many un-argued assertions, it can be understood as an idea clung to less for its verifiability than for the way it seems to eliminate contradictions too painful to confront. Had Swinburne been able to convince himself of the proposition, he'd have been able to transcend his dichotomy of autonomous and heteronomous principles of art.

Within a year of finishing the Blake study, though, Swinburne received a letter from the Italian revolutionary leader Giussepe Mazzini, urging him to give up "songs of egotistical love" such as those found in *Poems and Ballads*, and write "a series of lyrics for the Crusade" in Italy (Lafourcade 149). Swinburne's response, the long poem "A Song of Italy," seemed to indicate a definitive turn away from *l'art pour l'art*. But even in this late phase, having publicly rejected aestheticism, one still finds Swinburne vacillating with regard to autonomous art. Looking back on a mixed review of Victor Hugo's *Les Miserables* he'd written during his aestheticist phase, Swinburne wrote that he was, at the time, too much "under the morally identical influence of Gabriel Gautier and Théophile Rossetti [sic] not to regret...that a work of imagination should be colored or discolored by philanthropy, and shaped or distorted by a purpose" (Lang 207). The deliberate reversal of Gabriel Rossetti and Théophile Gauti-er's names asserts a kind of identity between English and French versions of *l'art pour l'art*, but what, exactly, is Swinburne's attitude to this multi-national movement? Does the philanthropy of a heteronomous art like Hugo's color or discolor the writing? Does a purpose beyond art itself shape or distort the aesthetic? It is impossible to say. And in this impossibility we see Swinburne's continued anxiety of the aesthetic, an anxiety that runs through the length of his writing career.

A similar anxiety finds its way into a later poet of British aestheticism, Arthur Symons. His famous 1893 essay "The Decadent Movement in Literature," for example, treats the movement he describes with deep ambivalence. Symons refers to Mallarmé quite positively as the "leader of the great emancipation," (141) and sees the freedoms proposed by Mallarmé as liberations from the heteronomous art of the moralizing bourgeoisie, for Mallarmé "has wished neither to be read nor to be understood by the bourgeois intelligence, and it is with some deliberateness of intention that he has made both issues impossible" (142). But even as he celebrates Mallarmé's commitment to artistic autonomy, Symons expresses uneasiness about an art apparently cut off from morality, politics, and any efficacy in the world of action. It is the literature, he says, of a moment "too languid for the relief of action, too uncertain for any emphasis in opinion or conduct" (136).

When Symons discusses the poetry of Mallarmé, his language is telling, in that it consistently indicates a sense of the limitations of the aesthetic / decadent project he describes. Mallarmé's latest poems, says Symons,

> ... consist merely of a sequence of symbols, in which every word must be taken in a sense with which its ordinary significance has nothing to do. Mallarmé's contortion of the French language, so far as mere style is concerned, is curiously similar to a kind of deprivation which was undergone by the Latin language in its decadence. It is, indeed, in part a reversion to Latin phraseology, to the Latin construction, and it has made, of the clear and flowing French language, something irregular, unquiet, expressive, with sudden surprising felicities, with nervous starts and lapses, with new capacities for the exact noting of sensation. Alike to the ordinary and to the scholarly reader, it is painful, intolerable; a jargon, a massacre. (142)

Even leaving aside the obvious reservations about "painful, intolerable" poetry, one is struck by the negative nature of Symons' description ("deprivation," "reversion," "nervous"). Most strikingly, Symons describes Mallarmé's project as "merely a sequence of symbols" as involving "mere style"—as if something of great substance was missing from the aesthete's work. While Symons is committed to the project of literary decadence, he is by no means an unanxious adherent of the movement.

Symons' ideas were influential on W. B. Yeats, a fellow member of the Rhymer's Club.[2] Many of Yeats' poems can be read as meditations on their own conditions of production, and reveal a consistent ambivalence with regard to the aesthetic movement's claims for autonomous aesthetics. "Fergus and the Druid," for example, poses a dialog between a figure of autonomous imagination (the druid) and a figure of worldly, political power (Fergus). Fergus initiates the conversation, remarking on the infinitely changing nature of the shape-shifting druid's existence. The druid then asks, "What would you, king of the proud Red Branch kings?" (7) and Fergus replies, saying that he feels trapped in his role as a figure of power, always feeling the crown upon his head. He laments the fixed nature of his own identity that leaves him unable to enjoy the freedoms of the druid's imaginative existence. But when Fergus tells the druid that he would "be no more a king, but learn the wisdom that is yours," (7) the druid replies in language reminiscent of Symons' claim that aestheticism was unhealthy: "Look on my thin grey hair and hollow cheeks / And on these hands that may not lift the sword, / This body trembling like a wind-blown reed" (7). The druid, for all his freedom, is a figure of weakness, impotence, and, significantly, a figure of no help to those in need. Autonomous aesthetics, while free of the rigidities of political responsibility, hardly appear ideal. When Fergus, despite the druid's warnings, opens the "little bag of dreams" and partakes of the druid's powers, he finds his experience curiously empty. The imaginative experience, cut off from the possibility of action, use, or productivity, is beautiful but nothing more. It leaves Fergus, to recycle Symons' words about the decadent movement in literature, "too languid for the relief of action, too uncertain for any emphasis in opinion or conduct" (136). That the poem is drenched in the exotic and archaic imagery

---

2. For a discussion of the mutual influence of Yeats and Symons, see Haskell M. Block, "Yeats, Symons and The Symbolist Movement in Literature," Yeats Annual 8 (1990): 9–18.

characteristic of the English decadent poets only serves to make more plain the source of Yeats' poem in his anxiously ambivalent response to the idea of autonomous art.

Other examples of the aesthetic anxiety are, of course, legion in the works of poets of the late nineteenth and very early twentieth centuries. Nor are the novelists of the period free of anxieties about autonomous art. The ambivalent fate of Des Essentes at the end of Huysmans' *Against Nature* and the horror of the aesthete's active, commercial doppelganger in Henry James' story "The Jolly Corner" provide just two of many examples of the period's anxieties. Along with their freedoms from bourgeois norms the artists of aestheticism found new fears of irrelevance and irresponsibility.

Having inherited this anxiety-ridden autonomous aesthetic, successive generations of twentieth century avant-garde poets would seek to assuage those anxieties while retaining the idea of artistic autonomy. Their means to this end would be systematically articulated versions of the idea that Swinburne had expressed in passing in his study of Blake: that autonomous artistic pursuits were, by virtue of their very autonomy, paths to moral or political utility.

Early twentieth century avant-garde movements were, of course, tremendously varied in their goals and their means of expression but, as a number of theorists have argued, the force uniting them was a general rejection of the limits of aestheticism. Peter Bürger, for example, tells us that with the avant-gardes of the 1920s "the social subsystem that is art enters the stage of self-criticism," a self-criticism based on a rejection of "the status of art in bourgeois society as defined by the concept of autonomy" (22). Avant-gardists of all stripes turned against the ideals of an aestheticism that, in their view, led not only to such positive things as artistic freedom, but also to "the other side of autonomy, art's lack of social impact" (22). Building on Bürger's analysis, Jochen Schulte-Sasse sees the project of the avant-garde movements of the 1920s as a matter of breaking free of social inutility:

> Aestheticism's intensification of artistic autonomy and its effect on the foundation of a special realm of aesthetic experience permitted the avant-garde to clearly recognize the social inconsequentiality of auton-

omous art and, as the logical consequence of this recognition, to attempt
to lead art back into social praxis. . . . [T]he turning point from Aestheticism to the avant-garde is determined by the extent to which art
comprehended the mode in which it functioned in bourgeois society,
its comprehension of its own social status. The historical avant-garde
of the twenties was the first movement in art history that turned against
the institution "art" and the mode in which autonomy functions. (xiv)

Schulte-Sasse's final point is significant: it is not that avant-gardists
rejected the idea of aesthetic autonomy, seeking to put their art at the
service of various causes, campaigns, and institutions: theirs was not
the path of agitprop or socialist realism. Rather, they sought a new way
for aesthetic autonomy to function socially.

"Can one, in fact, claim to emancipate men when one has begun by
betraying beauty and truth?" asks Ferdinand Alquié in *The Philosophy of
Surrealism* (66). Put another way, Alquié's question is this: can you have
political revolution without aesthetic autonomy? The surrealists attempted to put to rest any anxieties about the political utility of autonomous
art by asserting the identity of revolutionary politics and aesthetic
freedom. The assertion of this identity was difficult to maintain, causing
divisions within, and expulsions from, the surrealist movement. It was,
moreover, treated with skepticism by the French Communist Party, and
it raised unresolved questions about whether the kind of revolution
envisioned by the surrealists could be connected with any specific political program. Such was its appeal, though, that it was embraced by some
of the most vibrant artists and writers of Europe for decades.

When the Bureau of Surrealist Research issued its manifesto, the
"Declaration of January 27, 1925," it set out to do three things: to distance
itself from established ideas of literature that walled writing off from
social praxis; to affirm the autonomy of aesthetic activity; and to assert
the identity of that activity with revolution. "We have nothing to do with
literature," asserts the first of the declaration's clauses, while the final
clause tells us "surrealism is not a poetic form" (450). The need for
distance from "literature" and the "poetic" was urgent, because autonomous aesthetics had, it seemed to the signatories of the declaration
(Breton, Louis Aragon, Paul Éluard, Antonin Artaud, Philippe Soupault,

Benjamin Péret, and some twenty others) severed the vital links between art, on the one hand, and life and action, on the other. While the signatories rejected autonomous art's isolation, they affirmed its freedom from limits imposed by causes, institutions, and systems of morality, maintaining that their project would involve a "total liberation of the mind" (450). This liberation was to be connected to a larger project for, as they made clear, they were "determined to make a Revolution" (450).

Just what kind of revolution was entailed by the January 1925 "Declaration" was somewhat ambiguous at first, but it soon became clear that it was not to be limited to a revolution in style.[3] Indeed, by the time the third issue of *The Surrealist Revolution*—the journal associated with the Bureau of Surrealist Research—appeared in April of 1925, André Breton was asserting the inherent solidarity between surrealist revolution and the less radical (to his mind) revolutionary tendencies of the striking workers of France (Picon 73). This identification of aesthetic autonomy and a specifically leftist political revolution became a hardened position, and by March of 1928, with the eighth issue of *The Surrealist Revolution*, Breton, Péret, and Éluard united with the painter Pierre Unik in condemning Artaud for "seeing the Revolution as no more than a metamorphosis of the soul's inner conditions..." a subjectivist and aestheticist "dead end," as far as Breton was concerned (Picon 77).

In "Legitimate Defense," also from the eighth issue of *The Surrealist Revolution*, Breton addresses French Communist Party criticism of the surrealist version of revolution. While Breton firmly asserts the identity of aesthetic autonomy and political revolution, we can already see the first small cracks begin to appear in what he hoped would be a seamless ideology. Breton tells us that the author of a Communist party broadside has been

> accusing us of still vacillating between anarchy and Marxism and calling on us to decide one way or the other. Here, moreover, is the essential question he puts to us: 'Yes or no—is this desired revolution that of the mind *a priori* or that of the world of facts? Is it linked to Marxism, or

---

3. As Helena Lewis demonstrates in *Dada Turns Red: The Politics of Surrealism*, "revolution" for the surrealists "first meant the liberation of mind and spirit, but later came to include political and social revolution" (17).

to contemplative theories, to the purgation of the inner life?' This question is of a much more subtle turn than it appears to be, though its chief malignity seems to me to reside in the opposition of an interior reality to the world of facts, an entirely artificial opposition which collapses at once upon scrutiny. In the realm of facts, as we see it, no ambiguity is possible: all of us seek to shift power from the hands of the bourgeoisie to those of the proletariat. Meanwhile, it is nonetheless necessary that the experiments of the inner life continue, and do so, of course, without external or even Marxist control. (56)

The erasure of any division between imaginative freedom and political revolution is necessary to retain the surrealist position, a position the Communists had already come to look on with distrust. And in Breton's "meanwhile" and "nonetheless"—terms indicative of a coincident, rather than a causal or essential relation—we see his own language begin to express doubts about the possibility of maintaining an essential link between autonomous aesthetics and political revolution. The faintest ghost of the aesthetic anxiety remains, buried deep within the edifice of Breton's polemic.

The difficulties in maintaining the idea of an identity between aesthetic autonomy and political revolution went much further than a subtextual disturbance of Breton's prose, though. Such difficulties came in three principle forms: Communist insistence on heteronomous art, the gravitation of some surrealists toward aesthetic concerns at the expense of politics, and a growing skepticism about whether surrealism could be compatible with specific political projects.

Although that most heteronomous of aesthetic theories, socialist realism, didn't become state policy in the Soviet Union until 1932, surrealists, under pressure from French communists, had already felt pressure to put their art and writing directly at the service of the revolution. When, for example, Marcel Fourrier wrote in the seventh issue of *The Surrealist Revolution* that "once and for all, our business is to realize in full all that the working class represents, all that its revolution implies," he comes close to abandoning the aesthetic autonomy the surrealists had claimed in their "Declaration" (Picon 78). The value of autonomous art was always less clear to representatives of the French Communist

Party than it was to the surrealists themselves. As André Thireon, a representative of the Party, put it, "what could the Party have done with Max Ernst or André Breton to win over the miners of Lens?" (Haslam 161). Moreover, when Breton joined the Communist Party in 1927, he was shocked to find that the Party's idea of writing for the revolution did not involve any consideration of aesthetic autonomy: they asked him to work as a labor journalist, a task he refused on the grounds that it was a "dirty business" (Picon 79). "Surrealism," as Ferdinand Alquié put it, "found itself in the dilemma of having to choose between a social revolution that it wished to support but which discouraged freedom of expression, and a bourgeois society that it abhorred but which tolerated and even encouraged intellectual freedom" (59). While the majority of the surrealists upheld the identity of aesthetic autonomy and political revolution, their position was eccentric within communist circles. In 1930 the Kharkov Conference of the Association of Revolutionary Writers and Artists denounced Breton, and after 1932 stances such as his were considered heretical.

While the claims of heteronomy troubled surrealism from one side, the claims of an aestheticism without much direct concern for politics plagued it from another. As early as 1925 Louis Aragon had claimed that true surrealist work, work that addressed "the problems raised by the human condition," had "little to do with the miserable flicker of revolutionary activity which has appeared in the east in these last few years" (Picon 73). The 1933 folding of the journal *Surrealism in the Service of the Revolution*—the successor to *The Surrealist Revolution*, and a journal whose very name indicates the pressure the surrealists were under from the proponents of a heteronomous aesthetic—led to a further drift toward aesthetics at the expense of politics. When the journal closed many of the surrealists migrated to Albert Skira's new journal *Minotaure*. This was very much a journal of the art world, with beautiful production values, exquisite illustrations, and an overt restriction on the expression of political views. If political figures on the left wanted revolution without aesthetic autonomy, art-world figures like Skira wanted aesthetic autonomy without political revolution. The idea of the identity of the two was under attack from all sides.

In addition to these difficulties, the surrealists faced charges from both inside and outside the movement to the effect that their emphasis on aesthetic autonomy was not compatible with any specific revolution, but was, rather, a matter of perpetual critique or purely negative politics. Such charges came from within the movement very early on, and we have evidence (though, lamentably, no transcripts) of a vigorous debate on the issue. In 1925 Pierre Naville and others issued a statement in *The Surrealist Revolution* which declared that there had been a meeting of surrealists "to determine which of the two principles, Surrealism or revolution, ought best to guide their activity." Having "failed to resolve this question," though, they came to the understanding that "for the moment, they see only one positive point" on which all could agree: "that the Spirit is an essentially irreducible principle which cannot be fixed either in life or beyond" (Naville 15). The "Spirit," in this view, could not be embodied and fulfilled in any Marxian-Hegelian utopia. If this art was to be revolutionary, some of its practitioners felt it could not be tied to any specific revolution.

Similar arguments about the nature of surrealist revolution came from outside the movement itself, with one notable example issuing from the pen of Herbert J. Muller in 1940. The surrealists, he says,

> ... proclaim that their art is an application of dialectical materialism, a necessary counterpart of political revolution. This is nonsense. Surrealism is a glorification of the irrational, the unconscious; Marx invested his faith in rational analysis for the sake of conscious control. The Surrealists may contribute their mite to the destruction of the old social order; they can contribute nothing to the building of a new order. If anything like the kind of society they want does emerge from the war, it will be only because of a mighty collective effort, disciplined and controlled by conscious intelligence, and in this task attitudes like theirs would be at best a nuisance. (44)

Surrealism cannot be at the service of any specific revolution, says Muller: an autonomous art's politics can only be critical or negative, and can have no constructive part to play in the creation of revolutionary social order.

Despite criticisms of this kind, Breton clung steadfastly to the idea of the unity of aesthetic autonomy and political revolution, issuing a major restatement of the view in 1938's "Manifesto for an Independent Revolutionary Art," a document ostensibly co-authored with Diego Rivera, but actually written by Breton with the assistance of Trotsky. Breton's primary thrust in the manifesto is to denigrate the heteronomous art emanating from the Soviet Union and assert both the autonomy of art and its essential connection to revolution. The Soviet Union, he says, has "spread over the entire world a heavy twilight" and "in this twilight of filth and blood we see men disguised as intellectuals and artists who have turned servility into a stepping stone..." (473). Heteronomous art such as socialist realism is inherently servile, for "art cannot...without demeaning itself, willingly submit to any outside directive" (474). Citing Marx himself as a believer in autonomous art—"The writer does not in any way look on his work as a *means*. It is an *end in itself*"—Breton argues for the necessary freedom of artistic production (474). Such artistic autonomy must, by its nature, be a matter of constructive political revolution, declares Breton, reaffirming his position of 1925: "True art, art that...strives to express the inner needs of man and of mankind as they are today—cannot be anything other than revolutionary: it must aspire to a complete and radical reconstruction of society, if only to free intellectual creation from the chains that bind it" (473). The circularity of the passage is remarkable, indicating the inherent instability of a position that refuses to prioritize either art or politics over the other. Free art, following only the inner direction of the artist, must strive for political reform, "if only to free intellectual creation from the chains that bind it." Art serves politics to serve art. The argument chases its own dialectical tail.

Did the surrealist assertion of the essential identity of aesthetic autonomy and political utility assuage the old anxieties about art's isolation? Given the constant controversy about the identification of aesthetics and politics both within and around the movement, given the widespread rejection of surrealism by the representatives of the revolutionary forces with whom the surrealists sought to affiliate themselves, and given the drifting away from politics toward more purely aesthetic concerns by some surrealists, we can at best call their solution to the aesthetic anxiety a problematic one. Such is the appeal of their kind of solution to the aesthetic anxiety, though, that more recent avant-garde movements have followed similar, if less tumultuous, paths to that of the surrealists.

Since the 1970s the language poets have attempted to soothe the aesthetic anxiety in a manner much like that of the surrealists before them. Embracing a radical critique of capitalism, they have also stead-fastly maintained that theirs will be a poetry unbeholden to any limits on expression imposed by institutions, political parties, or audience expectations. They yearn for an art both autonomous and political and, like the surrealists, resolve these contradictory yearnings by effectively claiming that artistic autonomy is a path to the political.

Perhaps the most common version of the identification of autono-my and politics among language poets comes in the form of the assertion that a truly autonomous poetry will be unreadable by conventional means, and will therefore be uncommodifiable. Indeed, it will ideally resist incorporation into any part of the capitalist system (as product, as ideology, as entertainment property), and will constitute a kind of critique of that system. When the poet Abigail Child proclaims in capital letters that her poetry will consist of "UNITS OF UNMEANINGNESS INCORPORATED ANEW // VS. A COMMUNITY OF SLOGANEERS" (94) she makes an assertion of this kind. Against the practitioners of heteronomous writing (the sloganeers, apologists for the dominant social form), she holds up her own autonomous writing. In its very "unmeaningness" lies its politics: a refusal of commodification. Cana-dian poet David Bromige makes much the same case for an autonomous political art when he says "the profound vocation of the work of art in a commodity society: not to be a commodity, not to be consumed" (217).

Those who would claim that a truly political writing must put itself under certain restrictions, such as a simple language that can be under-stood by potentially revolutionary classes, face hostility from language poets. Charles Bernstein, the foremost polemicist among language poets, shows real frustration with this kind of criticism in a passage just a little reminiscent of Breton's refusal to act as a leftist journalist:

> I flip through this week's *Nation* (October 3, 1988) and notice a letter
> to the editor by their own small press critic. He suggests that the 'clarity'

that the *New York Post* 'demands of its sports writers' is a model that poets who wish to be political should emulate. Is it just my pessimism that makes me feel that this reflects an ever deepening crisis in our culture—a contempt . . . for intellectual and spiritual articulations not completely assimilated into and determined by the dominant culture's discursive practices? ("The Value of *Sulfur*" 105)

We get a clear sense of the way language poets have identified autonomy with politics here. Bending to the demands of a readership would, in Bernstein's view, be a form of heteronomy, in that the poet who does this is governed by a market, not by the demands intrinsic to art. But bending to the demands of a readership would also be a matter of assimilation to "the dominant culture's discursive practices." A refusal to conform stylistically is also a refusal to conform politically. The autonomous is the political to Bernstein.

Since this approach inevitably limits the reach of the writing to a relatively small number of readers, it often strikes the unsympathetic as counter-intuitive. Just as André Thireon wondered "what could the Party have done with Max Ernst or André Breton to win over the miners of Lens?" an American leftist might well wonder just what could be done with Abigail Child or Charles Bernstein to win over the displaced auto workers of Flint, Michigan. In more candid moments, some representatives of language poetry have expressed anxieties of these kinds. Susan M. Schultz, for example, states simply that "the questions of relevance, of audience, of efficacy, will always haunt us" (215).

Against such haunting doubts, how do language poets maintain a sense of the identity of aesthetic autonomy and political efficacy? For many, it begins with an elimination of the distinction between linguistic and material realities. Just as the Breton, in "Legitimate Defense," denies the division between inner and outer worlds, the pioneering language poet Ron Silliman, in his seminal 1977 essay "Disappearance of the Word, Appearance of the World," denies the division between the linguistic and the material. Silliman begins his essay with a long quotation from linguist Edward Sapir:

Human beings do not live in the objective world alone, nor alone in the world of social activity as ordinarily understood, but are very much at the mercy of the particular language which has become the medium of expression for their society. It is quite an illusion to imagine that one adjusts to reality essentially without the use of language and that language is merely an incidental means of solving specific problems of communication or reflection. The fact of the matter is that the 'real world' is to a large extent unconsciously built up on the language habits of the group. (123)

Endorsing Sapir's view that the real world is largely a matter of our accumulated language habits, Silliman finds himself in a position to turn linguistic activity into political activity. Asking himself whether the capitalist system has "a specific 'reality' which is passed through the language and thereby imposed on its speakers" Silliman replies in the affirmative.

But just what is this linguistic system of capitalism, and how is it to be challenged? For Silliman, capitalism seeks to make language invisible: the ideal capitalist text can be consumed with ease, and will present no language that draws attention to itself as language. "In its ultimate form," says Silliman, capitalism creates a linguistic situation in which "the consumer of a mass market novel . . . stares numbly at a 'blank' page (the page also of the speed-reader) while a story appears to unfold miraculously of its own free will before his or her eyes" (127). The language is transparent, unchallenging, and therefore pacifying. It gives no sense of itself as a created thing, and therefore implies it is a natural system, rather than the product of a particular ideological system. This, says Silliman, constitutes "an anesthetic transformation of a perceived tangibility of the word, with corresponding increases in its descriptive and narrative capacities," and these provide the "preconditions for the invention of 'realism,' the optical illusion of reality in capitalist thought" (125).

In Silliman's view, poetry has the possibility of breaking down the language system upon which capitalism depends. "The social function of the language arts, especially the poem," writes Silliman, "places them in an important position to carry the class struggle *for* consciousness to the level of consciousness" (131). The struggle, it is important to note, can be carried on without putting one's language in the service of mass movements. One need not follow the injunctions of *The Nation* to write with the simple clarity of sports journalists, still less need one follow the injunctions of some new Mazzini to write "lyrics for the Crusade." Acts of political resistance take the form of linguistic disjunction, the creation of the "unmeaningness" called for by Abigail Child. The satisfactions of such a belief are clear enough: one maintains total aesthetic autonomy, remaining above the dirty business of political journalism, and at the same time exorcizes the aesthetic anxiety.

It is far from clear, though, that Silliman is entirely successful in this exorcism. Toward the end of his essay we find a certain hedging of bets with regard to the efficacy of his brand of linguistic politics. After insisting on the political power of linguistic disruption, he makes the following statement:

> It is clear that one cannot change language (or consciousness) by fiat . . . First there must be a change in the mode and control of production and material life. . . . [P]oetry can work to search out the preconditions of post-referential language within the existing social fact. (131)

Linguistic disruption, it seems, will not bring about the revolution. Its role is in fact profoundly limited, and its political utility—the problem the essay set out to solve—turns out to be extremely, perhaps excruciatingly, limited: it can lay the groundwork for the kind of "post-referential" language that, presumably, will be used in poetry after a real, material revolution that changes the "mode and control of production." Silliman's essay was published twenty-eight years before Susan M. Schultz concluded that questions of efficacy will always haunt the language poets, but clearly her observation was as pertinent to the early years of the language movement as it was to be in the movement's twilight: Silliman's essay all but concedes the failure of its own thesis.

Like Silliman, Charles Bernstein insists on the identity of artistic autonomy and political action. He wants to write an autonomous poetry "that insists on running its own course, finding its own measures" ("State of the Art" 1), and champions poetry that "is political not primarily in its subject matter, or representation of political causes . . . but in the form and structure and style of the poems, and in the attitude toward language" ("The Value of *Sulfur* 107). Since Bernstein, like Silliman, accepts the notion that language systems define our relation the world, he can maintain that linguistic convention "is a central means by which authority is made credible," and that "conventional writing—with and without oppositional content—participates in a legitimating process" for existing systems of power ("Comedy and the Poetics of Political Form" 220, 221-2). A poem that radically breaks with convention, presenting situations where "linguistic shards of histrionic inappropriateness pierce the momentary calm" can, in this context, be political, because the war of linguistic convention against linguistic disruption pits "the authority of money versus aesthetic innovation" (220).

To his credit, Bernstein attempts to answer the question of just how the writing of linguistically radical poems would translate into radical political action. Bernstein makes the argument in a straightforward statement: "the poetic authority to challenge dominant social values, including conventional manners of communication, is a model for the individual political participation of each citizen" (219). Linguistic radicalism is to be an inspiration for political radicalism, a shattering of formal complacency that translates into a shattering of political complacency. For this argument to function, though, one still has to confront the question of readership, as a virtually unread poem would, in this model, have a negligible political impact. Unfortunately, though, Bernstein chooses to dismiss the question of audience altogether:

> Poets don't have to be read, any more than trees have to be sat under, to transform poisonous societal emissions into something that can be breathed. As a poet, you affect the public sphere with each reader, with the fact of the poem, and by exercising you prerogative to choose what collective forms you will legitimate. The political power of poetry is not measured in numbers: it instructs us to count differently. (236)

The analogy with forests hardly bears examination. To accept it would be to believe that an entire advertising campaign, or an enormous effort of political propaganda, could be undone simply by being understood and reworked in a poem, even if that poem were left forever in a desk drawer. Nor does the assertion that the legitimation of one or another "collective form" in a poem constitutes "political power" hold up. Questions of audience remain. Who gives poets the authority to legitimate discourse? Is this a matter of speaking truth to power, or to a few of the likeminded among the powerless? As to how we should "count differently," if we are not to count readers and those influenced by readers, Bernstein is silent.

Bernstein's contortions of reason are surprising, and one could be tempted to see in them an attempt to avoid confronting the aesthetic anxiety were it not for the fact that at one point in the same essay he confronts that anxiety directly. "Don't get me wrong," he writes,

> I know it's almost a joke to speak of poetry and national affairs. Yet in *The Social Contract* Rousseau writes that since our conventions are provisional, the public may reconvene in order to withdraw authority from those conventions that no longer serve our purposes. Poetry is one of the few areas where this right of convening is exercised." (225)

It is a little poignant that Bernstein sees this last assertion as a sign of hope rather than of despair, a sign of poetry's political efficacy rather than its marginalization.

"It is hard," writes critic Geoff Ward, "not to see a discrepancy between the aims and the achievements of Language poetry" (13). One can get a sense of this discrepancy not only from a look at our contemporary political situation, but from a look at our poetic situation as well. Language poetry postulated an essential identity between stylistic and political concerns, but an examination of the situation of poetry reveals that such a connection was by no means essential or inevitable. The stylistic devices of language poetry have become increasingly widespread since the mid–1980s, but in the process they have become increasingly divorced from the political radicalism the early language poets thought their corollary. Ken Edwards, editor of the avant-garde journal *Reality Studios*, was the first to note this trend. Writing in 1990, he looked back on 1983 as the year when the stylistic devices of language poetry started to be appropriated by poets who did not share their concerns with radical politics:

> By 1983 I had received, among the many eager unsolicited manuscripts arriving for *Reality Studios*, one from an American poet who enclosed some Surrealist-style poems with a note to the effect that if I didn't like them this person could send me some in a "Language poetry style," or

"like Charles Bernstein." This told me two things: one, the language poets (and Bernstein in particular) had definitely arrived; two, the movement had reached its culminating point or point of failure (that is, when people start imitating its effects without understanding its bases) remarkably early. Since resistance to reification is a central driving force for these poets, such a development gives rise to decidedly mixed feelings. (58)

The market proves to be a powerful solvent, dissolving the supposedly essential bond between style and politics the language poets thought they had found.

The critic Robert Baker concurs with the anecdotal evidence Edwards provides. Tracing the history of innovative poetic technique from the Romantics to the present day, Baker argues that techniques of the early twentieth century were picked up by poets in America after the second world war; then, "from the mid-seventies on," he argues,

Language Movement poets . . . radicalized these sorts of practices into a polemical art of the indeterminate and dispersive. In turn, and perhaps surprisingly, these practices have in recent years been loosely assimilated by many poets working in more traditional modes and only occasionally sharing the concerns—themselves extremely diverse—of these earlier modernist and avantgardist formations. Many contemporary poets, that is, appear to have adopted a similar distrust of inherited modes of narrative and thematic patterning . . . and a sort of programmatic disjunction . . . now appears to be taught in writing workshops around the country. (361–62)

The supposedly uncommodifiable style has become a commodity of sorts, provided by graduate writing programs intent on selling the latest, most advanced model of poetry.

It is interesting to note that surrealists were never quite able to establish a solid link between revolutionary politics and surrealist practice, and that the language poets were unable to establish a definitive link between textual disruption and resistance to capitalism. But what is more significant is to note just how long the urge to have both autonomous art and political efficacy simultaneously has endured. If nothing else, this should tell us that the anxiety of the aesthetic has been a condition of poetry from the mid-nineteenth century on, and that it seems likely to be with us as long as the idea of autonomous art endures. Whether there is a future to the particular illusion of the avant-garde (that autonomous art is inherently politically radical and politically efficacious) is dubious: that idea has worked its way through at least two full cycles now. Its durability has been proven, but so have its profound limitations.

Works Cited

Alquié, Ferdinand. *The Philosophy of Surrealism*. Ann Arbor: University of Michigan Press, 1965. Print.

Baker, Robert. *The Extravagant: Crossings of Modern Poetry and Modern Philosophy*. South Bend: University of Notre Dame Press, 2005. Print.

Bernstein, Charles. "Comedy and the Poetics of Political Form." *A Poetics*. Cambridge, Massachusetts: Harvard University Press, 1992. 218–28. Print.

——. "State of the Art." *A Poetics*. Cambridge, Massachusetts: Harvard University Press, 1992. 1–8. Print.

Bernstein, Charles. "The Value of Sulfur." *My Way: Speeches and Poems*. Chicago: University of Chicago Press, 1999. 104–07. Print.

Block, Haskell M. "Yeats, Symons and The Symbolist Movement in Literature." *Yeats Annual* 8 (1990): 9–18. Print.

Bourdieu, Pierre. *The Rules of Art: Genesis and Structure of the Literary Field*. Trans. Susan Emanuel. Stanford: Stanford University Press, 1996. Print.

Breton, André. "Legitimate Defense." *What is Surrealism?: Selected Writings*. Ed. Franklin Rosemont. Vol. 2. New York: Pathfinder, 2000. 46–60. Print.

Breton, André and Diego Rivera [Léon Trotsky]. "Manifesto for an Independent Revolutionary Art." *Manifesto: A Century of -Isms*. Ed. Mary Ann Caws. Lincoln, Nebraska: University of Nebraska Press, 2001. 472–77. Print.

Bromige, David. "My Poetry." *The American Tree*. Ed. Ron Silliman. Orono: National Poetry Foundation, 1984. 217. Print.

Bureau of Surrealist Research. "Declaration of January 27, 1925." *Manifesto. A Century of -Isms*. Ed. Mary Ann Caws. Lincoln, Nebraska: University of Nebraska Press, 2001. 450–51. Print.

Bürger, Peter. *Theory of the Avant-Garde*. Trans. Michael Shaw. Minneapolis: University of Minnesota Press, 1984. Print.

Cassagne, Albert. *La Théorie De L'Art Pour L'Art en France Chez les Derniers Romantiques et les Premiers Réalists*. Geneva: Slatkine, 1979. Print.

Cassidy, John A. *Algernon Charles Swinburne*. New York: Twayne, 1964. Print.

Child, Abigail. "Cross Referencing the Units of Sight and Sound/Film and Language." *The L=A=N=G=U=A=G=E Book*. Ed. Bruce Andrews and Charles Bernstein. Carbondale: University of Southern Illinois Press, 1984. 94–96. Print.

Edwards, Ken. "Language, the Remake." *fragmente* 2 (1990): 58. Print.

Flaubert, Gustave. Letter to George Sand, 29 Apr. 1871. *The George Sand-Gustave Flaubert Letters*. Trans. A. L. McKenzie. Chicago: Academy, 1979. Print.

Haslam, Malcolm. *The Real World of the Surrealists*. New York: Galley, 1984. Print.

Lafourcade, Georges. *Swinburne: A Literary Biography*. London: Russell and Russell, 1967. Print.

Lang, Cecil Y., ed. *The Swinburne Letters*. New Haven: Yale, 1962. Print.

Lewis, Helena. *Dada Turns Red: The Politics of Surrealism*. Edinburgh: University of Edinburgh Press, 1990. Print.

Muller, Herbert J. "Surrealism: A Dissenting View." *Surrealism Pro and Con*. Ed. Nicolas Calas, Herbert J. Muller, and Kenneth Burke. New York: Gotham, 1973. 44–64. Print.

Naville, Pierre, ed. *La Revolution Surrealiste*. New York: Ayer, 1955. Print.

Picon, Gaeton. *Surrealists and Surrealism, 1919–1939*. New York: Rizzoli, 1977. Print.

Schulte-Sasse, Jochen. Foreword. *Theory of the Avant-Garde*. Peter Bürger, trans. Michael Shaw. Minneapolis: University of Minnesota Press, 1984. vii–xlvii. Print.

Schultz, Susan M. *A Poetics of Impasse in Modern and Contemporary American Poetry*. Tuscaloosa: University of Alabama Press, 2005. Print.

Silliman, Ron. "Disappearance of the Word, Appearance of the World." *The L=A=N=G=U=A=G=E Book*. Ed. Bruce Andrews and Charles Bernstein. Carbondale: University of Southern Illinois Press, 1984. 121–32. Print.

Swinburne, Algernon Charles. *The Complete Works of Algernon Charles Swinburne*. Ed. Edmund Gosse and Thomas J. Wise. London: Heinemann, 1925. Print.

Symons, Arthur. "The Decadent Movement in Literature." *Aesthetes and Decadents of the 1890s*. Ed. Karl Beckson. Chicago: Academy, 1981. Print.

Yeats, W. B. *Selected Poems*. Ed. M. L. Rosenthal. New York: Scribner, 1996. Print.

Ward, Geoff. *Language Poetry and the American Avant-Garde*. Keele: British Association of American Studies, 1993. Print.

Public Faces in Private Places
Notes on Cambridge Poetry

My title comes from some lines of W. H. Auden's in *The Orators*: "Private faces in public places / Are wiser and nicer / Than public faces in private places" (5). Often, modern poets have presented their work as a matter of private faces in public places— that is, as the voice of private, authentic individual conscience entering the public sphere. Such a vision of poetry is, no doubt, fraught with its own problems and contradictions, but none of those concern me here. When we look at what has come to be known in some circles as Cambridge School poetry—the experimental poetry of Tom Raworth, John Wilkinson, and Jeremy Prynne, as well as Keston Sutherland, Andrea Brady, and Simon Jarvis, to name a few poets of the younger generation—we're faced with a very different conception of poetry. We find ourselves asking a question something like this: what ought we to make of a school of poetry that has a strong public concern, but no appreciable public presence? In Auden's terms, it is a poetry of public faces in private places.

Characteristically, poets of the Cambridge School have created a hermetic poetry, circulated outside the regular system of publication among a small group of cognoscenti. In some sense, this is a very private poetry, both in its formal qualities and in its support culture. On the other hand, the claims for this poetry represent it as anything but private: it is sometimes referred to as a poetry with a specific and far-reaching political goal and effect. In this sense, it is profoundly public poetry, at least in theory. The position is inherently contradictory, and has been complicated by the sometime refusal on the part of some of the Cambridge School's leading figures to allow their work to be published (that is, to become public) by commercial presses and prominent journals, even when it is sought out by editors. The choice of private publication—quite literally, since some of the most important work of the school has appeared in self-published pamphlets—defies the idea of a poetry of public, political significance.

This is the point for disclaimers, and I will not fail to provide one. I admit there is some debate about how much one can generalize about the Cambridge School of poetry. Not all of the poets are of a uniform view about the relationship of hermetic poetry and political efficacy. In fact, a good place to begin may be with a controversy between two poets associated with the Cambridge School, John Wilkinson and Peter Riley. In their debate, conducted over three issues of the *Chicago Review* in 2007, Wilkinson took what I understand to be the more orthodox Cambridge School position about the relationship of poetry and politics, while Riley took the apostate's position, a questioning of the norms of the group from within the group itself.

Although Wilkinson's initial salvo in this exchange took the form of a long review of Simon Jarvis' book-length poem *The Unconditional*, the publication of Jarvis' book was really just the occasion for a more significant project. The real intent of the piece was to introduce the Cambridge School to an American readership heretofore largely unfamiliar with it. Wilkinson begins with a brief description of Jarvis' book, in which he claims (not unreasonably) that "it would defeat rhetoric to overstate the peculiarity of Simon Jarvis' book *The Unconditional*" and that "must be among the most unusual books ever published." "Imagine if you can," Wilkinson continues, "a continuous poem of 237 pages, mainly in iambic pentameter, in which whole pages pass without a full stop." Jarvis' *The Unconditional*, says Wilkinson, is deeply challenging even to habitual poetry readers, as it is a poem "dedicated to a high level of discourse on prosody, critical theory, and phenomenology; all this conducted in a philosophical language drawing on Adorno's negative dialectics" and "a narrative language that is the unnatural offspring of Wyndham Lewis and P. B. Shelley." Moreover, Wilkinson tells us, the book is filled with a particularly unusual cast of characters. Resembling nothing so much as "refugees from an Iain Sinclair novel finally fed up with walking" and with "names like '=x' 'Agramant' 'Qnuxmuxkyl' and 'Jobless', the group starts out on a *Canturbury Tales*-like trip, but winds up in a dingy pub displaying unlikely degrees of alienation and erudition" (370). After this description, however, much of what Wilkinson has to say is really a more general statement of what he takes to be the program of common elements of Cambridge poetics.

As described by Wilkinson, one of the most significant elements of this program is the idea of poetry as "a special kind of cognition wherein knowledge and information cannot be distinguished from formal attributes" (370). The language of Jarvis and associated poets is anti-instrumental, and even anti-communicative, refusing to be at the service of communication or conceptual clarity. In a somewhat uncharacteristic passage within *The Unconditional*—a passage as close to authoritative statement as we'll find in a poetry that eschews authoritative statement—Jarvis gives us something close to his poetics, saying that he is

> willing a meaning to the edge of birth
> renewing thought in beating down all dearth
>   as when apparently from scraps of noise
> apparently not placed but simply thrown
>   or simply falling through the atmosphere
> a non-contingent pressure or a sense
>   patterns a ripple . . . (Wilkinson 375)

Poetry, it seems, should avoid giving a clear and paraphrasable meaning, by keeping meaning on 'the edge of birth.' The 'noise' of the poem, with all of its etymological and syntactic disturbances, keeps the patterns of meaning from becoming entirely clear. The goal of a poetry like this, says Wilkinson, is to avoid totalization or transferable meaning, lest it be appropriated into what he (echoing Adorno and the thinkers of the Frankfurt School) calls 'administrative reason.' All of this argument against utility or total comprehensibility leads to Wilkinson's statement that "aesthetic objects," in their anti-instrumentality, "constitute a special class" of things.

This is a surprising statement, though it wouldn't be surprising coming from the pen of a formalist or an aesthete. If, for example, you're hearing echoes of the American New Criticism, I think you are hearing aright: the contention that we can't separate the cognitive statement of the poem "from formal attributes" sounds a great deal like Cleanth Brooks' argument (in "The Heresy of Paraphrase") that it is not possible "to frame a proposition, a statement, which will adequately represent the total meaning of the poem" (205). Moreover, in Wilkinson's words you may hear echoes of an even more venerable tradition—the anti-utilitarian tradition of aestheticism. But there's a big difference between a Wilkinson and a Brooks, or any of a host of other writers who set themselves against paraphrasability and utility one could mention (one thinks of Mallarmé's essay condemning newspapers, or of Oscar Wilde and his "Preface" to The Picture of Dorian Gray or his "Decay of Lying"). Unlike those resolutely apolitical writers, Wilkinson insists on describing the work he advocates as a political poetry.

For Wilkinson, a poem can be political by insisting on the inseparability of its significance from its form. By so insisting, the poem embodies a resistance to the idea of being treated as a means to any end beyond itself. It can remain private in circulation and resistant to interpretation because its political role is not to enter the public sphere and persuade readers. Rather, its role is to challenge the kinds of language that are used in public persuasion by providing a counter-example in the form of a very different kind of language. It is, in a sense, an implicit critique of all forms of linguistic instrumentalization. Ideally, it will resist incorporation into any part of the political or economic system—incorporation as product, as ideology, as entertainment property.

Of course, ideas such as this are by no means original, nor are they exclusive to Wilkinson or the Cambridge poets he studies and advocates. Behind Wilkinson's insistence on the political relevance of the difficult and elusive work he describes lie sentiments like those of Adorno's famous footnote to Philosophy of Modern Music, where he claims that "the closed work of art belongs to the bourgeois . . . and the fragmentary work, in its state of complete negativity, belongs to utopia" (126 n.55). Indeed, Wilkinson sees Jarvis as upholding an Adorno-inflected "negative utopianism" as "the necessary horizon for art" (371).

The insistence on the non-communicative, the non-paraphrasable, and the non-instrumental lies behind a host of techniques associated with the Cambridge School, and is invoked to justify the sometime refusal of mainstream publication and the cultivation of private networks of distribution. We see such an insistence on non-communication in the works of all of the major figures of the Cambridge School, not just in the works of Jarvis, who serves as Wilkinson's representative figure. One common technique is the disruption of traditional sentence structure, in which (to cite the words of the critic Peter Middleton) "syntax retains a haunting awareness of what authoritative statement and authorial sincerity sound like, yet the fragmentation of sense compels this communicative bond to question itself repeatedly" (782–3). Another common technique, also described by Middleton, involves the creation of complex discursive contexts for individual words, in which it becomes difficult for the reader to know in just what sense a word is meant, since these words come to "carry the full weight of variant meanings and etymological connections' rather than settling into a single, primary denotation" (783). If there is a single dominant technique of the school, however, it involves what we might call a kind of striation of discourses, a mixing of poetic verbal registers with resolutely un-poetic kinds of language—scientific discourse, technocratic forms of language, and the like. We see this technique throughout the work of Jeremy Prynne, which the critic David Shepard has characterized as an attempt to "recombine a language fragmented into technical jargons," incorporating the vocabulary of specialized discourses into his poetry and thereby "return[ing] this knowledge to the public sphere from its sequestration in the ivory tower" (Shepard).

"L'Extase de M. Poher," a poem from the 1971 collection *Brass*, is perhaps the best example of a poem that both displays Prynne's most characteristic techniques and foregrounds his sense of poetry being properly concerned with public, rather than private, matters. The poem begins by invoking private experience, and juxtaposing it with a disorderly public world:

Why do we ask that, as if the wind in the
telegraph wires were nailed up in some
kind of answer, formal derangement of

the species. Days and weeks spin by in
theatres, gardens laid out in rubbish, this
is the free hand to refuse everything.
  No
question provokes the alpha rhythm . . . (161)

We're given two confined spaces of aesthetic experience—theaters and gardens—both of which are spaces traditionally reserved for private pleasures. Gardens, of course, are either private preserves or public spaces designed for recreation, and the French context of the poem invites one to think of Rousseau's take on theater in the famous *Letter to M. D'Alembert*, in which he argues that theater turns the public into a group of passive, atomized individuals privately consuming a spectacle. These spaces are set against disorderly public space: the gardens are surrounded by rubbish-strewn streets with roughly hung telegraph wires. As N. H. Reeve and Richard Kerridge put it in their reading of the poem,

> Gardens are contained pastoral spaces, in which artistic or natural freedoms apparently prevail, but they are decorative spaces in the midst of urban environments less successful in suppressing unwanted residues. Gardens are maintained by the larger social economy as recreation grounds, small worlds of contrived harmony whose connection with the larger economy is concealed. . . . [T]he 'free hand to refuse everything' enjoys an ideal freedom incompatible with any social or political existence. The 'alpha rhythm' is an effect which occurs when the brain is idling . . . (8)

Prynne's gardens are associated with a kind of pastoral experience: they are places from which one can dismiss larger concerns and the disorderly world of rubbish with a wave of the hand.

Prynne has, however, invoked the world of private, aesthetic, pastoralized experience only to dismiss it. No poetry of private experience will do, for him:

    No
poetic gabble will survive which fails
to collide head-on with the unwitty circus:
   no history running
    with the french horn into
     the alley-way, no

> manifest emergence
> of valued instinct, no growth
> of meaning & stated order:
> we are too kissed & fondled,
> no longer instrumental
> to culture in 'this' sense or
> any free-range system of time (161)

This is most certainly poetry that resists any authoritative interpretation or paraphrasability, but certain elements do emerge into signification. The poetry of private experience cannot survive because it fails to take on the "unwitty circus" of public life and public discourses. The charge against private poetry, say Kerridge and Reeve, "is summed up by the double sense of 'instrumental' here," because "Prynne would want a poetry neither useful to some manipulative power, nor providing musical accompaniment to a commodifying culture" (9).

Against pastoralism, Prynne turns in the remaining parts of the poem to what he calls "a verbal smash-up piled / underfoot"—that is, to a kind of verbal rubbish. This consists of deliberately unpoetic fragments of language from various scientific and technological discourses: one three-line section, for example, reads "1. Steroid metaphrast / 2. Hyper-bonding of the insect / 3. 6% memory, etc" (161). It's a turn to language from outside the sphere of private experience. Rather than embracing any particular scientific or technocratic language, however, Prynne makes a collage of fragments, rendering such language useless and sub-verting it from its usual instrumental function. Pastoralism of the garden and private life is a false resistance to such discourses of power. For Prynne, the *détournement* and decontextualization of such languages is a more positive engagement of them: he acknowledges them, but refuses to allow them to function in the service of power.

This is, unquestionably, very odd stuff, and after the initial bewilderment, quite engaging. The poem charges us to leave our gardens of private experience and to engage with and subvert the languages through which the larger world is run (that opening image of telegraph wires foreshadows the poem's later concern with communication). One wonders, though, just what the nature of the poem's politics could be.

One might think of this as a kind of Bakhtinian poetry of dialogism and polyvocality, although generally the different kinds of language are collaged together, not associated with different speakers, as in the novels Bakhtin so admired. But critical advocates of this kind of poetry tend to take things further. N. H. Reeve and Richard Kerridge's claim for work of this kind is grandiose, but far from atypical: for them, Cambridge poetry "collide[s] with the powerful instrumental discourses of the culture" with the effect of "smashing them into pieces" (9).

The same critics have also claimed that, in bringing together different kinds of language and placing them in contexts not normally their own, Prynne's work "break[s] out of the institutional space allotted to poetry and literature in late-capitalist culture" (9). This claim is important, and has entered into the most institutionally authoritative accounts of Cambridge School poetry—*The Cambridge History of Twentieth Century Literature*, for example, claims that such poetry "is capable of challenging the public sphere" (770). The claim should give one pause, though, because here we see a certain messianic role claimed for the poetry: it will escape the confines of mere aesthetic entertainment and change the world. This gives rise, or ought to give rise, to a number of questions, such as: *how?* and *for whom?* and *with what demonstrable consequence?*

The messianic role assigned to Cambridge School poetry by its more ardent advocates is all the more puzzling when one considers the publication venues and distribution networks that the poets tended to choose for their work. Prynne's publishing career is indicative of the general tendency among these poets to avoid prominent publishing: most poets of the school, argues Peter Barry, "learned their clinically modest stance from Prynne" (158). While the career trajectory of many more mainstream poets involves beginning with modest private printings or fugitive small-press publications, then moving on to larger academic and commercial presses, Prynne's career follows the opposite trajectory. His first collection *Force of Circumstance and Other Poems* appeared in 1962 under the Routledge and Kegan Paul imprint. Rather than celebrating what another kind of poet might see as an auspicious beginning, though, Prynne (who came to see the poems of the collection as too formally conservative) ordered all unsold copies destroyed (March-Russell).

Prynne's second book, *Kitchen Poems*, published by Cape Goliard in 1968, was the last work of his to appear from a conventional press until Bloodaxe published *Poems* in 2005. In the interim, nearly thirty small collections appeared from tiny presses such as Equipage, Barque, and Blacksuede Boot Press. Such presses lacked commercial distribution and their books were rarely reviewed by the popular press. Some of Prynne's most important collections, such as 1975's *High Pink on Chrome* and 1983's *The Oval Window* lacked even this degree of public presence and were privately printed and distributed.

It is important to note that this wasn't entirely a matter of a forced exile from the world of larger presses and prominent literary journals, but also a deliberate choice on Prynne's part. When Eric Mottram, the head of the prestigious Poetry Society, wrote to Prynne in 1976 asking for work to print in the Society's journal *Poetry Review*, Prynne demurred, writing:

> At the moment I do not have anything suitable, so that I cannot respond very positively; and I must admit that there are times when I do not feel altogether enthusiastic about publishing work in magazines. (Letter to Eric Mottram)

Prynne's reticence here is remarkable, especially given the political ambitions of his work, and the reticence isn't merely passing: Prynne refused to let his work be included in the *Oxford Anthology of British and Irish Poetry*, edited by Keith Tuma, a sympathetic advocate of experimental British poetry, in 2001.

Can poets who choose such marginal venues and who eschew the pursuit of a more popular distribution really challenge the public sphere? Can they liberate knowledge from the ivory tower and return it to the public sphere? Can they, with such a small reach, smash the powerful instrumental discourses of the culture into pieces? For much of its history, Cambridge School poetry seems not so much to have challenged the public sphere, but to have withdrawn from it.

In more recent years, though, the obscurity of the Cambridge School has been mitigated, and it has obtained a rather modest public presence. Peter Barry dates the change from the 1990s, when, he says,

> ... the avant-garde began to establish an above-ground presence, which is to say, one which was visible beyond the parallel infrastructure of low-tech, small-press publication and distribution networks and regionally-based reading circuits. The result is that the 'parallel tradition' of poetry now has more of a public identity (see, for instance, the reputation of J. H. Prynne, the success of Salt Publishing, the prominence of online journals like *Jacket*, and the interest in this work from British academics, as evidenced by the British Electronic Poetry Centre at Southampton). (179)

Even these small steps onto the public stage have been greeted with ambivalence from all sides. Representatives of the mainstream press and the Cambridge School alike have expressed skepticism about the development. In 2004, for example, *The Sunday Times* printed an article on Prynne by Maurice Chittenden with the headline "Oxbridge Split by the Baffling Bard." Chittenden's article, occasioned by strong praise for Prynne in a new volume of *The Oxford English Literary History*, began with an image of a Prynne as a very private poet before contrasting his work with that of one of the most public figures in modern British poetry:

> Late at night a man sits writing verse in a deserted Cambridge college library before heading home with his latest work in the basket of his bicycle. Could this really be Britain's greatest living poet? The belated discovery of J. H. Prynne, a bard who usually sells his work in pamphlets with print runs no more than 500, has split the worlds of academia and poetry.... The problem for many who read Prynne is that the words seem to swim over the page with no decipherable meaning. His abstract work contrasts with the more straightforward style of poets such as Larkin. (Chittenden)

The question animating Chittenden's article is whether one can be a great poet without cultivating a broad readership. Significantly, there is no discussion of the public themes or political implications of Prynne's work in Chittenden's article. Rather, he chooses to focus on Prynne's deliberate privacy: "Prynne," writes Chittenden, "usually shuns interviews and refuses to be photographed for the sleeves of his books." As far as the mainstream press is concerned, it is not Prynne's politics so much as it is his medium of publication and his eschewal of publicity that constitutes Prynne's message.

Ambivalence about the modest public presence of Cambridge School poetry since the 1990s comes from within the movement, too. One Cambridge poet, Tony Lopez, takes on the issue of growing publicity in his 2002 poem "About Cambridge." The poem exhibits one of the signature stylistic features of Cambridge poetry—the dialogic cross-cutting of different forms of discourse—in this case combining the language of commercial real-estate with stereotypical images of pastoralized academic privilege. Certainly there's a political point about the economic basis of such privilege in the poem, but there's more at work here. From the opening couplet ("About Cambridge they were never wrong / the old masters . . .") onwards, much of the Lopez's poem alludes to Auden's famous "Musée des Beaux Arts," a poem about the private nature of suffering in a busy and uncaring world. The concern with private versus public experience comes to the fore in the second half of the poem, most of which consists of an anaphoric incantation invoking a lost community of Cambridge poets. The idyllic community of poet-radicals seems to Lopez to have come to an end for a variety of reasons, including death, personal animosity, and significantly, the migration of some of the poets from the world of privately printed and circulated pamphlets to the larger world of more prominent, mainstream publishers. The community existed, says Lopez, "before Kelvin Corcoran left Reality"—that is, before the poet Kelvin Corcoran left the micro-press Reality Street Editions. It existed before other poets moved on, too:

> before Jeremy Prynne became a BLOODAXE poet
> before John James was collected by SALT
> before Peter Riley signed a transfer deal to CARCANET (Lopez)

and it existed before Tom Raworth and Rod Mengham went on to their modest public successes, "before the Raworth.com flotation / before Mengham was re-issued in PENGUIN." For Lopez, the movement toward a public presence by some poets associated with Cambridge is a fall from grace.

A similar ambivalence about the public presence of Cambridge poetry comes across in a statement by Keston Sutherland, a younger poet of the Cambridge School with a particular affinity for Prynne (Sutherland received a doctorate at Cambridge after completing his thesis, *J. H. Prynne and Philology*). In a 2008 discussion on a British Poetry email list devoted to discussion of experimental poetry, Sutherland engaged in an exchange with Chris Hamilton-Emery of Salt Publishing regarding Prynne's public image. Replying to Hamilton-Emery's claim that Prynne has developed a mystique even among those poetry readers ill acquainted with his poetry, Sutherland says:

> I suppose that's probably true, but before I went along with it I'd want to distinguish between readers and consumers. It must assuredly be true that lots of people have bought Prynne's books because they think he's a weird or fascinating figure, and I'm sure the great majority of those consumers do take a look inside and maybe get to the end once or even twice. I don't think I'm disparaging that use of the object if I say that for Prynne at least it wouldn't amount to "reading" the book, just as it wouldn't amount to knowing, or looking closely at, a painting if I just lingered in front of it at the National Gallery for a minute or two. On Prynne's terms, at least, and perhaps they are not uncommon among members of this list, being a reader of poetry means engaging closely and carefully with it, staking an intimacy on the work of interpretation, in some way perhaps even needing that intimacy or submitting to it as a sort of definition of oneself, or the component of a definition. (see Archambeau)

There's something like resentment here for the kind of reader who reads poetry casually. The only true reader of Prynne, Sutherland implies, is one who devotes his life to Prynne's poetry, letting that devotion become a central part of one's identity.

It is significant that Sutherland doesn't see this kind of intense devotion as something relevant to all kinds of poetry. "Some poetry demands and makes possible that sort of intimacy more than other poetry," he writes. While Sutherland tells us that he imagines many poets "are more interested in readers, even to the no doubt partly pathological extent that they'd prefer three readers to a hundred consumers," he draws a clear line between the poets who merit these true readers and those who'd prefer consumers: "leave out," he says, "the Andrew Motions and other ditzy glamour models of Oxford." There's a powerful sense of Prynne's work not belonging in the public sphere with that of Andrew Motion and his kind. Like Lopez, Sutherland looks longingly back on a time when Prynne's work (and that of many other Cambridge School poets) was privately published and circulated only among the truly devoted.

Clearly, the Cambridge move toward publicity doesn't sit easily with either the mainstream press or the poets themselves, no matter how public-spirited and political the concerns of those poets may be. As to the messianic role claimed for the poetry, it seems to bear relevance and consequence only for the tiniest of readerships. Such a limited reach isn't in itself of any particular importance—it is, after all, the condition of much poetry. The small size of its audience does present a powerful contradiction, however, if one of the main claims made for the kind of poetry in question is its ability to enter the public sphere and challenge the prevailing ideologies.

This contradiction is, in fact, one of Peter Riley's main concerns in his response to John Wilkinson. Riley challenges Wilkinson's claims for Cambridge School poetry, saying:

> For Wilkinson as for most other commentators on the forward side of things, to speak of poetical virtue is to speak of political virtue, there is no distinction. Poems and poetical thinking are politically good or they have no good in them. . . . The one big claim left to the poem, is that it (rather 'somehow') holds the answer or counter to political harm by occulted inference. . . . It is not just that the poet 'knows better' than the working politician . . . but that only the poet has the spirit to inhabit the sphere of total oppositional negation which is the only political register to be tolerated. Doesn't this mean that in a sense there is actually a withdrawal from politics, from the politics that happens and can happen, into one that can't possibly? An understanding of how politics works and how amelioration can be wrought through the science of it, of what the mechanisms are and so of what could be done—all this would be beneath us? To assume that you can go straight from aesthetics to ethics is worrying enough, but aren't the two here fused into one substance? (Letter, *Chicago Review* 222)

The contradictions of a publicly concerned poetry that works largely by negation and obscurity come to a head here. It isn't just the idea that such poetry doesn't so much engage politics as it withdraws from politics that bothers Riley, either: he's haunted by the sense that poets of this kind have become elitists. After the passage quoted above comes Riley's *cri de coeur*, directed toward the avant-garde community in which he himself has much standing: "How did we get to be so *haughty*?" (222).

In a reply to Riley in a subsequent issue of *Chicago Review*, Wilkinson's faith in the messianic political power of the Cambridge School appears to remain unshaken. He still maintains that the Cambridge mode of combining lyrical language with language from economic, scientific, and technological discourses—a poetry of "lyric writing tied to other modes of writing"—is "more likely to exert a political influence" than more traditional kinds of poetry (231). While Wilkinson doesn't directly address the question of whether there has been any actual political effect, he does seem to have been sensitized to the issue, and claims that the moment of truth is yet to come. Cambridge poetry, specifically the poetry of younger poets like Keston Sutherland and Andrea Brady, still has the possibility of bringing about real change, says Wilkinson, because "their poetry is being written at a point of historical convergence where it might exercise an incidental political potency" (232).

Wilkinson's view, though, seems more and more beleaguered. Among poets of the Cambridge School, Riley is not alone in his disaffection with the idea that obscure and formally difficult poetry has a significant political role to play. As Andrew Duncan, a poet and former student of Prynne affiliated with the Cambridge School recently put it "form as politics" is a "mirage" (244). Such criticism comes, increasingly, from beyond the Cambridge School itself. In the very same issue of *Chicago Review* in which Wilkinson defends himself against Riley, for example, we find a review of Prynne's *To Pollen* in which the author, the American poet Kent Johnson, addresses himself directly to Prynne. After comparing Prynne's project to that of American Language Poetry, Johnson says: "the political impulses of such writing are well rehearsed, and I believe you have done a bit of that yourself. But is it enough? Is it possible avant poetry has begun to hit its head against an increasingly comfortable and welcoming wall?" (223). It's an odd image, that comforting wall against which one hits one's head, but it is an apt one, giving us both the apparent futility of Cambridge School poetry's political ambitions and a sense of the comforting private confinement in which it has so often circulated.

Works Cited

Adorno, Theodor. *Philosophy of Modern Music*. Trans. Anne G. Mitchell and Wesley V. Blomster. London: Continuum, 2003. Print.

Archambeau, Robert. "Fit Audience Though Few: Cambridge Poetry and its Readers." *Samizdat Blog*. Robert Archambeau, 2 July 2007. Web. 11 Feb. 2013.

Auden, W. H. *The Orators: An English Study*. London: Faber and Faber, 1932. Print.

Barry, Peter. *Poetry Wars: British Poetry of the 1970s and the Battle of Earls Court*. Cambridge: Salt, 2006. Print.

Brooks, Cleanth. *The Well-Wrought Urn: Studies in the Structure of Poetry*. New York: Harcourt, 1956. Print.

Chittenden, Maurice. "Oxbridge Split by the Baffling Bard." *The Sunday Times*. Times Newspapers Limited, 22 Feb 2004. Web. 1 July 2010.

Duncan, Andrew. *The Failure of Conservatism in Modern British Poetry*. Cambridge: Salt, 2003. Print.

Johnson, Kent. Rev. of *To Pollen* by Jeremy Prynne. *Chicago Review* 53: 2/3 (2007): 218–25. Print.

Lopez, Tony. "About Cambridge." *Jacket* 20. John Tranter, 1 Dec 2002. Web. 1 Mar. 2008.

Mallarmé, Stéphane. "The Book: A Spiritual Instrument." *Critical Theory Since Plato*. Ed. Hazard Adams. New York: Harcourt, 1992. 674–76. Print.

March-Russell, Paul. "J. H. Prynne." *The Literary Encyclopedia*. The Literary Dictionary Company, 21 Jan 2005. Web. 10 June 2008.

Middleton, Peter. "Poetry After 1970." *The Cambridge History of Twentieth Century Literature*. Ed. Laura Marcus and Peter Nicholls. Cambridge: Cambridge University Press, 2004. 768–86. Print.

Prynne, Jeremy. Letter to Eric Mottram, 22 June 1976. The Eric Mottram Collection. King's College, London. Document: Mottram 4/2/52.

Prynne, Jeremy. *Poems*. Highgreen: Bloodaxe, 2005. Print.

Reeve, N. H., and Richard Kerridge. *Nearly Too Much: The Poetry of J. H. Prynne*. Liverpool: Liverpool University Press, 1995. Print.

Riley, Peter. Letter. *Chicago Review*, 53:1 (2007), 221–27. Print.

Rousseau, Jean-Jacques. *Letter to M. D'Alembert on the Theater*. Trans. Allan Bloom. Ithaca: Cornell University Press, 1960. Print.

Shepard, David. Rev. of *The Furtherance* by J. H. Prynne. *Verse*. English Department, University of Richmond, 20 Oct 2004. Web. 1 June 2008.

Sutherland, Keston. "J. H. Prynne and Philology." Diss. Cambridge University, 2004.

Wilde, Oscar. "The Decay of Lying." *Critical Theory Since Plato*. Ed. Hazard Adams. New York: Harcourt, 1992. 658–70. Print.

Wilde, Oscar. Preface. *The Picture of Dorian Gray*. Ed. Isobel Murray. New York: Barnes and Noble, 2003. xxiii–xxv. Print.

Wilkinson, John. Rev. of *The Unconditional* by Simon Jarvis. *Chicago Review*, 52: 2/3/4 (2007): 369–75. Print.
Wilkinson, John. Letter. *Chicago Review*, 53:2/3 (2007): 231–38. Print.

Negative Legislators
Exhibiting the Post-Avant

I s there such a thing as post-avant poetry? If so, what makes it post-avant? And why is it as it is? The answers, in the briefest form I can devise, are "yes," "reticence about large claims," and "generational experience," respectively. Such answers are, of course, brief and crude enough to be entirely indefensible. A slightly more extended treatment in the form of a series of exhibits will, I hope, be slightly less indefensible.

Exhibit A: Who You Callin' Post-Avant?

Reginald Shepherd, in an essay called "Who You Callin' Post-Avant?" offers as good a short definition of the post-avant as one is likely to find:

> 'Post-avant' (as in, 'post-avant-garde'—insider groups love shorthand) poets can be described as writers who, at their best, have imbibed the lessons of the modernists and their successors in what might be called the experimental or avant-garde stream of American poets, including the Objectivists (especially Oppen and Zukofsky), what have been called the New American Poetries (from Jack Spicer and Robert Duncan to John Ashbery and Frank O'Hara), particularly the Projectivist / Black Mountain School and the New York School(s), and the Language poets (including such poets and polemicists as Charles Bernstein and Ron Silliman), without feeling the need (as so many other poetic formations have) to pledge allegiance to a particular group identity. . . . Though

many of these poets have projects and even systems, there aren't a lot of programs. There's much prose writing and thinking about poetry, and many, many blogs (this is a very wired 'generation'), but not many manifestoes. (n.p.)

Post-avants are poets who tend to shy away from the autobiographical, anecdotal poetry that has made up the bulk of the poetry found in established American poetry magazines. "But," writes Shepherd, "they don't just discard the self as an ideological illusion." In addition,

> . . . they incorporate fracture and disjunction without enthroning it as a ruling principle. They are interested in exploring, interrogating, and sometimes exploding language, identity, and society, without giving up on the pleasures, challenges, and resources of the traditional lyric. Their work combines the lyric's creative impulse with the critical impulse of Language poetry. Theirs is a magpie-like eclecticism that draws from whatever materials, traditions, and techniques are of interest and of use, however seemingly incompatible, however ideologically opposed historically. They don't try to destroy the past for the sake of the future, or trumpet teleological notions (let alone grand narratives) of artistic 'progress' or 'advance' . . . (n.p.)

The eclecticism, the crossing of the lyrical with the non-lyrical, and the generally non-heroic sense of the poet's historical mission—I've seen these over and over in the works of the poets of my generation. The non-heroic, non-manifesto-writing ethos certainly applies to the post-avant sense of artistic progress—and this is different from several prior generations. When you read, say, Ezra Pound ("to break the pentameter, that was the first heave"), you get a sense that he really believes there's a kind of advance taking place (538). You get a similar sense from many critical accounts of what happened to poetry around the time of Robert Lowell's *Life Studies*: poets, it seemed, had suddenly *broken through* stuffy mid-century formalism and into a new, advanced form of freedom (in *Modern Poetry After Modernism* James Longenbach called this the "breakthrough narrative" version of American poetry). And although it has sometimes been satirized by some of the poets, there's often a heroic strain in language poetry polemics, a sense of intrepidly bearing the art forward to some New Jerusalem while fighting back the undead armies of tradition. There's little of this heroic sense in the post-avant. The post-avant has no significant interest in making grand claims of any kind. Not only does it eschew a sense of heroic poetic progress: it eschews large political or spiritual claims. For better or for worse, you just don't find anyone affiliated with the post-avant acting the revolutionary or guru the way Allen Ginsberg did.

Exhibit B: The Negative Legislator

It is no accident, then, that George Oppen has had a kind of renaissance among poets of the post-avant. Consider what James Longenbach says about him in what we'll call Exhibit B—a passage from a 2008 essay in *The Nation*:

> Neither before nor after his silence [a nearly three-decade hiatus from publishing poetry] was Oppen inclined toward didactic poetry; he considered the rhetorical excess of political poems—like the rhetorical excess of political meetings—to be 'merely excruciating.' In the early 1930s Oppen was associated with the Objectivist movement, a loose association of avant-garde poets that also included Louis Zukofsky, Charles Reznikoff and Lorine Niedecker. And while *Discrete Series*, his first book, is starkly elliptical, his later work combines Objectivist precision with a tender lyricism that his more staunchly experimental colleagues disdained.... However adamant Oppen's convictions, his meticulously shaped lines embody a music of deference—a constitutional unwillingness to dominate the world by virtue of having understood it. (n.p.)

Here, Oppen appears as a man with ethical qualms about making big claims. There's much truth to this representation of Oppen. After all, Oppen lived through the endless political wrangling of the American left of the 1930s: the splitting of Trotskyist hairs while the world burned, starved, and suffered horribly, often under the banner of one or another totalizing ideology. It's hard for most of us to imagine anything like the ideological pressure of a time when even so gentle and benevolent a soul as W. H. Auden found himself advocating political violence, as he did when he wrote of the need for "the conscious acceptance of guilt in the necessary murder" in his great-but-troubling (and later revised) poem "Spain" (425).

Oppen emerged from this context more honorably than did most, including Auden. Oppen never presented himself as having special political insight by virtue of his status as poet, nor did he sing praises to violence. One of the ways he expressed his qualms was at the level of form: his lyricism itself was often checked by various elisions and distancing strategies, preventing the reader from losing critical distance in the lyric moment, and preventing the poet from proclaiming any grand ideological truth. This isn't the poet as Shelley's visionary unacknowledged legislator announcing the laws of the future. This is, rather, the poet as a humbler figure, one who has absorbed the same lesson as had the Adorno of *Negative Dialectics*: to walk in fear of totalizing claims. In fact, the Oppen that Longenbach presents brings to mind that other saint in the post-avant poet's canon of forefathers, John Ashbery—especially the John Ashbery described by Stephen Stepanchev as a poet who "seems to fear too much coherence as being a form of dishonesty or falseness" because "an orderly syntax sometimes forces the poet to lie, to say easy things that he had not intended" (189).

This kind of Oppen-and-Ashbery reticence regarding statement, didacticism, prescription, visionary experience, and the like is itself a kind of ethical imperative. That is, there's an ethic to the "unwillingness to dominate the world" through didactic statement, and in the sense that "too much coherence [is] a form of dishonesty or falseness." The imperative here is negative, though: make no laws, tout no truth-claims, avow no total understanding. It is a kind of Hippocratic oath for poets, urging them to do no harm.

Exhibit C: Negative Legislation

Gregory Fraser's poem "Miles," from the collection *A Different Bother*, provides an example of many of the qualities of post-avant poetry:

> I piped the dizzy for who knows how, argued,
> *Without catacombs there can stand no town,*
> and one night slid my head through the crown
> at church, then followed a river glued

to its ember. Who couldn't predict my brass
would one day burst? That I, end-time, would stew
in a velvet folly? A bashful kid, I consented to
spoil the mildew's nap, decapitate the grass,

haul trash to the curb in bags that were, after
transport, trash themselves. Never once did I aid
the roaches treated like thugs in black suede.
By travel, I hoped to find not heaven, but a rafter

where mind and body hang, negating one another.
No such. Wind combed back the cattails, I
turned in a circle that wouldn't point. Why decry
the addict, who only seeks a different bother?

Someplace florid, a prince paints a topical picture.
Imagine—art about actual happenings! Of course,
of course, of course, of course,
the unathletic started in: *Old world with your*

lovely clarities, etc. Then I thought of the stars—
what trumpeted commotions fill their repertoires. (1)

The quatrains have a regular rhyme scheme (ABBA-CDDC etc.) culminating in a rhyming couplet at the end. The poem is a kind of extend-
ed-play Shakespearian sonnet, which itself shows something of the
historical openness of the post-avant. A hard-core avant-gardist of the
early twentieth century would sooner have been caught dining with a
petit-bourgeois policeman than have written such a thing, but the post-
avant is more open to such established forms. Such forms, after all, have
been problematized for so long there's no need to reject them as repressive norms. More importantly, though, the poem shows many of the
qualities Reginald Shepherd saw as typically post-avant. The poem
"problematize[s] and questions the notions of self and of personal
experience" without discarding "the self as an ideological illusion," as
Shepherd suggests the post-avant poem does. "I piped the dizzy for who
knows how" comes straight out of the John Berryman playbook, offering
an odd bit of diction and syntax that nevertheless obliquely suggest an
inner, emotional experience. And through the first few stanzas there's

a strong suggestion of Miles Davis' biography, albeit with a great deal of deliberate static on the channel. The post-avant poet, as Shepherd says, "incorporate[s] fracture and disjunction without enthroning it as a ruling principle"—and surely that's the sort of poet we have here: we see a developing self, and get a sense of its quotidian moments like taking out the trash. We also get a sense of the self in its social context—a troubled figure surrounded by those who can see the impending breakdown but don't do much to stop it ("who couldn't predict my brass / would one day burst"). There's a delicate balancing act going on between lyrical, confessional revelation and disjunction or fracture.

Moreover, the poem follows the project of the post-avant negative legislator: it refuses to judge, prescribe, or assume a position of moral authority—except, of course, inasmuch as such refusals are a kind of moral position. We see this most clearly toward the end, in lines like "Wind combed back the cattails, I / turned in a circle that wouldn't point. Why decry / the addict, who only seeks a different bother?" Turning in a circle that won't point: this is the negative legislator in his natural habitat, a kind of neo-negative capability, in which all contradictory positions and directions are explored, and none taken. That question about the addict adds to the impression of non-judgmentality: it implies a possible moral equivalence between the speaker and the junkie, each of whom is hooked into his own trip. On the one hand, the question seems to imply a "who's to judge?" position. On the other hand, it is a question, not a statement such as "Don't decry the addict . . ." so it remains ambiguous whether we're even meant to assume the relativism of "who's to judge?" We can turn around the circle all day, and it just won't let us end up pointing in a particular direction. This is the antithesis of didacticism or poetic legislation—except, again, for the possibility that a rigorous refusal to point in any particular direction is itself an ethical position, a kind of disinterestedness or even unworldliness.

Then there's the ending, where we're offered a glimpse of a different kind of art, one that *does* take up social positions, one that gets quite *litterature engagée* on us. The last six lines in which a "prince paints a topical picture," depict a kind of art concerned with actual happenings. But how does the poem coach us to feel about it? In a manner typical in post-avant poetry, it doesn't coach any one position. The fact that the topical picture is painted by a prince suggests a number of possibilities, most of them negative: that such art is antiquated; or despite any possible leftish sentiment, that it's ultimately the product of privilege; or that it's all a bit egomaniacal and self-important. Then again, there's the breathless "art about actual happenings!" which can read like a statement of envy at the prince's audacity, or as the opposite of that (in which case the breathlessness makes the line read as arch, as *faux-naif* excitement about a social project seen as banal). Then there's the wonderful "of course, / of course, of course, of course"—which signifies what? An admission that social engagement is needed, or important, or a necessary alternative to the kind of poem we're reading? Or perhaps it suggests a kind of impatient or world-weary dismissal of socially didactic art (one can read the phrases as if they were accompanied with a sigh). We're turning in a circle that won't let us point in any particular direction. Which is the point: it establishes the poet not as unacknowledged legislator, but as a negative legislator, whose one firm law is to make no other laws.

Exhibit D: Aeroflot Blue

> Her hair was totally 1950s Indiana Woolworth perfume clerk. You know—sweet but dumb—she'll marry her way out of the trailer park some day soon. But the dress was early '60s Aeroflot stewardess—you know—that really sad blue the Russians used before they all started wanting to buy Sonys and having Guy Laroche design their Politburo caps. . . . She really caught the sadness—she was the hippest person there. (Coupland 3)

There is, I think, a generational explanation for the post-avant embrace of negative legislation. If one came of age in the 1980s, one quite likely grew up with a distrust of grand narratives. We can find a sophisticated explanation of the phenomenon in Jean-François Lyotard's 1979 work *The Postmodern Condition: A Report on Knowledge*, in which he defines the mental condition of postmodern generations as "incredulity toward metanarratives" (xxiv). Or we can consider the experience of coming of age in Ronald Reagan's America—the spectacle of a nation full of flags, battleships, and the unalloyed joy and justice of the free market—a spectacle that, for many, didn't look like the country they lived in at all. The cognitive dissonance between the big narrative offered by Reagan's image factory and the harsher reality led to a skepticism about grand explanations. The condition was endemic, with large narratives seemingly under siege from all quarters. Did you believe Catholicism was a force for good? Suddenly one heard of all sorts of scandals involving the clergy. Were you a believer in Israel as a necessary haven for the victims of atrocity? Too many images of the treatment of the Palestinians were coming to light for that narrative to remain spotless. Was family the great saving force in a dark world? The boom in divorce put that belief in doubt. One reason Douglas Coupland's 1991 novel *Generation X* was such a success in its moment was how it captured the sense of disillusion. One of the opening images depicts a young woman at a party wearing a dress in a color that could only be described as "Aeroflot blue," and it captured the mood of the generation perfectly, with its washed-out reminder of a dead Grand Revolutionary Narrative. Growing up in the shadow of the failure of grand explanations, what course was left but to take the Hippocratic oath of negative legislation to practice one's art and do no harm?

Works Cited

Auden, W. H. *The English Auden: Poems, Essays, and Dramatic Writings, 1927–1939.* Ed. Edward Mendelson. London: Faber, 2001. Print.

Coupland, Douglas. *Generation X: Tales for an Accelerated Culture.* New York: St. Martin's, 1991. Print.

Fraser, Gregory. *A Different Bother.* Chicago: Beard of Bees Press, 2008. Print.

Longenbach, James. "A Test of Poetry." *The Nation.* The Nation, 11 Feb 2008. Web. 1 July 2011.

Lyotard, Jean-François. *The Postmodern Condition: A Report on Knowledge.* Trans. Geoff Bennington and Brian Massumi. Minneapolis: University of Minnesota Press, 1984. Print.

Pound, Ezra. *The Cantos.* New York: New Directions, 1996. Print.

Shepherd, Reginald. "Who You Callin' Post-Avant?" *Harriet.* The Poetry Foundation, 6 Feb 2008. Web. 1 July 2011.

Stepanchev, Stephen. *Modern American Poetry Since 1945: A Critical Survey.* New York: Harper and Row, 1965. Print.

When Poets Dream of Power

I t is difficult to know where to begin a discussion of poets and their relations to power: Longinus identified the decline of sublimity in Latin poetry with the political crisis of the Roman Republic; and Dante's hell is populated in large measure with figures consigned to the inferno as matters of political score-settling. Closer to our own age, and in our own language, we find the Elizabethan poets, many of whom were in one way or another members of the power elite of their time and place: Sir Thomas Wyatt, Henry Howard (the Earl of Surrey), Sir Edward Dyer, Sir Philip Sidney, Sir Walter Raleigh, Thomas Campion, Sir Henry Wotton, John Hoskins, Edmund Spenser. All those "sirs" give a picture of the situation: to a degree difficult for us to imagine, the literary elite and the power elite overlapped. Of the non-knighted and non-noble, Spenser rose from a humble background to become a significant landowner in Ireland, and Hoskins was a member of parliament. Campion, a successful physician, was an exception to the power elite rule. The overlap between power elite and poetry elite was considerable.

There was a long, slow differentiation of elites in the centuries that followed. But it is worth pausing in the eighteenth century, with Alexander Pope, among the first English poets to make money from putting poetry in the marketplace. He lived in a liminal period, when the system of relying on aristocratic patronage hadn't yet died off, and the market system was just beginning to show its potential for the right sort of author. The actual relation Pope had with power may, in fact, have been as a kind of housecat—one noble patron liked to stop Pope during readings and revise lines, such being the patron's prerogative. But Pope dreamed of himself as a kind of spiritual and moral advisor, not speaking directly on matters of immediate political urgency, but offering general principles that might inform the decisions of the powerful. Consider the opening of *An Essay on Man*:

> Awake, my St. John! leave all meaner things
> To low ambition, and the pride of kings.
> Let us (since life can little more supply
> Than just to look about us and to die)
> Expatiate free o'er all the scene of man;
> A mighty maze! but not without a plan;
> A wild, where weeds and flowers promiscuous shoot,
> Or garden, tempting with forbidden fruit.
> Together let us beat this ample field . . . (47)

The "St. John" is Henry St. John, Lord Bolingbroke, and one of Pope's most powerful friends. Pope envisions himself as a companion of the good Viscount Bolingbroke, and imagines the two of them engaged in aristocratic activities together (to beat the field was to send runners out into it with sticks to send birds flying up so they could be shot by the noble hunter and his companions). The tone is friendly, if a bit deferential, and the relationship to his Lordship is as philosophical guide: the world is a maze, but not without a plan—a plan the poet will explain to the Great Man in ways that will enable him to carry out his duties of state in a philosophically informed manner. If the deference might make some of us cringe, now, the proximity to power would make more than a few poets blanche with envy.

We start to get closer to a recognizably modern relationship of poetry and power with the Romantics—if only because the Romantics were often either radical bohemians with no direct influence on power (like Shelley) or government-sponsored former radicals whose views now appeared less threatening (like Wordsworth). The document of the time that seems most representative of the poet's dream of his relation to power is Shelley's "Defense of Poetry." It was never published in his lifetime, but has had a huge allure for generations of poets since—and why wouldn't it? It lets poets have their cake and eat it too. On the one hand, the poet is responsible only to his private vision, not the demands of the market or any kind of patron. On the other hand, the poet has enormous influence: his ideas shape the consciousness of the ages to come. All of this has its origins in Shelley's arguments with his father-in-law, the philosopher William Godwin: Godwin said philosophers were the primary thinkers of society, and poets should serve as publicists for philosophical ideas. Shelley turned the relationship around, saying that poets inspire everyone, including philosophers, to think in new ways. The process is gradual, spreading bit by bit from readers of the poet to those who are influenced at second or third or fourth hand. Hence the unacknowledged legislator. Of course there's no proof that the influence really takes place. One might say Shelley's dream of enormous influence is the product of a kind of alienation of the poet from power: Sir Walter Raleigh didn't look for such indirect influence on politics, and didn't need to. Nor did Alexander Pope look for some secret, long-term, possible-but-unprovable political influence: if he wanted political influence, he buttered Lord Bolingbroke's toast and made some subtle, inoffensive suggestions. You have to be far removed from actual legislators to pin your hopes on a small scale, but just possibly viral, influence on public opinion.

The alienation of the poet from power did not continue uninterrupted from the Romantics to our own time. "Tennyson," Eliot once wrote, was "the saddest of all English poets, among the Great in Limbo, the most instinctive rebel against the society in which he was the perfect conformist" ("In Memoriam" 295). Eliot is certainly right to sense a conflict at the heart of Tennyson. That conflict was, at its root, the conflict between the Romantic heritage of alienation and a social role on offer to the Victorian poet: the role of public moralist. Tennyson, in ways more instinctive than calculated, embraced this public role. Literary public moralists both propagated the values of the middle class and urged the amelioration of those values in an effort that, collectively, made a major contribution to the cementing of a social order

beneficial to that class. This public moralist is the Tennyson most famous
in his own day, the teacher of domestic order in *The Princess* and *Idylls of
the King,* the prophet of self-denial in *Maud* and *Enoch Arden,* the instiller
of faith in progress in "Locksley Hall," and the obedient servant of
empire in "The Charge of the Light Brigade." This public moralist
acting on behalf of the bourgeois order did not, and could not, sit at
ease with another side of Tennyson, the late-Romantic poet who'd loved
Keats' poetry, and who had carved "Byron is dead" into stone when, as
a youth, he'd heard of the great Romantic's passing. Part of Tennyson
was always loyal to one of the main Romantic ideas of the poet—that of
the poet as an alienated outsider. Tennyson spent a lifetime at war with
himself, his intellectual and aesthetic inheritance ever at odds with the
social role he was asked to play, and was so richly rewarded—in sales, in
status, in honors—for playing. Tennyson was far from insincere in his
moralizing on behalf of the triumphant Victorian bourgeoisie. He was,
after all, connected to the powerful class on whose behalf he wrote, and
he had seen enough of the social disorder of the 1830s and '40s to
understand the value of an orderly society. But he was far from uncon-
flicted.

Like the Romantics, the modernists tended to be alienated from
power, and to dream of worlds in which that alienation could be wished
away. Ezra Pound makes for an interesting case in point. He was always
concerned with the social role of the poet: in the essay "The Wisdom of
Poetry" he declared that "in former ages, poets were historians, gene-
alogists, religious functionaries" (*Selected Prose* 360–61). In his own day,
though, the role seemed rather less clear. Mass culture, Pound intuited,
had something to do with the change. "Hugh Selwyn Mauberley" expresses the alienation of the poet in the age of mass communications, incipient mass consumption, and the economic importance of the masses
whose tastes were so different from those of the elites poets had once
served:

> The age demanded an image
> Of its accelerated grimace,
> Something for the modern stage,
> Not, at any rate, an Attic grace;

Not, not certainly, the obscure reveries
Of the inward gaze;
Better mendacities
Than the classics in paraphrase!

The "age demanded" chiefly a mould in plaster,
Made with no loss of time,
A prose kinema, not, not assuredly, alabaster
Or the "sculpture" of rhyme. (61–62)

The poem was published in 1920. A year later, Pound offered his dream of a solution to the problem of the poet's role in modern times. As it turned out, it was a remarkably Shelleyan dream of indirect influence. Here's a passage from the article "How to Read," which ran in the *New York Herald Tribune*:

> The individual cannot think and communicate his thought, the gover-
> nor and legislator cannot act effectively or frame his laws without words,
> and the solidity and validity of these words is in the care of the damned
> and despised literati . . . when their very medium, the very essence of
> their work, the application of word to thing goes rotten, i.e. becomes
> slushy and inexact, or excessive or bloated, the whole machinery of social
> and of individual thought and order goes to pot. (*Literary Essays* 21)

In this dream of poetic influence on power, the "governor or legislator" probably has no idea that his language and his mental framework have been conditioned by the poet. But in controlling the meanings of words, poets have an enormous power as unacknowledged legislators. One might well argue that it isn't the literati who control the meaning of words, since their contribution to these matters is quantitatively minimal in relation to the products of mass culture. But arguments are for reasoners, and Pound isn't reasoning here so much as he's dreaming of a way for the things he loves to be important not just to him, but to the polity at large. There is a kind of will-to-power at work here, and a compensatory gesture—the sort of thing Seamus Heaney, in a very different context, would call "pap for the dispossessed" (47)—the dispossessed in the present instance being poets in modernity.

T. S. Eliot also dreamed of a closer relationship to power than was actually available to him. In fact, in his quiet, understated way Eliot actually dreamed of immense power for poets—or, at any rate, for the right kind of poet, the poet who was, like himself, a Christian intellectual. Like Pound, he dreamed of having enormous cultural authority; and like Pound, he had to find some kind of way to get past the fact of poetry's marginalization. He felt deeply that intellectuals should have some kind of leading role in culture, but, as he said in a letter to Philip Mariet: "the whole question of the popularization of ideas (and the avoidance of perversion of them) deserves our consideration, and I don't know where to begin" (Collini 314).

What to do, in a modern age that seemed to demand "A prose kinema, not, not assuredly, alabaster / Or the "sculpture" of rhyme"? Rather than directly facing the problem of modernity, Eliot does an end-run, and dreams of a return to the kind of pre-modern world where (he imagines) the poet and man of letters could take a leading role in culture and society. Eliot's most notorious presentation of this dream of pre-modernity comes in his book of criticism *After Strange Gods*. Here he tells us that "stability is obviously necessary" in society, and that the most stable kind of society is the agrarian. The modern industrial world is too fraught with perpetual change, and too prone to creating a culturally fragmented world. "The population should be homogenous," says Eliot, and "what is still more important is unity of religious background." He then makes his infamous comment about not wanting too many freethinking Jews in such a society (19–20).

Why is this social and religious homogeneity so important to Eliot? Not everyone is aware of how much commentary Eliot wrote for the specifically Christian press, but if we root around in this considerable body of work, we can come up with quite a clear picture of what a Christian society meant for Eliot. One thing it meant was this: a society that was to be guided, ultimately, by intellectuals. Eliot's book *The Idea of a Christian Society* makes it even more specific. Here, he tells us that the general populace should be thought of as a 'Christian Community.' This community should be led by a 'Community of Christians' composed of practicing Christians of intellectual superiority. This all sounds a little bit like the guardians in Plato's *Republic*, but Eliot hastens to clarify the informality of this community:

> The Community of Christians is not an organization, but a body of indefinite outline; composed of both clergy and laity, of the more conscious, more spiritually and intellectually developed of both. It will be their identity of belief and aspiration, their background of common culture, which will enable them to influence and be influenced by each other, and collectively to form the conscious mind and the consciousness of the nation. (43)

Like Pound and Shelley, Eliot dreams of influencing the consciousness of the masses, of being a kind of unacknowledged legislator. But instead of dreaming of an unrealistic power within the existing society, Eliot dreams of an entirely plausible kind of power—in a society that doesn't exist.

Robert Pinsky makes for an interesting contrast with Eliot, in that the kind of ideal society he imagines couldn't be more different from Eliot's. In contrast to Eliot's stable, homogenous, theologically oriented society, Pinsky celebrates the now-old ideal of the American melting pot. Pinsky's poem "The Figured Wheel" is about cultural syncretism, and "Ginza Samba," his poem in praise of the saxophone, is really a poem in praise of cultures mixing and melding (it is, after all, the tale of how a Belgian instrument became a jazz instrument—that is, an African-American instrument). This is progressive, compared to Eliot, though some might argue that it's a bit reactionary in the age of identity politics. Pinsky is not concerned with celebrating particularist identity, except at the scale of the nation as a whole. He's interested in the idea of America as a modern, polyglot place of cultural melding. It's not quite a utopia, though, especially because of the racial inequities— and it's in the discussion of race in the book-length poem *An Explanation of America* that we see Pinsky trying out different ideas of how the poet might relate to power.

Racial division, says Pinsky in *An Explanation of America*, makes America "as Malcom X once said, / A prison." "Living inside a prison, / Within its many other prisons, what / Should one aspire to be? a kind of chaplain?" he asks. The role of chaplain, the comforter of the people, appeals to him, but only momentarily. His faith in that role soon fades: "But chaplains, I have heard, are often powers, / Political, within their prisons, patrons / And mediators between frightened groups" (14). Consoling will solve nothing. Indeed, the very possibility of consolation seems beyond reach:

> No kind of chaplain ever will mediate
> Among the conquering, crazed immigrants
> Of El Camino and the Bergen Mall,
> The Jews who dream up the cowboy films, the Blacks
> Who dream the music, the people who dream the cars
> And ways of voting, the Japanese and Basques . . . (14)

The chaplain idea—the notion of being a mediator between different groups with conflicting interests—is more or less the role Matthew Arnold proposes for the literati in *Culture and Anarchy*. But if Pinsky dreams of having such a role, he's also skeptical of it, thinking it both impossible and prone to co-optation.

If Pinsky seeks something like a Victorian role for the poet, he does so in both literary and cultural circumstances that limit the possibilities for success. Firstly, the public moralist is didactic, and we live in a literary climate radically at odds with the notion of the didactic. Pinsky's early critical book *The Situation of Poetry* sets out to defend statement-oriented, discursive, and even didactic or moralistic poetry against fragmentation, hermeticism, and communication by image (the old modernist premises), but this is a reactive move, and no matter how much more didactic and discursive Pinsky is than the norm of our time, he doesn't come close to the didacticism of the public side of Tennyson. Everything has a bit of negative capability to it, even a trace of inconclusivity that makes public moralism difficult. But the more serious factors limiting Pinsky's ability to take on a kind of Tennysonian role are social: the reading audience now is more fragmented than in Tennyson's day, and one cannot speak to it with the confidence that one is voicing its views, echoing them back at their creators.

Whatever its feasibility in our time may be, perhaps the most admirable thing about Pinsky's dream of how he might make poetry relate to power is his doubting of his own dream, his consciousness of how even the most idealistic poets have betrayed their best selves through their co-optation by political power. His meditation on this issue is haunting. Urging us, in 1979, to think of the European poets, he says:

> Posed thoughtfully with their cigarettes or scarves
> As photographed for a fascist anthology
> Of forty years ago, above their verses
> About a landscape, tribe, or mystic shadow:
> Caught in the prison of their country's earth
> Or its Romantic potential, born of death
> Or of a pure idea " . . . *Italy*
> (Germany, Russia, America, Roumania)
> *Had never really been a country,"* a book
> Might say, explaining something. (30)

The "something" is ominous, hinting at extreme nationalism and worse. The fact that the phrase echoes the title of the book Pinsky's reader is holding—*An Explanation of America*—indicates just how acute Pinsky's self-consciousness about the possibility of co-optation can be. It is a self-consciousness that came too late to some of his modernist predecessors.

Works Cited

Collini, Stefan. *Absent Minds: Intellectuals in Britain*. Oxford: Oxford University Press, 2006. Print.

Eliot, T. S. *After Strange Gods: A Primer of Modern Heresy*. London: Faber, 1934. Print.

———. "In Memoriam." *Selected Essays of T. S. Eliot*. New York: Harcourt, Brace, and World, 1964. 286–95. Print.

———. *The Idea of a Christian Society*. London: Faber, 1939. Print.

Heaney, Seamus. *North*. London: Faber, 1985. Print.

Pinsky, Robert. *An Explanation of America*. Princeton: Princeton University Press, 1979. Print.

Pope, Alexander. *The Poetical Works of Alexander Pope*. Vol. 3. London: Roveray, 1804. Print.

Pound, Ezra. *Literary Essays*. New York: New Directions, 1968. Print.

———. *Selected Poems*. New York: New Directions, 1957. Print.

———. *Selected Prose, 1909–1965*. New York: New Directions, 1973. Print.

Can Poems Communicate?

"Where does one go in one's writing," the grand old poet-critic Donald Davie once wondered, "if the King James Bible has become a recondite source?" (21). The problem Davie framed is an old one, and was already eating away at W. B. Yeats in the 1890s, when he worried over whether there was a public language through which poems could connect with the wider world. What can a poet do when he or she can't expect a shared frame of cultural reference with an audience?

Yeats has taken a lot of criticism over the decades for his interest in the supernatural, but much of Yeats' thinking about magic was actually a way of thinking about the nature of symbolic communication, and the place of symbols in modern life. Consider the following passage from his 1901 essay on magic:

> I believe in the practice and philosophy of what we have agreed to call magic, in what I must call the evocation of spirits, though I do not know what they are, in the power of creating magical illusions, in the visions of truth in the depths of the mind when the eyes are closed; and I believe in three doctrines, which have, as I think, been handed down from early times, and been the foundations of nearly all magical practices. These doctrines are:—(1) That the borders of our mind are ever shifting, and that many minds can flow into one another, as it were, and create or reveal a single mind, a single energy. (2) That the borders of

our memories are as shifting, and that our memories are part of one great memory, the memory of Nature herself. (3) That this great mind and great memory can be evoked by symbols. (29)

There are two ways to read this passage. What we might call the strong interpretation would stress the supernaturalism. In this view, Yeats is talking about a kind of collective soul, or group dreaming, or telepathy, or symbols that radiate throughout creation. I prefer what we might call the weak interpretation of the passage. In this view, Yeats is saying something not too different from what people like Jung or Northrop Frye or any number of structural anthropologists have said: that there are large cultural systems of symbols and images, that these symbols and images inform our thinking and unite groups of people in terms of their assumptions and ideals, often in ways those groups do not apprehend consciously. Of course in actuality both strong and weak readings apply. Yeats wants to get away from Arnoldian skepticism, and the atheism of his Darwinian father: hence the supernaturalism. He also wants to get away from the individualism that the triumphant late-Victorian bourgeoisie rode down the boulevards of the capitals of Europe like a giant white pachyderm: hence the interest in collective experience.

The weak reading, with Yeats trying to articulate his sense that communication depends upon large, enduring sets of collectively apprehended symbols, is the reading relevant for present purposes. The problem, for him, was that modernity had become inimical to such symbolic systems. Just after the passage above he writes:

> I often think I would put this belief in magic from me if I could, for I have come to see or to imagine, in men and women, in houses, in handicrafts, in nearly all sights and sounds, a certain evil, a certain ugliness, that comes from the slow perishing through the centuries of a quality of mind that made this belief and its evidences common over the world. (30)

Yeats' disgust with modernity has many sources. The most unpleasant moments of his childhood took place in then hyper-modern London, where he was despised for his Irishness. He identified modernity with the English oppressors of Ireland. In addition, the intellectual atmosphere of his childhood home was saturated with Pre-Raphaelitism, with the medievalism of Ruskin, and with William Morris, who wondered, in his great essay "How I Became a Socialist," whether modern civilization was "all to end in a counting-house on the top of a cinder-heap?" (280). But the problem is also one of communication, and, ultimately, of cultural cohesion. In Yeats' view, we were once united by a "centuries old quality of mind" that modern, urban, industrial capitalism has somehow swept to the sidelines.

A better sense of the endangered world of shared symbols emerges in Yeats' essay "What is 'Popular' Poetry?" which first appeared in print a year after the essay on magic, and is collected with it in the volume *Ideas of Good and Evil*. Here, Yeats distinguishes between three types of poetry: popular poetry, coterie poetry, and poetry of the unwritten tradition. For Yeats, the "unwritten tradition" (10) is the oral folk tradition, still viable in the more out-of-the-way parts of Ireland in his lifetime (indeed, he took a lot of inspiration from the folk songs and tales he heard around his mother's family's place in Sligo). The true poetry of the people, whether written or oral, says Yeats, comes from this unwritten tradition, and gains its power and resonance from a framework of allusions, echoes, and references that are, at some level, familiar to the whole community. The words of such a poetry "borrow their beauty from those that used them before" (7) and the full resonance of the poems comes from seeing the events they depict or the emotions they express as if they were:

> ... moving before a half-faded curtain embroidered with kings and queens, their loves and battles and their days out hunting, or else with holy letters and images of so great an antiquity that nobody can tell the god or goddess they would commend to an unfading memory. (7)

The tapestry image is a Pre-Raphaelite-inflected way of describing the archive of collectively remembered past usage, a reservoir of meaning that would give poems resonance for the community. But the large idea at stake here is something like a set of archetypes, or at least of points of reference. This kind of poetry has power because it comes out of points of reference that have been shared by a community over time. It communicates rich and complex meanings because it doesn't just have a simple denotative meaning: it references a whole shared archive of connotations. What Yeats is claiming for written or oral poetry that rises up out of the "unwritten tradition" is something like what George Steiner claims when, in *On Difficulty*, he writes:

> Poetry is knit of words compacted with every conceivable mode of operative force. These words are, in Coleridge's simile, 'hooked atoms,' so construed as to mesh and cross-mesh with the greatest possible cluster of other words in the reticulations of the total body of language. The poet attempts to anchor the particular word in the dynamic mould of its own history, enriching the core of its present definition with the echo and alloy of previous use. . . . The poet's discourse can be compared to the track of a charged particle through a cloud-chamber. An energized field of association and connotation, of overtones and undertones, of rebus and homophone, surround its motion, and break from it in the context of collision . . . Multiplicity of meaning, 'enclosedness,' are the rule rather than the exception. We are meant to hear both solid and sullied, both toil and coil in the famous Shakespearean cruces. Lexical resistance is the armature of meaning, guarding the poem from the necessary commonalties of prose. (21)

Over against this kind of poetry, Yeats places "popular poetry," which for him is a stunted and attenuated thing, less the property of the people *per se* than of the modern bourgeoisie. He despises it. "Popular poetry," says Yeats, "never came from the people at all" (6). Rather, it came from and spoke to "a predominant portion of the middle class, of people who have unlearned the written tradition which binds the unlettered, so long as they are masters of themselves" (6). The middle classes, having disinherited themselves, have started to disinherit the general populace, as the peasants move into the cities and become proletarianized. This kind of poetry communicates immediately and easily, but does so at a terrible cost: it loses all the frames of reference (and therefore all the subtlety) of poetry that comes from the unwritten tradition. Its main features are "the triviality of emotion, the poverty of ideas, the imperfect sense of beauty of a poetry whose most typical expression is Longfellow." And Longfellow, says Yeats, "has his popularity, in the main, because he tells his story or his idea so that one needs nothing but his verses to understand it" (7). There's no tapestry of ancient kings and battles behind this kind of writing: just the plain, cheap wallpaper of a Victorian parlor, cast in the harsh glare of gaslight.

The third type of poetry—the poetry of the coteries—is the unpopular poetry of Yeats' time, poetry that works by literary reference and codes of allusion, perhaps ultimately derived from unwritten traditions, but filtered through layer after layer of bookishness and flavored with a strong dash of aestheticism. It is the poetry of the Rhymer's Club, of Dowson and Symons and the other poets Yeats visited when he was living in London. It has the same allusive quality built into its words as does the poetry of the unwritten tradition, and is, in some sense, that tradition's ally. It may seem like a bit of a stretch, this linkage of the peasant's oral tradition and the deeply cloistered and rather hothouse poetry of London aestheticism in the 1890s, but Yeats claims (perhaps more out of psychological need than factual accuracy) that the two go hand in hand because of their allusive richness. And they have common enemies, these two types of poetry—the modern middle class and the commercial world that came into being with that class:

> . . . it is certain that before the counting-house had created a new class and a new art without breeding and without ancestry, and set this art and this class between the hut and the castle, and between the hut and the cloister, the art of the people was as closely mingled with the art of the coteries as was the speech of the people that delighted in rhythmical animation, in idiom, in images, in words full of far-off suggestion, with the unchanging speech of the poets. (13)

The cloister of coteries (the modern version of monasticism), the aristocracy, and the peasants are all allied, for Yeats, in their cultural traditions—traditions that propose a language and a poetry of depth and resonance. Against them we see the world of the counting house, a world of efficient, shallow communication, and of poetry that does little but entertain vapidly.

There's something a bit questionable in the linking of the realm of erudite, remote, vaguely *symboliste* poetry with the poetry of the oral tradition. And there's something a bit questionable in the valorizing of the hierarchical, narrow world of agrarian society, too. But what Yeats is reacting against is real enough: there's an enormous transformation afoot in his lifetime, a transformation involving the rise of mass literacy, cheap books sold in high volume (making the selling of poetry economically marginal for publishers), and the displacement of poetry as a respected medium for knowledge. Yeats doesn't have a particularly clear socio-historical understanding of the events happening around him, but he's right about the general trend of things, and right about what it means for the language of poetry: with the dissolving of old agrarian communities and the rise of complex, diverse social formations, the old frames of reference that gave poetic language such power and resonance start to fall apart. Only a coterie audience of mandarins (and, in Yeats' nostalgic view, a hardy peasantry) still feel connected to those frames of reference.

This brings us to Donald Davie's *cri de coeur*. Where do you go in your poetry when the old frames of reference have become the property of coteries? T. S. Eliot, at least early on in his career, dramatized the conundrum ("these fragments have I shored against my ruins"). Other poets, deliberately or intuitively, went in the direction of popular culture, though the gains there may be temporary: nothing fades as fast as pop—not because it is inherently bad, but because pop is a business of fashions. Other poets discarded the idea of resonance-with-historical-usage and adopted a play of syntax and formal properties (the "new sentence" of language poetry being a late version of the phenomenon). Still others adopted poetics that eschews matters of meaning and historically reso-nant language (Merz, say, or Zaum). Others have soldiered along with the poetics of allusive and resonant language, either content with a coterie audience, or filled with uncomprehending rage at a reading public with whom they have difficulty communicating.

What would Yeats do, were he with us? I imagine he'd embody all of the contradictory responses in poems that argued against each other. That is, after all, what he did in the period from which the essays I've quoted come. The results—the poems of *The Wind Among the Reeds* and *In the Seven Woods*—include some of the finest in the Yeats canon. He dra-matizes and embodies the contradictions of poetry in an age when its ability to communicate is questionable. To judge from the results, this might not be a bad way to go in one's poetry in an age when the King James Bible has become a recondite source.

Works Cited

Davie, Donald. "A Son of Ezra." *Sons of Ezra: British Poets and Ezra Pound*. Ed. Michael Alexander and James McGonigal. Amsterdam: Rodopi, 1995. 15–30. Print.

Morris, William. *The Collected Works of William Morris*. Vol. 23. London: Longmans, 1915. Print.

Steiner, George. *On Difficulty*. Oxford: Oxford University Press, 1980. Print.

Yeats, W. B. *Ideas of Good and Evil*. London: Bullen, 1903. Print.

The Poet in the University
Charles Bernstein's Academic Anxiety

Ask an American poet where his or her paycheck comes from, and the most common answer, by far, will contain the word "university." The phenomenon of the poet as professor is not new, but the predominance of the phenomenon has become striking, and it raises a number of questions. What is the effect on poetry? What happens to poetry's reputation-making machinery when it becomes linked to America's hierarchical system of academic institutions? What will the logic of publish-or-perish do to poets? How will promotions and tenure committees adapt evaluation criteria designed for more scientific fields to poetry? I can answer none of these important questions. I do hope, however, to put forward a hypothesis about a related question: how does the confluence of poetry and academe change the poet's self-definition? Or perhaps that is too grand a claim. Perhaps what I really hope to offer are some thoughts about how entering academe affects the self-image of poets who established their reputations before entering the academy. Charles Bernstein has made that transition more successfully than any other American poet of his generation, but it did not come without a cost, paid in the currency of anxiety.

A Short and Easy Commonplace Book

The critic Gerald Bruns keeps a small selection of quotations, labeled

"A Short and Easy Commonplace Book," on his website. Here's the first of the quotations:

> The world has become chaos, but the book remains the image of the world: radicle-chaosmos rather than root-cosmos. A strange mystification: a book all the more total for being fragmented. At any rate, what a vapid idea, the book as the image of the world. In truth, it is not enough to say, "Long live the multiple," difficult as it is to raise that cry. No typographical, lexical, or even syntactical cleverness is enough to make it heard. The multiple *must be made*, not by always adding a higher dimension, but rather in the simplest of ways, by dint of sobriety, with the number of dimensions one already has available—always $n-1$ (the only way the one belongs to the multiple: always subtracted). Subtract the unique from the multiplicity to be constituted; write at $n-1$ dimensions. A system of this kind could be called a rhizome. A rhizome as subterranean stem is absolutely different from roots and radicles. Bulbs and tubers are rhizomes. Plants with roots or radicles may be rhizomorphic in other respects altogether: the question is whether plant life in its specificity is not entirely rhizomatic. Even some animals are, in their pack form. Rats are rhizomes. Burrows are too, in all of their functions of shelter, supply, movement, evasion, and breakout. The rhizome itself assumes very diverse forms, from ramified surface extension in all directions to concretion into bulbs and tubers. When rats swarm over each other. The rhizome includes the best and the worst: potato and crabgrass, or the weed. Animal and plant, couchgrass is crabgrass. (6)

The passage comes from Gilles Deleuze and Felix Guattari's *A Thousand Plateaus*, and has become a kind of touchstone for many critics and theorists concerned with the heterogenic and non-hierarchical nature of thought.

The next quote is also concerned with heterogenic and non-hierarchical ways of thinking:

> Within the academic environment, thought tends to be rationalized—subject to examination, paraphrase, repetition, mechanization, reduction. It is treated: contained and stabilized. And what is lost in this treatment is the irregular, the nonquantifiable, the nonstandard or nonstandardizable, the erratic, the inchoate.
>
> Poetry is turbulent thought, at least that's what I want from it, what I want to say about it just here, just now (and maybe not in some other

context). It leaves things unsettled, unresolved—leaves you knowing less than you did when you started.

There is a fear of the inchoate processes of turbulent thought (poetic or philosophic) that takes the form of resistance and paranoia. A wall (part symbolic, part imaginary) is constructed against the sheer surplus of interpretable aspects of any subject. You fix upon one among many possible frames, screens, screams, and stay fixed on that mode mono-maniacally. Such frame fixation is intensified by the fetishizing of dispas-sionate evaluation not as a critical method but as a marker of profes-sional competence and a means of enforcing a system of ranking. (43)

That's from "What's Art Got To Do With It?"—Charles Bernstein's plenary address to the Northeast Modern Language Association (NEMLA) conference in 1992. One can see why Bruns placed it next to the passage from *A Thousand Plateaus*: like Deleuze and Guattari, Bernstein waves the banner of interpretive and evaluative irresolution.

The third quote, while much briefer and considerably more cryptic, is another statement in support of thought that does not seek resolution. It's a single, uncharacteristically short sentence from Adorno's *Aesthetic Theory*: "Only what does not fit into this world is true" (76). Here we see a gesture toward the idea of negative dialectics—toward, that is, the idea that any whole or totalizing system of thought leaves something out, that (in Adorno's famous inversion of Hegel) "the whole is the false" (*Minima Moralia* 50). Truth, in this view, can't appear whole in this world—it is something evasive, excessive, and ultimately beyond representation. It can't be reduced to formulae, or made manifest in any final way.

As admirable as the ideas represented in Bruns' commonplace book are, and as congruent with one another, there is nevertheless something odd about the list. We see Bernstein, contrasting the "turbulent thought" of an open-ended poetry against the kind of thought we get in "the academic environment"—thought which, in his view, fears irresolution and multiplicity in favor of "paraphrase, repetition, mechanization, reduction." For Bernstein, academic thought is devoted to the quanti-fiable and the standard, and it walks in fear of the inchoate. What's odd about finding this in Bruns' list is that both of Bruns' other quotes in support of what Bernstein calls "turbulent thought" come, at least in part, from academics. When Adorno wrote the book that would be published after his death as *Aesthetic Theory* he was a professor at Frankfurt. Gilles Deleuze spent the early part of his career at the Sorbonne, and held a post at the University of Paris VIII (Vincennes / St. Denis), where he wrote the book from which Bruns' drew a quotation. Felix Guattari was no academic, though he did spend most of his career at the La Borde Clinic, which was both a functioning clinic and something of a para-academic institute, where research was conducted and where training took place in philosophy, psychology, ethnology, and social work. More strikingly, Charles Bernstein had been the David Gray Professor of Poetry and Letters at SUNY—Buffalo for more than two years when he skewered academic thinking as devoted to reductive standardization.

Here's the rub: if Bernstein is right about academic thinking, then we have to see him as a non-academic. We'd also have to be able to see the others that way, and Deleuze and Adorno are by no measure marginal academic figures. In their own lifetimes, and certainly by the time Bernstein made his NEMLA plenary address in 1992, Adorno, Deleuze, and Guattari had become some of the most influential figures in academe, making a huge impact on multiple disciplines in the humanities and social sciences in many nations. And they didn't just speak about the kind of thinking that exploded reductive, standardizing, paraphrasable interpretations: like Bernstein, they wrote in styles that set out to frustrate attempts at reduction, standardization, and paraphrase. Bruns' point in bringing the three quotations together was, in all probability, simply to emphasize and advocate the kind of thinking the various thinkers admired and had in common. But the juxtaposition (perhaps fittingly) doesn't allow us to settle easily into approval of all three statements. We are faced with a choice: either Bernstein is wrong about the nature of academic thinking, or Bernstein, Deleuze, Guattari, and Adorno have to be defined as non-academic figures.

It has been argued that Bernstein, despite having held prominent academic appointments for more than twenty years, is not truly an academic. In the article "Charles Bernstein and Professional Avant-Gardism," for example, Alan Golding has made an argument for Bernstein as having a non-normative status in academe, largely on the basis of Bernstein reflecting critically on his own academic status in his poetry and critical writing. Golding's article is provocative, and his readings of Bernstein are both subtle and insightful. But it is difficult to accept the notion that Bernstein is somehow not quite academic because he parodies, and is critical of, academe in his writing—if one accepts this line of argument, one would have to say that David Lodge was never really academic because he has written satirical campus novels like *Trading Places* and *Small World*. But even if we can make the argument that Bernstein is not truly academic, we'd have a far more difficult argument to make in putting Adorno, Deleuze, and Guattari outside academe. In addition to their training and (with the partial exception of Guattari) their careers, there's the matter of their enormous academic influence, as some of the most cited figures in several fields. To understand what's at stake when Bernstein sets academe up as something it does not seem to be, we need to take a closer look at the Bernstein essay from which Bruns drew his quotation.

Bernstein Tells the Northeast Modern Language Association About Academe

The lines of battle are clearly drawn in Bernstein's NEMLA plenary address of 1992. On the one hand, we have the "professionalism" of "the university environment," where thinking is inherently reductive and as such "antipoetic" (42). The procedure of academic thought, according to Bernstein, is "to elect one interpretive mode and apply it, cookie-cutter like, to any given phenomenon" (43). If you want to think like a professor, according to Bernstein all you need to do is this: "You fix upon one of many possible frames" (43). This insistence on single-minded, narrow, method-driven frame of thought leads to an "academic culture of imposed solutions at the expense of open-ended explorations"—perhaps because Bernstein's academics want to reduce phenomena to determined meanings and grow uneasy when they see "the sheer surplus of interpretable aspects" of their subjects (43). Against these unappealing academics, Bernstein places a poetic tradition, in which thought is much more open. "The poetic," says Bernstein, "is both a hypoframe, inhering within each frame of interpretation, and a hyperframe, a practice of moving from frame to frame" (44). Unlike academics proper, the poet is multidisciplinary in his individual thoughts, and is happy moving from one frame of reference to another: his thinking is a "an art of transitioning through and among frames." He has "context sensitivity" and "allows different contexts to suggest different interpretive approaches while at the same time flipping between different frames" (44). This gives one pause, in that Bernstein's dichotomy seems to make a straw man out of academe.

One can, of course, find some instances of the cookie-cutter approach Bernstein sees as endemic to academe. I think immediately of one of the most misguided publishing ventures of recent memory, the Bedford Critical Editions of classic literary texts. These were an attempt to emulate the success of the Norton Critical Editions. Unlike the Norton editions, though, the Bedford editions didn't collect prominent pieces of existing criticism to package with the text itself. Rather, they published commissioned essays, each of which was meant to represent a particular theory— a feminist reading, say, or a Marxist reading. But the very fact that Bedford failed to make significant inroads against the Norton editions, with their less mechanical, more intuitively interdisciplinary and miscellaneous commentaries, is an indicator that academic culture is not predominantly a phenomenon of the kind Bernstein claims it is. Moreover, Bernstein's characterization of academe is at odds with the work of a figure Bernstein actually cites in his essay: Stanley Fish. While Bernstein sees Fish as an academic of the reductive sort, we need look no further than the opening pages of one of Fish's most famous essays, "Interpreting the Variorum," to see how far off-base Bernstein has gone. "Interpreting the Variorum," which appeared in *Critical Inquiry* in 1976, was a review of a collection of several centuries worth of commentaries on Milton's poetry. Fish surveys the long conflict of interpretations, and the deep history of different forms of interpretation ("frames" in Bernstein's terms), and tells us that the problems of interpretation simply do not lend themselves to resolution:

> In short, these are problems that apparently cannot be solved, at least not by the methods traditionally brought to bear on them. What I would like to argue is that they are not meant to be solved, but to be experi-

enced (they signify), and that consequently any procedure that attempts to determine which of a number of readings is correct will necessarily fail. (149)

Fish can hardly be seen as without influence in academe, and like those other influential academics Deleuze and Adorno, he believes in a multiplicity of meanings, supports a multiplicity of frames of understanding, and welcomes the inchoate and inconclusive. One could wear oneself out citing academics, prominent when Bernstein gave his address, whose ways of thinking are utterly unlike the reductiveness of Bernstein's academic straw man. Even the New Critics, antiquated and marginalized by the 1990s when Bernstein wrote, did not believe that meanings must be "subject to . . . paraphrase," famously finding paraphrase heretical. Or, moving to "The Humanistic Intellectual: Eleven Theses," an essay that appeared in 1989 (the year Bernstein entered the academy), one could point out that no less prominent an academic than Richard Rorty argued that the social function of academics in the humanities was "to instill doubts in the students about the students' own self-images and about their societies"—a goal best accomplished by "keep[ing] the humanities changing fast enough so that they remain indefinable and unmanageable" (130). This is hardly the academic world Bernstein depicts, and it is an image of the academic humanities upheld by no marginal figure, but by one of the most influential thinkers of the late twentieth century.

Reducibility, Emergence, Scientific Knowledge

Bernstein's misrepresentation of academic thought isn't just limited to humanistic thinking. Even those figures we in the humanities suspect of rigidly programmatic thought—the scientists—do not, as a rule, want to reduce everything to a single, unified theory, a single master frame. Here's what Peter Medawar, an expert on these matters, has to say about the notion that science is all about reducing multiple frames of understanding to a single frame (the statement comes from his book *Induction and Intuition in Scientific Thought*, which appeared in 1969—the view being long established by the time of Bernstein's complaint about academe):

Reducibility; emergence: If we choose to see a hierarchical structure in Nature—if societies are composed of individuals, individuals of cells, and cells in their turn of molecules, then it makes sense to ask whether we may not 'interpret' sociology in terms of the biology of individuals or 'reduce' biology to physics and chemistry. This is a living methodological problem, but it does not seem to have been satisfactorily resolved. At first sight the ambition embodied in the idea of reducibility seems hopeless of achievement. Each tier of the natural hierarchy makes use of notions peculiar to itself. The ideas of democracy, credit, crime or political constitution are no part of biology, nor shall we expect to find in physics the concepts of memory, infection, sexuality, or fear. No sensible usage can bring the foreign exchange deficit into the biology syllabus, already grievously overcrowded, or nest-building into the syllabus of physics. In each plane or tier of the hierarchy new notions or ideas seem to emerge that are inexplicable in the language or with the conceptual resources of the tier below. (15–16)

Even the lab-coated researchers with good calculators in their pockets resist being categorized as the hidebound, narrow-minded thinkers that populate Bernstein's imagined academe. They're as interested in multiple frames, and as wary of reducing matters to single-framed, cookie-cutter thinking as are the humanists and social scientists.

Status Shifting and Self Doubt

So why does Bernstein present such a distorted version of academic thinking? It's possible that he's simply ignorant of academic thinking, but that hypothesis seems both extremely uncharitable and unlikely to the point of near impossibility. In fact, Bernstein cites plenty of academic thinkers in his NEMLA plenary address. The strange thing is that when he approves of them, he positions them as outsiders, at war with what he imagines to be academic thought. So when he tells us he admires Roland Barthes (from the Centre national de la recherche scientifique and the Collège de France), Stanley Cavell (who was Bernstein's thesis advisor at Harvard), Erving Goffman (from the University of Chicago), Michel de Certeau (from the University of Paris—VII, and other institutions), and Luce Irigaray (from the Centre national de la recherche scientifique) he has to pretend they aren't creatures of the academy, and to deny their status as some of the most influential academic thinkers of our time. Why? Bernstein works in academe, and seems to admire the kind of thinking that academics do—but he refuses to see it that way. Instead, he mischaracterizes academe as a place inimical to the kind of thinking he admires—which he claims is the special province of poetry, and of a few thinkers who, despite their status as stars of academe, are somehow meant to be non-academic.

When we find that someone's statements about the world are inaccurate without being ignorant, one course of action is to stop looking for explanations in the world outside that person, and look instead for some inner cause. That is: if Bernstein is wrong about academe, but has knowledge of academic thought, the explanation probably lies in some inner need, on Bernstein's part, to present a distorted view of academe. If I had to venture a hypothesis about why Bernstein distorts academe, I'd look at his unusual career trajectory into the academic world. Unlike most academics, who go to graduate school with the hope (however farfetched in recent years) of going on to a career as a professor of physics or French or creative writing, Bernstein began his career as a poet outside of academe. He wrote his books and led an active poetic life while working from the early 1970s to 1989 as a medical writer and an arts administrator, and only then found his way into academe. While he'd been an engaged student as a Harvard undergraduate, he didn't enter academe by the usual route of doctoral study, and this shows in his attitude to academe, which seems fraught with the kind of anxiety one might expect when someone leaves one status behind and takes up another, without the usual certification.

The sociologists Richard Sennett and Jonathan Cobb get at this sort of status-anxiety issue in their study *The Hidden Injuries of Class*. Here they examine the psychological consequences of changing work status, mostly by examining blue collar workers who transition into low-level white collar work. It's not that Bernstein has changed social class *per se* (medical writers, arts administrators, and English professors all fall within the professional classes), but he did shift from one status system (that of corporations and non-profit agencies) to another (the world of the universities, which is stratified in different ways, and by different criteria).

And what happens to Bernstein seems very like what happens to the workers described by Sennett and Cobb. Consider the case of Frank Rissarro (not an actual name: Sennett and Cobb change the names of their subjects to protect their privacy). Rissarro's father was a laborer, and he himself held a job as a meat-cutter for most of his working life. At one point, after he failed to raise the capital to start his own small business, a friend introduced him to a local bank manager, and he got a job in the office helping people fill out the loan forms that a higher-level official would review for approval. In many ways, Rissarro is satisfied with his new life—but because he arrived among the other bank workers by a non-standard route, he feels the need to defend the kind of life he left behind, and to denigrate the norms of the system he's joined. "I'm working, like I said, with fellows that are educated, college boys, in the office," says Rissarro, "I go in at nine, I come out at five. The other fellows, because they got an education, sneak out early and come in late. The boss knows I'm there, a reliable worker. 'Cause I had the factory life..." (21). Even though Rissarro chose to leave his old life for a new opportunity, he sees his old life as having a kind of legitimacy that the lives of those around him in his new career don't have. "These jobs aren't real work where you make something," says Rissarro, "it's just pushing papers" (21). This is how Rissarro deals with the anxiety of not being a 'real' banker (an anxiety caused by his non-standard, and late, entry into the field). He needs to denigrate the new norms, even as he conforms to them. It's how he can feel legitimate: he's a representative of his old set of values in this new world of mere paper-pushers. The analogy with Bernstein is this: like Rissarro, he enters a new field late in life, without the usual educational certification. Like Rissarro, Bernstein associates virtue with the way of life he's left behind (for Bernstein, this is the world of extra-academic poetry). Like Rissarro, Bernstein decides to read the kind of work he sees being done in his new environment as more-or-less worthless. Rissarro's paper-pushers become Bernstein's narrow-minded, "cookie-cutter" thinkers. There's a kind of self-doubt in both cases, and a distortion of the activities of those around them, which serves as a way to compensate for these anxieties and doubts. Rissarro's doubts in the banking world are, it seems, the same doubts of one kind of poet upon entering the university.

Works Cited

Adorno, Theodor. *Aesthetic Theory*. Trans. Robert Hullot-Kentor. London
Continuum, 2004. Print.
———. *Minima Moralia*. Trans. E. F. N. Jephcott. London: Verso, 2005. Print.
Bernstein, Charles. "What's Art Got To Do With It?" *My Way: Speeches and Poems*.
Chicago: University of Chicago Press, 1999. 36–51. Print.
Deleuze, Gilles, and Felix Guattari. *A Thousand Plateaus*. Trans. Brian Massumi.
Minneapolis: University of Minnesota Press, 1987. Print.
Fish, Stanley E. "Interpreting the Variorum." *Is There a Text in this Class? The
Authority of Interpretive Communities*. Cambridge, Massachusetts: Harvard
University Press, 1982. 147–73. Print.
Golding, Alan. "Charles Bernstein and Professional Avant-Gardism." *Talisman*
36/37 (2009): 28–42. Print.
Medawar, Peter. *Induction and Intuition in Scientific Thought*. Philadelphia: Ameri-
can Philosophical Society, 1969. Print.
Rorty, Richard. *Philosophy and Social Hope*. Harmondsworth: Penguin, 1999.
Print.
Sennett, Richard, and Jonathan Cobb. *The Hidden Injuries of Class*. New York:
Norton, 1993. Print.

The State of the Art

The year is 1712, and the state of the art of American poetry is, in a word, provincial. The best-known and best-selling American poem remains Michael Wigglesworth's *The Day of Doom: A Poetical Description of the Great and Last Judgment*, written some forty years earlier and currently in its fifth edition. A bumpy, ballad-meter ride through Calvinist theology, it will remain popular for decades. When Francis Jenks writes about it in the *Christian Examiner* in 1828, he'll remind his audience how much this strange, homespun work once meant to their countrymen. It was, says Jenks, "a work which was taught our fathers with their catechisms, and which many an aged person with whom we are acquainted can still repeat, though they may not have met with a copy since they were in leading strings." It was, moreover, "a work that was hawked about the country, printed on sheets like common ballads," and it presented, in language often graceless but equally often vivid "the common theology of New England at the time it was written" (537).

The Day of Doom represents a kind of poetry at the service of religion, written by men who do not consider themselves to be, first and foremost, poets. Wigglesworth, having turned down the presidency of Harvard, held the title "teacher at Malden Church in New England," and saw himself as a man of God who happened to write poetry, not as a poet who happened to believe in God. When he died in 1705, there was not much by way of American institutions to support poetry, and his work found its way to readers through the primitive market for written works, carried by peddlers down the roads and river valleys of the land.

Poetry in England, of course, is much more sophisticated than in the humble cottages of New England: it's been just a year since the publication of Alexander Pope's *An Essay on Criticism*, a critical exercise the precocious poet had written in orotund heroic couplets back in 1709, at the tender age of 21. Stuffed to bursting with learning from Virgil, Homer, Aristotle, Horace, and Longinus, Pope's poem holds the classics up as the greatest models for poetry, spurning the rustic form and grim pieties of Wigglesworth. Disdaining novelty for its own sake ("Regard not then if wit be *Old* or *New* / But blame the *False*, and value still the *True*"), Pope hews to the standards of Horatian decorum, in which the parts of a work unite into a seamless whole, which should both delight and instruct (47).

Unlike Wigglesworth, Pope doesn't see himself as a man who happens to write poetry, he is something new: he's a poet, in the sense of being a specialized kind of professional writer with a particular place in the evolving literary ecosystem. He's benefitted from the old system of noble patronage, but he's had enough success in England's rapidly growing literary marketplace to take jabs at those literary men who sit "at the Great-man's Board, / To fetch and carry Nonsense for my Lord" (47). Indeed, he's done well enough with his new mock-epic *The Rape of the Lock* to see how a reading public, flush with new wealth from the financial revolutions of the last two decades, hungers for entertaining works that have the kind of classical sheen that could, through the appearance of refinement, lift the mere money-grubbing merchant who reads it into the rising class of cultivated gentlemen. He's at work on a translation of Homer that will soon make him rich, and in a few years he'll move to a villa at Twickenham where he'll set to rewriting Shakespeare, regularizing the verse of the plays and excising errant lines so as to bring the bard closer to the correctness of classical writing. When these projects are complete, the state of the art of English poetry will be what Virgil would have wanted—had Virgil been, like Pope's typical reader, status-conscious and market-rich, an *arriviste* Londoner looking to show that he knew an ode from an octave and a fish-fork from a fingerbowl.

But it is not 1712. It is 1812, and the embodiment of the state of the art of American poetry lies in a desk drawer in Cummington, Massachusetts, in the eighty-one lines of William Cullen Bryant's "Thanatop-sis." The poem, written by the teenaged Bryant, combines the old Puritanical sense of the brevity of life, of the ever-present grave, with something new, picked up from the poems of an earlier generation of English poets: the worship of nature. Daringly, Bryant suggests that our final home and spiritual destiny rests not in Heaven, but in the ever-living bounty of nature, into which we will merge when we die. Bryant's poem echoes Wordsworth, anticipates the American Transcendentalists, and in a few decades will be lavishly praised by Poe in the great essay "The Poetic Principle." But Bryant's poem won't see print for another five years, when his father sends it to the first literary journal in America, the recently founded *North American Review*.

Bryant's reticence about sending his poem out into the world makes sense. He understands that he won't be able to support himself as a poet: there's no real patronage system in the American republic, and writing poetry doesn't pay. After stints as a lawyer, and in the equally demean-ing role of hog-reeve for the town of Great Barrington, Bryant will embark on a career as editor of various literary journals. Perhaps it is not coincidental that these journals will not survive: the break between the beliefs of literary men like Bryant, with their nature-worship and Romanticism, and the more conventional beliefs of the reading public, is becoming ever more apparent. While Michael Wigglesworth's *The Day of Doom* echoed the public's beliefs back to them, Bryant seeks, in his poetry, new kinds of truth, and exotic kinds of meaning. Bryant will finally come to fame and fortune not through poetry, but through his work as a newspaper editor. These labors will make him one of the leading opinion-brokers in the nation, but they will also temper his imagination. Among his last published works, in the 1870s, will be a two-volume set he edited called *Picturesque America*, a kind of coffee-table book *avant-la-lettre*, which finally merges his love of nature with topics the ever-growing, ever more democratic reading public could appreci-ate: armchair tourism and the spirit of nationalism.

Of course even Bryant, with his newfangled sense of a divine nature, would be behind the times in England, where the Romantics are pushing, quite fearlessly, into new terrain. It is 1812, and Lord Byron gives his politically heretical address to the House of Lords in praise of the machine-breaking Luddites. He also publishes the first installments of *Childe Harold's Pilgrimage*, that great hymn to the glory of the individualist, "the most unfit / Of men to herd with Man; with whom he held / Little in common," a man "proud in desolation" who will not "yield dominion of his mind to spirits against whom his own rebelled" (47). If the nature-religion of Wordsworth or the young Bryant quietly put the poet in opposition to popular belief, lines like these announce that opposition in fiery letters in the sky. The poem is a scandal to the mainstream reader, but also a best seller, especially in continental Europe, where the Napoleonic betrayal of revolutionary ideals left thousands of angry young men alienated and in need of rebellious pages over which to brood.

In terms of immediate impact, Byron's work is clearly the state of the art of English verse, but in terms of eventual influence, Byron's writing will be eclipsed by the ongoing work of another, older Romantic: Coleridge. 1812 is the year Coleridge gives his lectures on Shakespeare, introducing the idea of organic form, which dictates that the work of art mustn't follow mechanically imposed rules, but generate its own rules from within. It is a great rebuttal to the neoclassical followers of Aristotle (among them one Alexander Pope). In the decades ahead the idea will open vast new continents for poetic experimentation. Just as important will be a poem of Coleridge's that has been circulating in manuscript for years, but that won't see publication until 1816. "Kubla Khan" gives us a speaker trying to make sense of a mysterious visionary experience. By presenting us with a series of suggestive, polysemous, and at times indeterminate symbols, it places its readers in a position similar to that of its speaker, trying to grasp an elusive yet powerful significance. If the state of the art of poetry has to do with its influence on the future, "Kubla Khan" is surely the state of the art of English verse in 1812. It is also a poem that recognizes the great problem poets will face in the years ahead: the problem of audience. At the end of the poem the visionary is confronted by crowds who cry "Beware! Beware! / His flashing eyes, his floating hair!" and close their eyes with "holy dread," fearing this outsider who has tasted the milk of some exotic paradise (108). William Cullen Bryant's "Thanatopsis" may have given some readers a shiver with its unorthodox views of God and nature. But Coleridge had already conceptualized the problem that Bryant encountered, the problem of the poet whose views are at odds with those of the mainstream of his society. Coleridge's own bohemian life has shown him that the poet had, essentially, become homeless in society. He will spend years dreaming of a subsidized class of intellectual humanists, called the Clerisy, as a solution to the problem of modern intellectuals without patrons or significant markets for their works. Here, again, he anticipates the future, and the vast growth of universities in which so many poets will find their place and their pay.

But it is not 1812. It's 1912, and everybody's been talking about progress: technological progress has been so rapid that a new term—"state of the art"—was introduced two years ago in Henry Harrison Suplee's engineering manual *Gas Turbine: Progress in the Design and Construction of Turbines Operated by Gases of Combustion*. Social progress has been rapid, too, especially when it comes to communications and transportation. International travel and the availability of books and journals from other countries have started to make national distinctions in literature less meaningful: Americans write in Paris, and the leading poet among the well-informed English is an Irishman, W. B. Yeats. There's been a great deal of progress in literacy, too: the number of literate people in the English-speaking world has roughly tripled over the past half-century, and well over 90% of the population has at least rudimentary reading skills. One might think poets would celebrate this rise in reading, but many view the development with suspicion. A decade ago, in the essay "What is Popular Poetry?" William Butler Yeats lamented the effects of modern literacy. The old oral tradition of the peasantry, Yeats said, was the "true poetry of the people," and it gains its resonance from a framework of allusions familiar to the whole community. The words of this poetry "borrow their beauty from those that used them before," and their full power comes from depicting events as if they were "moving before a half-faded curtain embroidered with kings and queens, their loves and battles" (365–66). Modern life and modern mass literacy cut people off from their old folk beliefs, and deprive poets of the means to communicate with any kind of subtlety. The poet is driven to private references, delicate hermetic symbols, and personal mythologies: an exaggerated version of the visionary's position at the end of "Kubla Khan." It's a desperate situation. What to do?

All over the Western world the response of the sort of poets we might think of as "state of the art" has been to start pushing language away from shared reference, and toward an emphasis on sound and the formal properties of language. If you can't count on communicating with the new mass public, why not turn away from the kind of communication that depends on shared reference? Sure, you could dream of shoring up the fragments of old systems of reference against the ruins—but you could also start exploring the non-referential parts of language, and thinking of them as the essence of poetry. In a year's time the Russians will invent *zaum*, a poetry of sound alone, and a few years after that Hugo Ball will read "Karawane," a poem of leaping, senseless syllables, at the Cabaret Voltaire. And just this very year, Gertrude Stein, holed up in bohemian Paris, will finish *Tender Buttons*, whose strange little loops of language don't aim at the kind of resonant expression Yeats finds so difficult in the modern age.

Stein has the financial wherewithal to be a writer unconcerned with the financial success of her works, which is just as well: when *Tender Buttons* finally appears in 1914, it will be under the imprint of Claire Marie Press, described by Mabel Dodge as an "effete and decadent" enterprise, bohemian and "absolutely third rate" (Mellow 178). The book will sell poorly, but steadily, to a very specialized, self-consciously literary audience, high on the heady fumes of formal experimentation. The book will continue to sell slowly for decades, and still be in print in a century's time—ignored by the broad public, treasured by the elect few.

Of course, the year isn't 1712, 1812, or 1912. It's 2012, and you are probably among the hyper-literate elect who still read *Tender Buttons*. You've read "Kubla Khan," too, and maybe a canto or two of *Childe Harold's Pilgrimage*. "Thanatopsis" and Pope's *Essay on Criticism* may or may not have been something covered in your undergraduate literary survey, but they probably aren't among the poems you turn to for pleasure. And all the bookies assure me that the odds are heavily against *The Day of Doom*—so popular for so long—having been a part of your literary education.

Our way of relating to the past tells us more about ourselves than it tells us about the past, and it's significant that most of us don't find much immediately appealing in Pope, still less in Wigglesworth. The direct influence of either on our poetry is rare. A few current formalists admire Pope, but even with them, there's often a certain pastiche quality to their more Popian work: one thinks of R. S. Gwynn's *Narcissiad*, a pastiche of Pope's *Dunciad*, itself a pastiche of Homer. I can't think of a single contemporary poet ever mentioning the importance of *The Day of Doom* to his or her development. But what does this tell us? American poets, nowadays, tend to be specialists, writing poetry *as poets*. That is, they're just not like Wigglesworth, who wrote poems only as a means of serving some larger cause. For us, poetry is an autonomous art, not a subordinate art like political poster printing, or the carving of altar pieces, or the filming of commercials. But American poets aren't specialists the way Pope was. Pope was a market-oriented specialist, serving the needs of a newly rich public anxious to fit in with the established gentry, yearning for English versions of the classics and easily grasped norms of taste. Poetry in our time and place very rarely serves the needs of the kind of mass-audience that would make it viable in the marketplace, and rare is the poet who will tell you, with a straight face, that she's writing with an eye on making the best-seller lists.

What we admire from the past is just as significant as what we ignore. "Kubla Khan" is a perfect poem for those who think of poetry as discontinuous with ordinary language, as a special form of writing that isn't just prose plus special effects, like rhyme and meter. "Kubla Khan" gives us language that resists straightforward communication, language inviting ongoing interpretation, language that makes special demands on the reader: demands for careful attention, and for the tolerance of ambiguity and indeterminacy. These demands aren't different, in kind, from the demands the poems of *Tender Buttons* make. And it matters that so many more contemporary American poets know and admire these poems than know and admire Wigglesworth, or even Pope. It tells us something about where we are: we are in the realm of the poem as autonomous creation, demanding to be seen as a language art, not a medium for religion or a means of joining an established social elite, or a means of making money.

The emphasis on the freedom of poetry to revel in its role as a primarily linguistic artifact, and the emphasis on the poet as a non-commercial specialist in an unpopular art form, go hand-in-hand. They both fit neatly into the institutional framework in which a plurality of American poets finds their home: the university. Like its German model, the American university is built on the assumption that there are discrete, autonomous areas of knowledge, each with its special object of study and methods appropriate to those objects. Initially, the university model presented a problem for poets and poetry critics, whose object of creation and study seemed to have so many dimensions: political, social, religious, linguistic, and so forth. What could be more inimical to the departmental model of knowledge than a poem? But in the late 1930s, American poets and poetry critics found the keys to the magic kingdom of academe. In 1938 John Crowe Ransom claimed that, unless poetic form and poetic language became central concerns, the American English department might "almost as well announce that it does not regard itself as autonomous, but as a branch of the department of history, with the option of declaring itself occasionally a branch of ethics" (Graff 148). Much has happened since the late thirties, including a kind of hybridizing of literary studies with history and sociology. But the notion of poetry as an independent academic specialty has remained, and, if anything, been strengthened by the growth of creative writing programs: no university worthy of its quadrangle is without a specialist in modern poetry, and another specialist in the writing of poems.

Given the emphasis of academe on discrete fields of knowledge, it should come as no surprise that the dominant kind of poem produced by the poets in—or emerging from—the American academy emphasizes the special nature of poetic language, rather than, say, the poem as a means to religious salvation. Elliptical poetry, after all, offers us a kind of disjunction and obliquity very much at odds with the communicative norms of ordinary language. It is no coincidence that the very term "elliptical poetry" comes into use shortly after Cleanth Brooks and Robert Penn Warren define the modern, autonomous study of literature, when Warren uses the term to describe poems without "definition of situation, movement of narrative, logical transition, factual description" in his 1942 essay "Pure and Impure Poetry" (130).

Contemporary elliptical poets may or may not have strong religious or political convictions; they may or may not yearn for success in the marketplace. The kind of work they create, though, is most notable for being a special use of language. Consider Anne Carson's "Sleepchains," in which we read:

> Who can sleep when she—
> hundreds of miles away I feel that vast breath
> fan her restless decks.
> Cicatrice by cicatrice
> all the links
> rattle at once.
> Here we go mother on the shipless ocean.
> Pity us, pity the ocean, here we go. (24)

As Stephen Burt put it when he quoted the poem in his seminal essay "The Elliptical Poets," "syntactical slips and breaks and un-accompanied suggestion do all the work" (346). Language operates in a special, poetic sense and in this regard it is perfectly adapted to its academic home in the English department.

The sociologists of culture have some useful terms for describing what has happened to American poetry: the "heteronomous principle," the "autonomous principle," and the "idea of specific capital." The heteronomous principle of art maintains that the success of art is measured in terms outside of art itself: success in the market, in the field of politics, or in the field of religion, for example. The autonomous principle maintains that success in an art is a matter of succeeding in terms specific to that art. Poetry has traveled a long way from the heteronomous principle of poetry in 1712 toward a more autonomous principle. Coleridge certainly saw poetry as largely governed by the autonomous principle. Yeats lamented the decreasing ability of poetry to make an impact in fields beyond the literary, and Gertrude Stein more-or-less set up housekeeping in the field of autonomous art, with success measured in terms of dazzling linguistic innovation more than anything else. Under the auspices of the university, poets have come to accept the autonomous principle of success: large sales of poems based on market success, such as those of Jewel or Shel Silverstein, are often viewed as failures in terms of the autonomous principle. Poems that forefront language play, formal innovation, and the post-Ashbery special poetic language of ellipsis have a greater legitimacy under the contemporary autonomous principle of poetry. If the rewards of the market come in the form of economic capital, the rewards of an autonomous field, not subject to other fields, come in the form of capital specific to that field: prestige among other producers. That is the capital available to, and often cherished by, many American poets today. It is also the capital embodied in letters of recommendation written by other poets, the capital tallied up in the publication lists on *curricula vitae*, and the capital conferred (along with some economic capital) by anthologists and prize committees.

But there's something else going on in American poetry, circa 2012, something related to the emphasis on poetry-as-language and the poet-as-specialist. There is also the urge to be *au courant*—something quite foreign to, say, Alexander Pope, who wanted to affirm the classics as lasting verities. There's an accelerating replacement of one movement by another, in prestige if not in actual poetic practice. Confessional poetry? Long gone, replaced by a variety of identity-politics inflected forms of writing. Language poetry? Very hip, until the post-avant and ellipticism arrived. And the dominant ellipticism is now challenged, by "the new thing," a term coined in a *Boston Review* article by Stephen Burt for the poets publishing with the Cultural Society (18); and, more prominently, by what Marjorie Perloff has christened "the conceptual generation" (84). Pierre Bourdieu calls this process of premature displacement "the social aging of art," and notes that it comes about when the rewards of making art have taken the form of specific capital (146–48). Hollywood screenwriters write for the market and are relatively unconcerned with labeling their elders out-of-date. But American poets in 2012 tend not to have a market, or a heteronomous principle of valuation. They seek validation of a kind specific to the poetic field, and the way to gain it quickly is to delegitimize the older, more dominant practitioners. From this follows a flurry of movements, something approaching the condition of (to steal a phrase from the critic Jed Rasula) "every day another vanguard" (v).

Kenneth Goldsmith, in a 2007 essay called "The End of History," gives us a remarkably candid testament about what it feels like to participate in this process of the social aging of art. Poetry, says Goldsmith, is "the epicenter of nonmaterial gain"—a field with its own specific capital, removed from the market. A former visual artist, Goldsmith recounts a conversation he'd had with a collector about why he was leaving the relatively more remunerative art world to become a poet. "While I was a successful artist," he'd said, "I knew in my heart that I'd never be an important artist; I knew that . . . I'd never be able to change the history of the field." "So you went for history rather than money?" asked the collector. "Yeah," Goldsmith responded, "I think that if you ask any artist, they'll tell you that a primary motivator to their becoming an artist would be to make history, not money." And how does one make history, and claim one's share of the specific capital available in the poetic field? By insisting on the rapid social aging of art. "A very close friend who has been called the most radical of the first generation Language Poets," says Goldsmith, turned out to have "some very conventional ideas about poetry." Unwilling to take "the next step" and embrace "the next generation's writing, conceptual writing," this poet was, in Goldsmith's view, consigning himself to the past. In pioneering conceptualism, with its aesthetic of cut-and-paste and the found text (Goldsmith's best known work, *Traffic*, consists of unedited transcripts of traffic reports), Goldsmith explicitly seeks to claim a space for himself in history by superseding the more "conventional" past. "Novelty" was a term of blame for Alexander Pope, but that term's close cousin, "innovation," has become a term of praise in our own time. One might think of Pope and Goldsmith as opposites, but in some sense they are quite the same: each is poetically responding to the social conditions of his time in a manner quite likely to earn him a place in literary history.

The conditions faced by Pope and the conditions faced by Goldsmith are, of course, quite different. Not only was there little interest in novelty in the neoclassical era of Pope, the very term "state of the art" lay two centuries in the future. We live a full century into the life of that term, and it now applies in fields quite distant from the realm of the gas turbine, for which it was invented. Indeed, perhaps the most salient feature of our own moment in the history of poetry is the prominence, and the durability, of the notion of a state of the art, of the perpetual replacement of one vanguard by another. This, itself, tells us a great deal about where we are in the history of American poetry, and where, in the immediate future, it may be going.

Works Cited

Bourdieu, Pierre. *The Rules of Art: Genesis and Structure of the Literary Field*. Trans. Susan Emanuel. New York: Columbia University Press, 1996. Print.

Burt, Stephen. *Close Calls with Nonsense: Reading New Poetry*. St. Paul: Graywolf: 2009. Print.

———. "The New Thing." *Boston Review*. Boston Review, May/June 2009. Web. 19 Jan. 2012.

Byron, George Gordon, Lord. *Selected Poetry and Prose*. London: Routledge, 1995. Print.

Carson, Anne. "Sleepchains." *Metre 5* (1998): 24. Print.

Coleridge, Samuel Taylor. *Selected Poems*. Boston: Heath, 1905. Print.

Goldsmith, Kenneth. "The End of History." *Harriet*. The Poetry Foundation, n.d. Web. 1 Feb. 2012.

Graff, Gerald. *Professing Literature: An Institutional History*. Chicago: University of Chicago Press, 1989. Print.

Jenks, Francis. "Dr. Beecher Against the Calvinistic Doctrine of Infant Damnation." *Christian Examiner*. Vol. 5. 1828: 229–63, 316–40, 506–42. Print.

Mellow, James R. *Charmed Circle: Gertrude Stein and Company*. New York: Henry Holt, 1974. Print.

Perloff, Marjorie. *Unoriginal Genius: Poetry by Other Means in the New Century*. Chicago: University of Chicago Press, 2010. Print.

Pope, Alexander. *Selected Poetry and Prose*. London: Routledge, 1988. Print.

Rasula, Jed. *Syncopations: The Stress of Innovation in Contemporary American Poetry*. Tuscaloosa: University of Alabama Press, 2004. Print.

Warren, Robert Penn. "Pure and Impure Poetry." *Praising it New: The Best of the New Criticism*. Ed. Garrick Davis. Athens, Ohio: Ohio University Press / Swallow Press, 2008. Print.

Yeats, William Butler. *The Yeats Reader*. Ed. Richard J. Finneran. New York: Scribner, 2002. Print.

To Criticize the Poetry Critic

Seeing the New Criticism Again

Once upon a time there was a small group of men who cared about poems, but not much else. They wanted to discuss poems in terms of their form, and such was their love for poetry they wanted these poems to be perfect, for every detail to balance out every other, and for the poems to come together in wonderfully ironic wholes. They worked hard reading those poems, searching for unities and ironies and balances, and they called this hard work "close reading." This was all a terrible mistake, but they didn't know it, because Derrida had yet to come down from his mountain with the ten commandments of deconstruction. And the men so loved poems that they didn't want the messiness of the world to enter into the poems, so they read the poems they loved without reference to context. They worked hard to avoid looking at history and ethics and politics, and they called this hard work "formalism." This too was a terrible mistake, but they didn't know it because Greenblatt had yet to come down from his mountain with the ten commandments of the New Historicism. But these men, misguided as they were, came to dominate our English departments, because something called the G.I. Bill came along, leading behind it a long line of eager and ambitious people, a new generation of students who hadn't been prepared for college at fancy prep schools. Someone had to find a new way to teach them, a way that didn't depend on the students having prepped for college at Groton or Choate or some provincial equivalent. And the New Critics came forward and said they didn't need for their students to do anything but closely read a few short poems and all would be well. But all was not well until the New Critics were driven from the land by Derrida and Greenblatt—may their swords never rust, may their books remain in print forever.

This, more or less, was the story I was told about the New Critics when I was a graduate student in the 1990s. The people telling me this story considered themselves enemies of the New Critics, but in the years since leaving their seminar rooms, I've discovered that, where partisans of the New Criticism still exist, they tell a remarkably similar story. And I'm not sure who's done more damage to the New Critics: their detractors or their defenders. Detractors condemn the New Criticism as ahistorical and unconcerned with ethics or politics, and defenders generally don't disagree with this depiction. They just value it differently, hoisting it high like a tattered flag under which to rally the scattered remnants of the pre-identity-politics, pre-continental-theory literary intelligentsia. As in so many fiercely fought debates, though, beneath the clamor the two sides really agree more than they differ: both, after all, see the New Critics as formalists, and set them up against a set of politicized, post–1960s approaches to literature. But does the consensus lying beneath the squabble offer an accurate view of things? My contention is that is does not, and that both detractors and defenders insist on unity where there is none to be found. Like the cartoonishly simplified New Critics in the story above, they take a contradictory and dissonant thing and hammer it into something coherent, with all the parts are subordinated to an interpretive whole.

The challenge in reading the New Critics again is to try to see them without any of the preconceptions that underlie the debate between their detractors and their defenders. When we meet this challenge, we see in the New Critics a more diverse, less strictly formalist movement than we find in the distorted version so often invoked by both sides of debate. It may be of some service to us, as we attempt to wipe several decades' worth of preconceptions off our critical lenses, to remember that none of the New Critics actually saw themselves as locked in battle with the nascent forces of deconstruction, cultural studies, and identity politics. One of the things that becomes clear when we reread the New Critics is that they weren't a rearguard action, but an advance force, launching raids against a host of other critical movements. Although the New Critics are often taught at the beginning of the literary theory seminar, as a kind of point of origin for modern literary theory, they didn't emerge in a vacuum, but in a battlefield.

The New Critics turned their critical artillery, first and foremost, on early-twentieth century academic scholarship, which they saw as a dull and dutiful business of the establishment of context: all dusty philology and dry bibliography. The New Critics fought, too, against the impressionistic criticism found in the journalistic world. Such criticism was a debased form of Walter Pater's impressionism and, in the New Critical view, diverted attention from the work of literature to the consciousness of the individual reader. But it wasn't just against the practices of the academics and the journalists that the New Critics struggled. Although all-but-forgotten now, colossi of literary theory like Max Eastman and Irving Babbitt towered over the literary scene in the early twentieth century, their tomes promulgating psychological and moralistic approaches to literary study, respectively. And the 1930s wasn't only the period in which the John Crowe Ransom, Allen Tate, Robert Penn Warren and company, their Vanderbilt apprenticeships behind them, set out to reinvent criticism: it was also a time haunted by the specter of Marxist criticism, the decade of Christopher Caudwell and the young George Orwell, voices heard on both sides of the Atlantic.

Emerging as it did in the context of more established, competing theories, it's understandable that the New Criticism put polemical emphasis on its differences from historical, impressionistic, moralistic, and political approaches to literature. But we do a disservice to the New Criticism if we see it as turning its back on the insights offered by these approaches. Indeed, the goal of the New Criticism, more often than not, wasn't to spurn history, politics, ethics, or psychology, but to bring these things back into contact with the specific formal qualities of the literary work. Synthesis, rather than aesthetic separatism, was the main project, a fact too often overlooked by both the defenders and the detractors of the New Criticism.

To see this, we have to make an effort to rescue the moral or ethical side of the New Criticism from oblivion. Many figures are important in this connection—John Crowe Ransom, Randall Jarrell—but none more so than Yvor Winters. For Winters, the poem was primarily a rational statement about the world, not an aesthetically autonomous balancing-act in which formal elements were put together in an intricate puzzle. The ideal poem would coordinate its rational and emotional content, and base both of them on an appropriate motivation in the world: that is, the poem would show us appropriate emotional and intellectual responses to specific experiences. For Winters, the critic's job in assessing how well a poem succeeds depends on a method that takes us far from the kind of irony-hunting formalism most of us associate with the New Criticism: "What then is the nature of the critical process?" asks Winters:

> It will consist (1) of the statement of such historical or biographical knowledge as may be necessary in order to understand the mind and method of the writer; (2) of such analysis of his literary theories as we may need to understand and evaluate what he is doing; (3) of a rational critique of the paraphrasable content (roughly, the motive) of the poem; (4) of a rational critique of the feeling motivated—that is the details of style, as seen in language and technique; and (5) of the final act of judgment . . . (84)

Readers who think of the New Criticism as pure formalism, whose sense of its range is defined by catchphrases like "the verbal icon" and "the heresy of paraphrase" may find this paragraph a bit of a shock. Items one and two in Winters' list tell us we need to know about context to understand a poem, and items three through five insist on both a moralistic and a stylistic assessment of the poem in question. This is neither moralism pure and simple, nor is it anything like pure formalism—it is a fusion of the two.

There are some who may take Winters' emphasis on moral judgment as grounds for excluding him from the New Critical movement, but this is a kind of retrospective limiting of the range of the New Criticism to fit our stereotypes. Those who would cast Winters out of the movement would do well to remember that none other than John Crowe Ransom, whose New Critical credentials couldn't be in better order, included Winters in his 1947 book *The New Criticism*. But even if we kick Winters out of the New Critical canon, there's still plenty of evidence that the New Criticism often sought to incorporate, rather than exclude, moral or ethical criticism. Consider the uncontroversially New Critical Allen Tate, who tells us, in "Miss Emily and the Bibliographer," that while "the specific property of a work of literary art which differentiates it from mere historical experience" is something that a pure moralist like Irving Babbitt "could never understand," morality nevertheless finds its way into poetry (44). "It gets in," says Tate, "not as moral abstractions but as form, coherence of image and metaphor, control of tone and rhythm, the union of those features" (44). Certainly there's formalism in Tate's thinking, but it doesn't involve an eschewal of ethical concern. The critic must make what Tate calls "a total judgment," (44) a judgment of the fusion of moral and formal elements. As with Winters, so also with Tate: in both critics we see old, moralizing criticism taken up in and fused with a new sensitivity to form.

Re-reading the New Critics also helps us see the limits of the idea that the New Criticism was an anti-historicist phenomenon. Certainly there are moments when particular New Critics deny the relevance of historical context—in the essay just cited, for example, Allen Tate tells us "the literature of the present begins . . . with Homer" (47). But there are just as many moments when the New Critics insist on the relevance of history to the study and judgment of literature. Often this is a matter of asserting the importance of literary tradition—Eliot's "Tradition and the Individual Talent" echoes throughout the essays of the New Critics. At other times, though, the references to history are much less matters of literary tradition, and much more matters of politics and economics. One could be forgiven for thinking it was Fredric Jameson who wrote the sentence "how could anyone fail to realize that the excesses of modernist poetry are the necessary concomitants of the excesses of late-capitalist society?" But it wasn't Jameson, it was Randall Jarrell (219).

It also shows us some of the things the New Criticism can offer us as we try to understand our own literary situation. Those who think that elliptical poetry was invented by John Ashbery, for example, may be surprised to find Robert Penn Warren writing on the topic of elliptical poetry in his essay "Pure and Impure Poetry." Warren tells us that elliptical poetry is a kind of writing that leaves out "definition of situation, movement of narrative, logical transition, factual description, generalization, [and] ideas" (130)—a description that could apply to the contents of any number of literary journals today. While our contemporary debate about elliptical poetry tends to devolve into crude assertions of approval or disapproval, Warren draws a distinction between two different kinds of elliptical poetry. On the one hand, there is an elliptical poetry that, despite the appearance of sophistication, is intellectually vapid, excluding as it does any meaningful engagement with ideas. In such poems, says Warren, ideas take no part. On the other hand there is another kind of elliptical poetry, best represented by Eliot's *Waste Land*. Eliot, says Warren, has "purged away statement of ideas" because he wants the ideas "to participate more fully, intensely, and immediately" in the poem. Poets like Eliot "are trying to carry the movement of mind to the center of the process" of poetry. Their ellipses aren't vague, but exploit "precision, complication, and complicated intellectual relation to the theme" (132–33). Whether or not we agree with Warren's particular conclusions, if we followed his example in distinguishing between different types of elliptical poetry the contemporary debate would be much improved.

Given the variety of the New Criticism, and the potential usefulness of little-discussed New Critical concepts in understanding our own literary scene, the question arises: how did such a crude caricature of New Criticism as a matter of pure formalism come to be so dominant? The answer comes when we examine a phenomenon that can only be referred to as something like an unspoken pact between universities and New Critics, in which New Critics justified literary study in terms universities could appreciate: as an autonomous field of intellectual endeavor.

The common story of the rise of the New Criticism emphasizes the democratizing of higher education in postwar America, and there is much truth to this. But there is a second factor in the success of the New Critics, a factor based on the foregrounding by many—but not all—such critics on the autonomy of literary study, and their accompanying emphasis on the autonomy of the literary object. The American university, like its German model, is predicated on the assumption of discrete and autonomous areas of knowledge, and was therefore receptive to ideas of literary study as an autonomous endeavor. The division-and-department administrative model of the university was one that favored the idea of autonomous areas of inquiry. This idea of clearly divided and administered knowledge-areas implies, as Gerald Graff puts it in *Professing Literature*, "the isolation of literature as its own autonomous mode of discourse with its own autonomous 'mode of existence.'" Moreover, as Graff points out, the English Department's mode of discourse and existence must, in this view, be "distinct from that of philosophy, politics, and history" and put a premium on "methods that seemed systematic and could easily be replicated" (145).

This predisposition of the American university to autonomous rather than heteronomous views of knowledge predates the New Criticism considerably, having its origins as far as the founding of Johns Hopkins University on German educational models in 1867. By and large, though, literature departments lagged behind the sciences and social sciences in developing autonomous principles for the study of their subject matter. But by the mid–1930s—just as New Critics like Brooks and Warren were launching their fledgling academic careers—the institutions were ready for change. R. S. Crane of the University of Chicago, for instance, looked to reform his own department on the autonomous principle, calling, in 1935, for a faculty that did not subordinate formal to political or moral concerns:

> . . . men of the type of the older impressionists we could hardly use, and as for the remnants of the Humanists, there is little to be hoped for from the kind of principles—essentially political and ethical rather than esthetic in character—for which they mainly stood. (4)

Crane may not have known exactly what he wanted, but he knew what he didn't want: heteronomous principles of literature, the prevalence of which seemed to threaten to subordinate literature to politics and ethics.

It should come as no surprise that three years later, in the year of *Understanding Poetry*'s first edition, John Crowe Ransom would look back on Crane as a visionary, and praise him as a great reformer in the famous essay "Criticism, Inc." By 1950, many proponents of heteronomous principles of literature and literary study in the academy had come to feel that the reformers had them up against the ropes. MLA president and Harvard professor Douglas Bush's address to the MLA two years earlier ("The New Criticism: Some Old Fashioned Queries") had been less an act of resistance than an angry surrender to an enemy that dismissed his own ethical and humanistic views as nothing more than "the didactic heresy" (19–20). Then, as at many an MLA conference since, the desperate pleas of the president were ignored by the eager young assistant professors, ready to make names for themselves by following the next new thing.

In an institutional environment that called out for a method of study based on autonomous principles of literature, critics like Tate and Ransom were there to supply what was needed. This is not to say that they were nothing more than opportunists, merely that some of the ideas they produced happened to fit the demands of the academic/literary marketplace of the time, and they put this side of their work forward. Then again, one can sometimes detect a whiff of opportunism in private correspondence, as when Ransom writes to Tate in 1937, saying that "I have an idea that we could really found criticism if we got together on it" and that "the professors are in an awful dither trying to reform themselves and there's a big stroke possible for a small group that knows what it wants in giving them ideas and definitions and showing the way" (Young 85).

Regardless of how deliberate any particular New Critics may have been in exploiting the universities' need for a theory of literature as an autonomous object of study, those who prospered most seemed to embrace the idea that both the method and object of literary study were autonomous. Ransom's "Criticism, Inc.," for example, echoes R. S. Crane's criticism of non-autonomous methods of literary study in claiming that the unreformed English department could "almost as well announce that it does not regard itself as autonomous, but as a branch of the department of history, with the option of declaring itself occasionally a branch of ethics" (Graff 148). A year later, in 1939, Cleanth Brooks would write in *The Well-Wrought Urn* that, without an insistence on formalist methods, professors of literature would wake up one day to find that they had been "quietly relegated to a comparatively obscure corner of the history division" or were being "treated as sociologists, though perhaps not as a very important kind of sociologist" (235). Against these dire consequences, Brooks held up a strictly formal method of literary study. By 1951, he felt able to codify the method in a number of "articles of faith" published in *The Kenyon Review* under the title "The Formalist Critic." No minor sociologist he, but a professional practitioner in a proper field of inquiry.

In discovering, and speaking in terms of, the logic of the mid-century research university, some New Critics emphasized the formalist element of their ideas. But we need not take up uncritically their self-representations, or misrepresentations. Indeed, it is the imperative of the critical intellect to question such representations. If we do so, we may find that we can return to the New Criticism and see it again, as if for the first time.

Works Cited

Bush, Douglas. "The New Criticism: Some Old-Fashioned Queries." *PMLA* 64 Supplement Part 2 (March 1949): 18–21. Print.

Brooks, Cleanth. "The Formalist Critic." *The Kenyon Review* 13 (1951): 72–81. Print.

Brooks, Cleanth. *The Well-Wrought Urn: Studies in the Structure of Poetry*. New York: Dobson, 1968. Print.

Crane, R. S. *The Idea of the Humanities*. Vol. 2. Chicago: University of Chicago Press: 1967. Print.

Graff, Gerald. *Professing Literature: An Institutional History*. Chicago: University of Chicago Press, 1989. Print.

Jarrell, Randall. "The End of the Line." *Praising it New: The Best of the New Criticism*. Ed. Garrick Davis. Athens, Ohio: Ohio University Press / Swallow Press, 2008. 213–23. Print.

Ransom, John Crowe, *The New Criticism*. Norfolk, Connecticut: New Directions, 1941. Print.

Tate, Allen. "Miss Emily and the Bibliographer." *Praising it New: The Best of the New Criticism*. Ed. Garrick Davis. Athens, Ohio: Ohio University Press / Swallow Press, 2008. 39–48. Print.

Warren, Robert Penn. "Pure and Impure Poetry." *Praising it New: The Best of the New Criticism*. Ed. Garrick Davis. Athens, Ohio: Ohio University Press / Swallow Press, 2008. 117–37. Print.

Winters, Yvor. "Preliminary Problems." *Praising it New: The Best of the New Criticism*. Ed. Garrick Davis. Athens, Ohio: Ohio University Press / Swallow Press, 2008. 75–84. Print.

Young, Thomas Daniel. *John Crowe Ransom: An Annotated Bibliography*. New York: Garland, 1982. Print.

Poetry / Not Poetry

Where do we draw the line between what is poetry and what isn't poetry? Or, to put the question another way, what makes a poem a poem? Ask a poet like Howard Nemerov, and you'll get a beautiful answer, in the form of a poem called "Because You Asked about the Line between Prose and Poetry":

> Sparrows were feeding in a freezing drizzle
> That while you watched turned into pieces of snow
> Riding a gradient invisible
> From silver aslant to random, white, and slow.
>
> There came a moment that you couldn't tell.
> And then they clearly flew instead of fell. (125)

I imagine many poets will like the answer: it's elegant, and it pays a compliment to poetry, making it fly, while prose merely falls. But in the end Nemerov's answer about the nature of poetry is evasive, offering little more than the "I'll know it when I see it" argument that people used to invoke in debates about pornography. I don't really have a better way to answer the question, except to say that the only real way to answer anything is to quit looking for trans-historical, absolute truths and start rooting around in contexts, in the history of how a question has been answered, and the reasons those old answers made sense at the time.

Turning the question in this direction, I think we can say that something changed in the way we answered the question "how is poetry different from prose" right around the beginning of the nineteenth century, and that, with some small modification, the new answer poets came up with at that time is still with us. The new answer arrived with Romanticism, and we're far from done with it.

Roland Barthes, in his great, early study *Writing Degree Zero,* makes a statement about poetry before Romanticism. He tells us that for poets of the pre-Romantic period, there was a fundamental similarity between good poetry and good prose. "Poetry is always different from prose," writes Barthes, but in the neo-classical eighteenth century "this difference is not one of essence, it is one of quantity. It does not, therefore, jeopardize the unity of language, which is an article of classical dogma" (41). In other words, the neoclassical or Augustan writer doesn't grant poetry one of the rights that we moderns and postmoderns grant it: the right to follow rules significantly different from those governing discursive prose. It is more or less the same as prose, but with the added use of particular literary devices such as rhyme and meter. Consider Alexander Pope's poem *Essay on Man*: it is more or less what it sounds like it is—a discursive, explanatory essay. It just happens to add versification. In the neoclassical paradigm, prose and poetry are involved in the same sort of things: explaining, talking, arguing, narrating. And why did people write poems? Many reasons, of course: but they tended to be the same sorts of reasons one writes prose, utilitarian reasons such as personal advancement, money, getting the girl, social improvement, or didacticism. Prose and poetry were close cousins formally—one just had extra verse elements—and close cousins in terms of their *telos* or purpose.

Then things became strange. They became strange right around the time the Romantics hit the stage—not that this is a bad thing: indeed, it's the beginning of everything I most love in poetry. Suddenly, poetry wasn't more-or-less continuous with prose, or prose-plus-special-effects: there was a new discontinuity of language. Poetry was reborn as something very different from prose, and different from verse, too.

Consider Coleridge's famous definition of poetry in the *Biographia Literaria*. Here, we learn that poetry, unlike prose, generates its own rules.

We learn that the poem, unlike prose, looks inward upon itself, seeking an inner co-ordination of all parts to the whole. And we learn that the statement or use-value or *telos* of the poem is secondary to its formal composition. Poetry, says Coleridge, is a kind of communication "opposed to works of science, by proposing for its immediate object pleasure, not truth; and from all other species . . . it is discriminated by proposing to itself such delight from the whole, as is compatible with a distinct gratification from each component part" (II, 10). The poem, Coleridge continues, gives us parts that:

> . . . support and explain each other; all in their proportion harmonizing with, and supporting the purpose and known influences of metrical arrangement. The philosophic critics of all ages coincide with the ultimate judgment of all countries, in equally denying the praises of a just poem, on the one hand, to a series of striking lines or distiches, each of which, absorbing the whole attention of the reader to itself, becomes disjoined from its context, and forms a separate whole, instead of a harmonizing part; and on the other hand, to an unsustained composition, from which the reader collects rapidly the general result unattracted by the component parts. (II, 10)

For Coleridge, the feeling that there is a fusing of all parts into a whole is the defining element of the poetic work. All works in which we feel the presence of this kind of fusion, even those in prose, achieve the status of poetry, and many works in verse do not. Pope, for example, is no poet as far as Coleridge is concerned:

> . . . in *The Rape of the Lock*, or *The Essay on Man* . . . still a point was looked for at the end of each second line, and the whole was, as it were, a *sorites* [a form of logical proposition], or, if I may exchange a logical for a grammatical metaphor, a conjunction disjunctive, of epigrams. Meantime the matter and diction seemed to me characterized not so much by poetic thoughts, as by thoughts translated into the language of poetry. (*Biographia Literaria* I, 11)

The important thing is that a true poem offers a feeling of parts coming together into a larger whole, rather than a set of discrete observations. And it is important, too, that this co-ordination takes place not by some formula, but by rules generated with each new poem. As Coleridge says in "Shakespeare's Judgment Equal to His Genius," "no work of true genius dares want its appropriate form, neither is there any danger of this," because "genius cannot be lawless; for it is even this that constitutes genius—the power of acting creatively under laws of its own creation" (432).

All of this has consequences for the meaning of poetry. Since the feeling of a fusing of parts is so important, and so total, a true poem cannot be paraphrased. If it could, then whatever it has to say would be sayable without the poem's particular coordinating of parts—that is, without the poetry. In a sense, the true meaning of the poem isn't any extractable content, but the very fact of the fusing of parts, the sense the reader has of something coming together in the reading process.

Coleridge's idea of the symbol is connected to this. Unlike the allegory, with its one-to-one relation of sign and meaning, the symbol is polysemous, offering endless suggestive possibilities. Interpreting the symbolic work is an ongoing coming-toward and escaping-of full apprehension—think of Coleridge's own "Kubla Khan," pregnant with meaning, but frustrating attempts to ascribe to it any particular meaning. We feel that something significant is present, that the parts are coming together into some greater whole, but the whole remains, finally, elusive. This is very different from the poem as a vehicle for a discursive statement. As Coleridge states in an appendix to *The Statesman's Manual*, "discursive understanding, which forms for itself general notions and terms of classification" can only give us "Clearness without Depth" (Appendix C, xii). Poetry, when it is symbolic, gives us depth without clarity. We can never quite say what it means, or what it proposes to accomplish in the world.

Poetry of this kind, tends to become a bit of an embarrassment in modern utilitarian society. Poets operating under a paradigm like Coleridge's weren't meant to try to say particular things, or to make things happen: they were to chase mysterious symbols, and create works that promised to bring all parts together into elusive organic wholes. Poetry became not a kind of ornamented prose, but something that played by different rules, and was written for different, murkier reasons.

While these things may have started with Romanticism, they continued after the Romantic movement in new permutations and combinations. The French *symboliste* movement was in some sense an intensification of the idea that the poem was beyond paraphrase, beyond utility, beyond the logic of means-and-ends. And, despite some of their anti-Romantic rhetoric, the American New Critics in the twentieth century made huge intellectual investments in Coleridge's ideas: "The Heresy of Paraphrase" is a rehashing of Coleridge, and New Critical ideas of irony and balance are just Coleridge's fusion of parts to whole revisited and made more static, emphasizing an achieved and identifiable fusion where Coleridge emphasized the ongoing experience of parts coming together.

The Romantic paradigm remains with us even now, even though we tend not to know it. Indeed, some of the most thoughtful poets of the last few decades have been practicing a kind of modified or inverted version of Romanticism. Consider elliptical poetry: so much of it is concerned with showing a lack of formal coherence that one might think of it as the farthest thing from Coleridge's fusion of parts or its New Critical offshoot, the well-wrought urn. But the deliberate incoherence of elliptical poetry is often out to accomplish the same sorts of things Coleridge outlined. Firstly, elliptical techniques foreground the differentiation of poetry from prose: poetry is different, we see, because it doesn't try for prose coherence. And in the deep ambiguities and incoherencies of elliptical verse we can see effects similar to those Coleridge thought of as belonging to the symbol: we avoid paraphrasable meaning, we escape the utilitarian logic of means-and-ends. As Stephen Burt put it, elliptical poetry makes use of "all the verbal gizmos developed over the last few decades to undermine the coherence of speaking selves" (47). This is very much in line with the general trend of thinking that runs from Coleridge through Mallarmé, and even through the New Critics.

So where do we draw the line between poetry and not-poetry? It seems that we've been doing it by insisting on poetry's autonomy, its freedom from use-value, its freedom from specific meaning. Poetry is poetry because it is unlike prose: it is more free, and stands somehow (we like to think) outside of the utilitarian world—as an escape from that world, or possibly as a critique of it. This seems to be the best answer we've come up with in the two centuries since the poets left off praising popes and princes in exchange for patronage. There will come a moment when this will cease to be our answer, but when that will be, no one can tell.

Works Cited

Barthes, Roland. *Writing Degree Zero*. Trans. Annette Lavers and Colin Smith. New York: Hill and Wang, 1977. Print.

Burt, Stephen. "The Elliptical Poets." *American Letters and Commentary*. 11 (1999): 45–55. Print.

Coleridge, Samuel Taylor. *Biographia Literaria*. Ed. J. Shawcross. 2 vols. Oxford: Oxford UP, 1949. Print.

———. *The Statesman's Manual*. London: Gale and Fenner, 1816. Print.

Nemerov, Howard. *The Selected Poems of Howard Nemerov*. Ed. Daniel Anderson. Athens, Ohio: Ohio University Press / Swallow Press, 2003. Print.

The Death of the Critic

The most imposing obstacle facing anyone foolhardy enough to ask whether an avant-garde artistic praxis is possible under postmodern conditions is the much-contested nature of the terms themselves. Since my claim here will be that a postmodern avant-gardism is not only possible but manifest in that most conservative of arts, the art of criticism, I hope I may be forgiven for deferring a demonstration of that claim until I've established just what I mean by 'avant-garde' and 'postmodern' in this particular context.

The Linguistic Skepticism of the Avant-Garde

A classic definition of avant-gardism, one that seems to serve as a kind of accepted folk-wisdom among many poets of what Ron Silliman calls the post-avant, was articulated by Renato Poggioli in his 1968 study *The Theory of the Avant-Garde*. Poggioli proposes that avant-gardism proceeds from the assumption that languages and systems of expression are, by their nature, entropic. Avant-garde artistic and literary praxis are, in this view, inevitable reactions to "the flat, opaque, and prosaic nature of our public speech, where the practical end of quantitative communication spoils the quality of the expressive means." For Poggioli, the "conventional habits" of expression in a bourgeois, capitalist society are subject to a "degeneration," and the role of the avant-garde must be the renewal of whatever language (literary, visual, etc.) the artist chooses as a field of operations (37).

This idea, of course, does not originate with Poggioli, but derives from a long tradition of thinking about experimental art, much of it from the era of the historical avant-garde itself. Poggioli's point about linguistic entropy was already present in Victor Shklovsky's seminal article of 1917, "Art as Technique." Here, Shklovsky presents the problem of linguistic entropy as a problem of ever-decreasing experiential returns: "If we start to examine the general laws of perception," he writes,

> we see that as perception becomes habitual, it becomes automatic. Thus, for example, all of our habits retreat into the area of the unconsciously automatic; if one remembers the sensations of holding a pen or speaking in a foreign language for the first time and compares that with his feeling at performing the action for the ten thousandth time, he will agree with us. (753)

In this view, ordinary life in modern society is inherently a matter of alienation, not merely from one's labor, but from one's every action: ". . . life is reckoned as nothing. Habitualization devours works, clothes, furniture, one's wife, and the fear of war" (754). Only the artist devoted to new forms of representation can overcome this alienation. If, as Shklovsky claims, "the purpose of art is to impart the sensation of things as they are perceived and not as they are known," then the technique of art must be "to make objects unfamiliar, to make forms difficult, to increase the difficulty and length of perception . . ." (758). The artist, in this view, should be an innovator who works against habit and banality.

This view of the avant-gardist's role as the eternally vigilant regenerator of languages, symbolic systems, and modes of experience, appears in countless manifesti of the historical avant-garde, and is handed down to us through thinkers like Poggioli and Clement Greenberg (whose *Avant-Garde and Kitsch* made the idea central to American academic thinking about the avant-garde). So thoroughly normalized has this view now become that an American academic can, at a reputable scholarly conference, casually remark of an experimental poet like Michael Palmer, "the writer's task is to challenge received ideas about signification, to undermine authoritative modes of discourse" (Finkelstein), and meet no response other than approval. Approval is, of course, entirely merited: this is a vital element of art's role in our time. But while this view of the avant-garde is correct as far as it goes, it is limited by its formalism and aestheticism, by the deep-seated tendency to see art as independent of its institutions and social embeddedness.

The Institutional Skepticism of the Avant-Garde

One irony of Victor Shklovsky's status as a kind of patron saint of the avant-garde is that the examples he chooses to illustrate his idea of defamiliarization are not drawn from the powerful currents of avant-garde practice that flowed through Russia in 1917. Suprematism and Zaum are absent, Mayakovsky does not appear, and there is only the briefest mention of Khlebnikov. Instead, Shklovsky derives his most extended and convincing examples from classic nineteenth-century Russian writers such Tolstoy and Gogol. This, in itself, indicates the insufficiency of the reinvigoration of entropic language systems as a defining characteristic of the avant-garde. Indeed, as Jochen Schulte-Sasse points out, skepticism about language's ability to remain fresh and retain meaning was already present in the late eighteenth century (ix), the period in which Schiller and Goethe wrote:

> All dilettantes are plagiarizers. They sap the life out of and destroy all
> that is original and beautiful in language and in thought by repeating
> it, imitating it, and filling up their own void with it. Thus, more and
> more, language becomes filled up with pillaged phrases and forms that
> no longer say anything . . . (313)

If the avant-garde is to be understood as something distinct from the artistic and literary traditions that preceded it, it must possess some quality or propose some project other than defamiliarization and linguistic regeneration. Schulte-Sasse (following the theorist Peter Bürger) maintains that this quality is to be found in the avant-garde's questioning of the institutions of art. Schulte-Sasse begins with the premise that the late-nineteenth century Aesthetic movement was predicated on Kantian notions of aesthetic disinterest and autonomy. While the movement constituted a kind of critique of the bourgeois, utilitarian world, it was a dead-end in that it removed art from the world of power. Art became otherworldly, incapable of intervening in civil society, and its critique of capitalist values became a matter of an impotent refusal rather than a force for active intervention (xiv). Rather than being primarily concerned with the regeneration of language, the essence of the avant-garde was institutional critique. The avant-garde, in this view, turned against the institutions of art (literary forms of publication, art galleries, museums, good taste and connoisseurship, etc.) and the theory of art (autonomous, disinterested, Kantian) that underwrote those institutions. It is in this respect, Schulte-Sasse says, that the avant-garde differed from modernism:

> Modernism may be understandable as an attack on traditional writing techniques, but the avant-garde can only be understood as an attack meant to alter the institutionalized commerce with art. The social roles of the modernist and the avant-garde are, thus, radically different. (xiv)

The Bürger/Schulte-Sasse position is certainly adequate as a solution to the problem of how we can separate the avant-garde from earlier movements devoted to defamiliarization and linguistic skepticism. Moreover, the carefully uncommodifiable, deliberately unbeautiful nature of much avant-garde work can be taken as signs of the Bürger/Schulte-Sasse thesis in action: the scandal of such works is aesthetic, but it is more than that: it is a scandal to the very institutions of art, to the gallery-museum-publishing house system, and the whole philosophical apparatus that made such a system possible.

Postmodern Pastiche and the Project of the Avant-Garde

At least one project of the avant-garde—its regeneration of entropic language through defamiliarization—has been dismissed as impossible in postmodern conditions. Frederic Jameson, for example, argues that attempts at defamiliarization have become "meaningless," and their emphasis "on the vocation of art to restimulate perception, to reconquer a freshness of experience back from the habituate and reified numbness of everyday life in a fallen world" cannot function in our cultural climate (*Political Unconscious* 121).

Central to Jameson's concept of the postmodern is the idea that we have moved into an era in which the idea of the modern self has been largely undermined, and with it the notion of individual literary or artistic style. "The old individual or individualist subject," he writes, "is dead." Indeed, from a postmodern and poststructural point of view, "the bourgeois individual subject" is "not only a thing of the past: it is also a myth" that "never really existed in the first place; there have never been autonomous subjects of that type" ("Postmodernism and Consumer Society" 285). Defamiliarization, accomplished through heroic feats of individual style, is impossible in the face of this realization, because it depends on the now-lost illusion that a new, individual view can come into being and release us from ossified thought and clichéd perception. The avant-garde, in Jameson's view, is impossible, because it depends on the myth of the artist as individual stylist, a view that is unsustainable.

Jameson is not alone in thinking the bourgeois subject is dead, and the heroic artist along with it. Roland Barthes' seminal essay "The Death of the Author," for example, argues along similar lines, claiming that our idea of the individualist author is a myth of the modern era now coming to an end:

> The *author* is a modern character, no doubt produced by our society as it emerged from the Middle Ages, influenced by English empiricism, French rationalism, and the personal faith of the Reformation, thereby discovering the prestige of the individual, or, as we say more nobly, of the 'human person.' (1131)

With the death of the mythical author, Jameson and Barthes both see a new emphasis on socially determined codes of meaning. Instead of individual artists regenerating language with unique feats of style, they see artists capable only of working within established symbolic codes. Unable to make "an original gesture" the postmodern artist (or "scriptor," in Barthes terminology), can only "mingle writings." Even when the scriptor "seeks to *express himself*, at least he knows that the interior 'thing' he claims to 'translate' is itself no more than a ready-made lexicon" (1132).

Barthes sees a mingling of writings from an existing cultural matrix or lexicon as the inevitable mode of postmodern writing. Jameson departs from Barthes' view only by coloring it with the dark tint of political melancholy. Whereas artists of the historical avant-garde would quote traditional texts in an attempt to parody them, postmodern writers have, in Jameson's view, seen the futility of the avant-garde project. They "no longer 'quote' such texts, as a Joyce might have done . . . they incorporate them" (283). They have lost the faith that there is a proper way of seeing that degraded, entropic language has distorted, and that avant-garde work can redeem:

> Pastiche is, like parody, the imitation of a peculiar or unique style, the wearing of a stylistic mask, speech in a dead language: but it is a neutral practice of such mimicry, without parody's ulterior motive, without its satirical impulse, without laughter, without that still latent feeling that there exists something *normal* compared with which what is being imitated is rather comic. (284)

No drawing of moustaches on the Mona Lisa can save us, in Jameson's world. We are doomed to empty acts of repetition.

I do not dispute the death of the author, nor do I make any claims for the revival of parody. But I do wish to draw attention to two examples of work by writers I am calling critic-pasticheurs—literary critics working through pastiche—because this work seems to me to accomplish exactly what Jameson would see as impossible. It continues, through postmodern pastiche, both the linguistic and the institutional projects of the avant-garde. It defamiliarizes through pastiche, and in the process challenges the institutions of writing and their philosophical bases.

The Critic-Pasticheur and Defamiliarization

Who, then, are the critic-pasticheurs? There are a number of examples, but let me name two: David Kellogg and Benjamin Friedlander. Both are American literary critics and, perhaps not coincidentally, poets. Both have written works of literary criticism that are, in whole or in part, deliberate imitations of pre-existing source texts. Their works don't set out to parody those source texts: rather, they imitate them, using pillaged phrases and sentence structures as means of creating new insights.

The opening of Kellogg's essay "The Self in the Poetic Field," offers a compact example of what the technique looks like. It is composed of a pastiche made up of (in his words) "a line by line rewriting, with a few sentences removed, of J. D. Watson and F. H. C. Crick's 'A structure for Deoxyribose Nucleic Acid' published in the journal *Nature* in 1953" (97). The original essay begins like this:

> We wish to suggest a structure for the salt of deoxyribose nucleic acid (D.N.A.).
>
> This structure has novel features which are of considerable biological interest. A structure for nucleic acid has already been proposed by Pauling and Corey (1). They kindly made their manuscript available to us in advance of publication. Their model consists of three intertwined chains, with the phosphates near the fibre axis, and the bases on the outside. In our opinion, this structure is unsatisfactory for two reasons: (1) We believe that the material which gives the X-ray diagrams is the salt, not the free acid. Without the acidic hydrogen atoms it is not clear what forces would hold the structure together, especially as the negatively charged phosphates near the axis will repel each other. (2) Some of the van der Waals distances appear to be too small.
>
> Another three-chain structure has also been suggested by Fraser (in the press). In his model the phosphates are on the outside and the bases on the inside, linked together by hydrogen bonds. This structure as described is rather ill-defined, and for this reason we shall not comment on it. (737)

Kellogg's essay makes only minor variations:

> I wish to suggest a structure for contemporary American poetry (C.A.P.). This structure has novel features which are of considerable critical interest.
>
> A structure for poetry has already been proposed by Eliot. He has kindly made his manuscript available to the world for the last eighty years. His model consists of an enveloping tradition, with the dead near the center, and the individual talent on the outside. In my opinion, this structure is unsatisfactory for two reasons: (1) I believe that the material that provides the poetic structure is the living community of readers, not the dead. Without the stack of coffins, it is not clear in Eliot's model what forces would hold the structure together, especially

as the variously interpreted bodies near the center will repel each other. (2) The self of the poem is extinguished along with the poet.

Another dynamic structure has been suggested by Bloom. In his model the dead are on the outside and the living individuals on the inside, linked together by Freudian anxieties. This structure is rather loosely described, and for this reason I shall not comment on it. (97–98)

The goal, here, is far from parody. Kellogg is not out to mock the ambitions of scientific inquiry, nor does he wish to cast any doubts on the validity of the source-text. Instead, his project, here and in the remainder of the essay, is to defamiliarize our usual ways of looking at literary history, and the relation of the poet to his or her work.

Benjamin Friedlander's project is more ambitious. In *Simulcast: Four Experiments in Criticism*, he undertakes a massive rewriting of source texts. Here, as in the opening of Kellogg's essay, his goal is not parody. Instead of seeking to undermine the authority of a source text, he sets out to follow the verbal contours of his texts as a means of discovery. He outlines his experimental critical project as follows:

> I describe these works as experiments because all four are based on source texts and thus inaugurate a species of criticism in which the findings only emerge after struggle with predetermined forms. Sometimes this struggle took shape as an exercise in translation, not unlike the re-creation of a sonnet's rhyme scheme and meter. Often, translation was impossible, and the struggle resolved itself instead in an act of controlled imagination—not unlike the sonnet's original creation. In each case, the production of my text had less in common with the ordinary practice of writing an essay than it did with the composition of metrical verse. . . . [the book's] somewhat scandalous methodology [involves] the creation of criticism through the strict recreation of an earlier critic's text (or, more precisely, through as strict a re-creation as the discrepancy between my source text and chosen topic would allow). Thus, my "Short History of Language Poetry" follows the arguments (and even wording) of Jean Wahl's *A Short History of Existentialism*, while "The Literati of San Francisco" takes Edgar Allan Poe's *Literati of New York City* as its template. . . . Although I was predisposed in each of these pieces to certain arguments and conclusions, I willingly abandoned these when they became incompatible with the critical approach demanded by my source. (1–2)

What is particularly interesting here is the way that Friedlander's work embraces postmodern notions of the writer as a scriptor, and works against traditional notions of authorship. Friedlander's book is not the product of his informed, critical reflections on his topics prior to writing. In fact, sometimes the book's assertions are, as he says, at odds with his own convictions. He does not record his observations, does not paint the landscape of his pre-existing literary knowledge. There is no individual intelligence creating insight through heroic reflections. Hesitating to call the book's often stimulating insights the assertions of a critic or author, one falls back on the old idea of the book's *speaker*, here. But even this idea seems to imply the creation of a consistent character, one who might hold the views on offer, and this is not what happens in Friedlander's work. There is a strange sense in which the assertions of *Simulcast* belong to no personality or character possessing traits or existing prior to the text itself. We don't so much have a speaker as a Barthesian scriptor. The scriptor, after all, isn't defined only as the combiner of existing discourses, but as a creature simultaneous with the text. As Barthes puts it,

> The Author, when we believe in him, is always conceived as the past of his own book: the book and the author take their places of their own accord on the same line, cast as a *before* and an *after*: the Author is supposed to feed the book—that is, he pre-exists it, thinks, suffers, lives for it; he maintains with his work the same relation of antecedence a father maintains with his child. Quite the contrary, the modern writer (scriptor) is born simultaneously with his text; he is in no way supplied with a being which precedes or transcends his writing, he is in no way the subject of which his book is the predicate; there is no other time than that of the utterance, and every text is eternally written here and now. This is because (or: it follows that) to write can no longer designate an operation of recording, of observing, of representing, of "painting" . . . (1132)

The technique is clearly the product of the postmodern world of the scriptor and of pastiche. But unlike the emptiness of Jameson's postmodern pastiche, this work results in a kind of defamiliarization.

Indeed, both Kellogg and Friedlander turn to their source-texts as critical tools to take them away from their own instinctive thoughts about literature, and force them into new insights different from their own critical predispositions. The project shares a great deal with the creative works of the Oulipo, which would use deliberate, systematic forms of writing, carried through with some rigor, to break past our habitual, ossified modes of composition and thinking.

What makes this particularly effective is the turning to source-texts from discourses at a remove from the norms of critical prose in our time. Kellogg leaves the humanities behind and seeks out a scientific source-text, while Friedlander turns to temporally remote, belletristic criticism (Poe), or to a philosophy currently out of fashion in the academy (Existentialism). The discourses are alien enough to break our usual norms of thinking, but familiar enough to generate insights that are still comprehensible, if not uncontroversial, to readers embedded in our current discursive environment. As the critic Vincent Sherry once said of the intertextual poetry of John Matthias, which draws from arcane historical source-texts, "on the one hand, the pedagogue offers from his word-hoard and reference trove the splendid alterity of unfamiliar speech; on the other, this is our familial tongue, our own language in its deeper memory and reference" (29). Critic-pasticheurs like Kellogg and Friedlander offer us an estrangement of thinking, based on a revival and re-examination of disused discursive strategies. It is simultaneously postmodern pastiche and avant-garde linguistic regeneration.

The Death of the Critic

The critic-pasticheur doesn't just accomplish the linguistic goals of the avant-garde, he accomplishes the institutional goals of the avant-garde as well. Unlike the historical avant-garde, though, the critic-pasticheur doesn't challenge the institutions of autonomous art. Rather, he challenges the institutions and assumptions of professional criticism.

Perhaps the most deeply embedded principal of professionalized literary criticism is the idea of the critic's responsibility as a knowing subject standing behind his or her methodologically grounded truth-claims. The critic has, in this view, a method or technique that can be applied to texts, and that will yield results that the critic stands behind as a matter of professional pride and integrity. In 1966, for example, the American Association of University Professors made the following statement about the professional's knowledge a part of its creed:

> ... guided by a deep conviction of the worth and dignity of the advancement of knowledge, he recognizes the special responsibilities placed upon him. His primary responsibility to his subject is to seek and to state the truth as he sees it ... (see Robbins 36)

In this view the critic is to be an earnest and sincere subject, standing behind his written words. The speaker of the book is identical with the author: indeed, the author stands in relation to the words of the book in the "author-God" position so thoroughly debunked by Barthes.

When Friedlander calls his methodology "scandalous," the scandal to which he refers can only be a scandal of professionalism. When he chooses to abandon the "arguments and conclusions" that he personally believes to be true in order to follow the textual contours of his sources, he strikes a blow at the very idea of the critic as a knowing subject standing behind his words. What is more, he undermines the idea of critical writing as the presentation of existing and established knowledge. Instead, he proposes the critic's work as a matter of generating new and challenging insights through the defamiliarization of habitual modes of thought.

One answer to the question of whether avant-gardism is still possible under postmodern conditions, then, must be yes. But in this latest iteration of the avant-garde impulse, some of the primary actors are not the artists, but the critics.

Works Cited

Barthes, Roland. "The Death of the Author." *Critical Theory Since Plato*. Ed. Hazard Adams. New York: Harcourt Brace Jovanovich, 1992. 1130–33. Print.

Bürger, Peter. *Theory of the Avant-Garde*. Trans. Michael Shaw. Minneapolis: University of Minnesota Press, 1984. Print.

Friedlander, Benjamin. *Simulcast: Four Experiments in Criticism*. Tuscaloosa: University of Alabama Press, 2004. Print.

Finkelstein, Norman. "The Problem of the Sacred in the Recent Poetry of Michael Palmer." Twentieth-Century Literature Conference. University of Louisville. 24 Feb. 2006. Conference Presentation.

Goethe, Johann Wolfgang Von. *Werke*. Ed. Paul Raabe. Vol. 47. Weimar: Weimarer Ausgabe, 1990. Print.

Jameson, Frederic. *The Political Unconscious: Narrative as a Socially Symbolic Act*. Ithaca, New York: 1982. Print.

——. "Postmodernism and Consumer Society." *The Continental Aesthetics Reader*. Ed. Clive Cazeaux. London: Routledge, 2000. 282–94. Print.

Kellogg, David. "The Self in the Poetic Field." *Fence* 3.2 (2000–2001): 97–108. Print.

Poggioli, Renato. *The Theory of the Avant-Garde*. Trans. Gerald Fitzgerald. Cambridge, Massachusetts: MIT Press, 1968. Print.

Robbins, Bruce. *Secular Vocations: Intellectuals, Professionalism, Culture*. London: Verso, 1993. Print.

Sherry, Vincent. "The Poetry of John Matthias: 'My Treason and My Tongue.'" *Word Play Place: Essays on the Poetry of John Matthias*. Ed. Robert Archambeau. Athens, Ohio: Ohio University Press / Swallow Press, 1998. 26–34. Print.

Shklovsky, Victor, "Art as Technique." *Critical Theory Since Plato*. Ed. Hazard Adams. New York: Harcourt Brace Jovanovich, 1992. 751–59. Print.

Schulte-Sasse, Jochen. "Theory of Modernism versus Theory of the Avant-Garde." Foreword to Bürger, Peter. *Theory of the Avant-Garde*. Trans. Michael Shaw. Minneapolis: University of Minnesota Press, 1984. vii–xlvii. Print.

Watson, J. D. and F. H. C. Crick. "A Structure for DNA." *Nature* 2 Apr. 1953: 737–47. Print.

Marginality and Manifesto

Can the manifesto matter? Or is it an outdated weapon in the arsenal of the poets, a rusted blunderbuss only to be displayed under glass in the museum of cultural oddities? Questions like these seem to lurk just below the surface in "Eight Manifestos," a special section of the February 2009 issue of *Poetry*, a feature edited and introduced by Mary Ann Caws, the unquestioned dean of manifesto studies. On the one hand, the section gestures toward the idea of the manifesto as a museum piece, both figuratively and literally: a note tells us that the section commemorates the centennial of F. T. Marinetti's "Futurist Manifesto," and if we read all the fine print we find that several of the poets who wrote items for the section presented them at New York's Museum of Modern Art. On the other hand, what we have aren't essays on the nature and history of the manifesto: they're manifestos proper, or seem to be. If the manifesto is indeed an old blunderbuss, the poets seem to have pried it out of its display case and fired off a few live rounds.

Even a cursory look at the nature of the manifestos, though, raises some doubts about how much faith poets still place in the manifesto. By and large, the manifestos are either parodic, or dead-set against the historical roles manifestos have played in history, or elegaic about the death of the manifesto. Joshua Mehigan's contribution, "The Final Manifesto," parodies the Oedipal struggle inherent in the writing of manifestos by stripping away any specific theoretical content and offering only such statements of naked generational ambition as "You are a museum of irrelevance," "We are here and now," and "History will forget you and salute us." It really doesn't matter what specific poetic program a manifesto offers, Mehigan seems to say: they're really just a means for young poets to slay the old monarchs and make names for themselves. Much of Thomas Sayers Ellis' manifesto seems more sincere, but he raises some doubts about this sincerity with comments about how followers of his manifesto's program adhere to it in part to keep their "professional opportunities (in publishing and employment)" open. In the end, he makes a case much like Mehigan's, highlighting the barefaced careerism of some manifesto writers. Other poets reject the ideas of progress and innovation so dear to the hearts of most manifesto writers in history. Ange Mlinko, for example, argues that when it comes to styles, "the pendulum swings back and forth," and rejects the prophetic, authoritative role of the manifesto writer, saying that she "can't really say anything more definite for the time being." A. E. Stallings actually does speak in the voice of assured authority, but does so not in the name of a break with the past, but in the name of continuity, tradition, and unabashed rhyme. "Rhymes do not need to be hidden or disguised," she declares, "they are nothing to be ashamed of." She takes the bullhorn voice of the manifesto to argue against the content of a thousand experimentalist manifestos. Another set of poets argue, in different ways, against the idea of group action inherent in the idea of the manifesto. "Shouldn't there be a greater variety of life, a greater variety of art, a greater variety of poetry than what gathers in schools?" asks D. A. Powell; while Michael Hofmann assures us that "there are no plurals" in poetry, except for mere "functionaries" and "hacks." Even Charles Bernstein, the poet in the "Eight Manifestos" selection most likely to be associated with a group, denies the possibility of group action. Midway into his manifesto he pauses to define Language Poetry as "a loose affiliation of unlike individuals." Finally, Joshua Clover and Juliana Spahr (writing "on behalf of Hate Socialist Collective") lament the demise of the manifesto. They admire many of the things manifestos stood for—innovation, social criticism, and as the moniker "Hate Socialist Collective" indicates, group action. But everything in their contribution is anger and elegy. They feel keenly the loss of a time when, in their view, the openness of political possibilities fostered an openness of poetic possibilities. "The manifesto is dead," they declare, and "we will not celebrate the end of that era with you." Poor Marinetti, my dead king!

Taken as a whole, the manifestos—or anti-manifestos—amount to an implicit statement of the exhaustion of the manifesto, a sense that the old blunderbuss has served its purpose and, while we may want to take it out and look it over as a historical artifact from time to time, it is best left under glass, a relic of an earlier time. Some relish this situation, others decry it, but it does seem to be as close to a consensus as you'll get in a gathering of poets.

Why this sense of exhaustion? Have the conditions that brought about a flourishing of manifesto writing a century ago really changed? Is there really nothing left at which to carp? To arrive at any kind of an answer, we need to remember just what motivated the writers of manifestos in the heyday of the genre. Broadly speaking, writers of poetic manifestos in the early decades of the twentieth century aimed at one of two kinds of things: to challenge the marginalization of poetry in society; and to challenge the center of poetry from the margins of the art. Dada and surrealism provide examples of the first kind of challenge. If there's any generalization one can make about such unruly movements, it's this: that they set out to break down the barriers between art (including poetry) and life. Poetry had become marginal to society because it had been cordoned off by the institutions of literature, by journals and anthologies and professors, and the febrile manifestos of Dada and surrealism claimed that dissolving those institutions, and the very idea of art and literature as distinct areas of human activity, would return poetry to the broader life of the people. Other groups had the more modest (but still, when one thinks about it, rather grandiose) goal of reforming literature, challenging moribund orthodoxies from the margins and making literature new. Imagism is a good case in point: it's well-known dicta were meant to clear away the dominant modes of Georgian verse and elevate the taste of a small group of neophytes into a new literary standard. The center, hoped the Imagists, would not hold, and their aesthetic would be loosed upon the world.

In at least two senses, the conditions that led to the flourishing of manifesto writing do, in fact, still obtain. Take the matter of the marginality of poetry in society. According to the 2004 NEA report "Reading at Risk," only 12% of the adult American population read any poetry in the year prior to the survey (National Endowment for the Arts). The same report found that poetry's readership was in decline. In absolute terms, there are still quite a few American poetry readers—about 25 million. But if you've ever spent an evening tipping a glass of wine with a group of poets, you'll get a pretty clear sense that most poets consider the situation a bit grim, and don't feel that their work is central to the culture.

The question of whether there's a center to American poetry, one that could be challenged from the margins, is a bit murkier, but in the end the answer has to be yes. The question is made murky by the sheer number of publishing poets. It's difficult, and maybe even impossible, for any one reader to get a full sense of just what's going on in all of the provinces of American poetry. Ron Silliman took a dim view of the possibility of seeing American poetry steady and seeing it whole in 2007, when he wrote "as MFA programs pop up like mushrooms in a damp forest climate, and as the number of publishing poets in the USA moves beyond 10,000 toward the 20,000 mark or thereabouts, nobody will have any hope whatsoever of reading even a fraction of what is being written . . ." It's made murkier still by the reluctance of many of the most prominent American poets to accept the idea that they are in any sense central figures. Robert Hass, for example, once asked me what I planned to name the book about him and his old Stanford classmates I was working on. When I told him it was called *Laureates and Heretics* the two-time Poet Laureate looked downcast, muttering, "I *knew* I'd pay for it when I took that job!" In the upside-down world of American poetry "laureate," it seems, is a term of dishonor, and "heretic" a term of praise. It's not just prominent poets who take this tack: in *The Believer*, for example, an interview with John Ashbery is introduced with a short essay in which the interviewer mentions Ashbery's many prizes, his considerable influence on younger poets, and the dinner date with James Tate he was set to go on after the interview. Despite all these signs of centrality and integration into a community of poets, the interviewer insisted on describing Ashbery as "an outsider." One imagines he did this out of politeness, that the idea of centrality seemed too like an affront. Perhaps it's because poetry is itself a marginal art in our society that the idea of centrality seems like a betrayal of the art. It reminds me of the way my friends and I would talk about punk rock in high school: the most prominent bands always seemed like they were somehow betraying punk's deliberate marginality, and the very notion of prominence was viewed with the narrowed, suspicious, sidelong eyes of the sullen teen.

A final murkiness comes from the fact that there's really no single dominant poetic school in American poetry. Think of some of the most prominent poets, and immediately we see a range: Robert Pinsky's discursiveness, John Ashbery and Jorie Graham's elliptical verse, the formalism of Kay Ryan or Donald Hall, the surrealist-inflected work of Charles Simic, the identity politics of Adrienne Rich or Rita Dove, the experimentalism of Charles Bernstein. Their work can't be said to constitute a single dominant style in any meaningful sense. Certainly there are kinds of poetry (and kinds of poet) that are excluded from prominence, and we should remain sensitive to this, and alert to the inequities of the current institutional arrangement. But we really don't have an official culture like that of the old Soviet Union, nor do we have the narrow establishment taste of, say, France in the age of salon painting.

Despite all this murkiness, though, we can roughly discern the shape of a center in American poetry—but it's a center defined less by style than by institutional considerations. It's significant, I think, that Jed Rasula begins *The American Poetry Wax Museum*, his study of poetic canonization, not with a survey of stylistic possibilities but with a parodic representation of the institutions that make or break poetic reputations. He imagines:

> . . . an American Poetry Wax Museum, operated by the MLA and subsidized by the nationwide consortium of Associated Writing Programs. Special galleries would be dedicated to corporate benefactors, including *The New York Times Book Review, The New Yorker, Poetry,* and *American Poetry Review.* (1)

Access to the prominent journals, publishing houses, and the syllabi and faculty appointments of academic programs (one's access, or that of one's supporters) makes for prominence and centrality—which is not to say that such prominence and centrality correspond entirely, or even approximately, to the quality of any particular poet's work. An excellent, and prominent, young poet-critic clarified the idea of centrality-by-institutional-access for me one night after a literary conference. I'd been going on about how a certain older poet was down in the dumps because he wasn't as well-known as he'd like to be. "Look, he's great, but he's as prominent as he *can* be," replied the poet-critic, "without a New York publisher and elite grad students." Unlike some earlier, less plural eras in poetry, you can become a prominent poet by working anywhere across a fairly wide spectrum of styles, but you can't become central without access to the complex apparatus of publicity, recognition, funding, and canonization that has grown up around American poetry over the generations.

It's here, with this notion of a poetic centrality defined less by stylistic conformity than by institutional access, that we begin to see the reason for the relative dearth of manifestos in contemporary poetry. As Pierre Bourdieu argues in *The Field of Cultural Production*, when an art form becomes divorced from institutional support—when it is without, say, a financially sustaining market niche, or a set of aristocratic or ecclesiastical patrons—the battle for position becomes a battle about innovation in style. If there are no court-sponsored positions to fill, no market from which to gain riches, no state ministry of culture grants available, then an artist or poet will seek position by challenging existing formal orthodoxies. What we end up with in such conditions, says Bourdieu, is an ongoing "revolution of the young against the old and the 'new' against the 'outmoded'" (187). This is exactly the sort of struggle for position Joshua Mehigan parodies in his "Final Manifesto," but it's important to note that this sort of revolution needn't be merely cynical on the part of the young: in fact, it tends to be all the more sincere when motivated by material necessity. And conditions in the early twentieth century, when manifesto-writing ran rampant, were certainly difficult for unestablished poets: it was a time when the old aristocratic patronage system had all-but disappeared, the emerging book market didn't support poetry any better than it does now, and the complex system of grants, prizes, residencies, and academic appointments we take for granted existed only in nascent form. Things have changed. While the plight of the adjunct writing prof scraping together yet another contest entry fee is real enough, fewer poets starve in garrets than was once the case, and we can afford a certain *laissez-faire* attitude toward style. Of course there will still be the spectacle of poets striving to be noticed as the latest thing. Indeed, it remains every bit as intense as it was in the early twentieth century, and seems to be connected with the lack of a broad, non-specialist audience for poetry. But in terms of institutional support from universities and foundations, there's room at the inn for Rae Armantrout and Billy Collins, Amiri Baraka and Dana Gioia, just as there's room in *Poetry* for Thomas Sayers Ellis, Charles Bernstein, and A. E. Stallings. There are new vanguards all the time, but there is material support for far more poets than there has ever been, and poets of many persuasions have found comfortable perches from which to write. And this largesse, relative to other historical periods, matters when it comes to the writing of manifestos, which has become something of a lost art. The flourishing of manifesto writing, it turns out, was a symptom of a climate of material and institutional scarcity.

Works Cited

Ashbery, John. "An Interview with John Ashbery." *The Believer.* The Believer, Feb. 2009. Web. 1 July 2011.

Bernstein, Charles. "Manifest Averions, Conceptual Conundrums, & Implausibly Deniable Links." *Poetry.* The Poetry Foundation, n.d. Web. 15 June 2011.

Bourdieu, Pierre. *The Field of Cultural Production.* Ed. Randal Johnson. New York: Columbia University Press, 1999. Print.

Ellis, Thomas Sayers. "The New Perform-a-Form: A Page vs. Stage Alliance." *Poetry.* The Poetry Foundation, n.d. Web. 1 July 2011.

Hate Socialist Collective. "Leave the Manifesto Alone: A Manifesto." *Poetry.* The Poetry Foundation, n.d. Web. 15 June 2011.

Hofmann, Michael. "Manifesto of the Flying Mallet." *Poetry.* The Poetry Foundation, n.d. Web. 2 July 2011.

Mehigan, Joshua. "The Final Manifesto." *Poetry.* The Poetry Foundation, n.d. Web. 1 July 2011.

Mlinko, Ange. "The Eighties, Glory of." *Poetry.* The Poetry Foundation, n.d. Web. 28 June 2011.

National Endowment for the Arts. "Reading at Risk: A Survey of Literary Reading in America." National Endowment for the Arts, n.d. Web. 10 June 2011.

Powell, D. A. "Annie Get Your Gun." *Poetry*. The Poetry Foundation, n.d. Web. 1 July 2011.

Rasula, Jed. *The American Poetry Wax Museum: Reality Effects, 1940–1990*. Urbana: NCTE, 1995. Print.

Silliman, Ron. "Untitled Blog Entry." *Silliman's Blog*, Ron Silliman, 15 Sept. 2007. Web. 5 July 2011.

Stallings, A. E. "Presto Manifesto!" *Poetry*. The Poetry Foundation, n.d. Web. 29 June 2011.

Poets and Poetry

A Portrait of Reginald Shepherd
as Philoctetes

hiloctetes, sadly, has never been a favorite character of Greek
legend. He gets only a brief mention in the *Iliad*, and missed his
chance for greater acclaim when the last manuscript of Proclus'
Little Iliad, where he may have played a greater role, was lost to history.
The Greek tragedians liked him—he's the subject of a play by Aeschylus
and another by Euripedes, and two by Sophocles—but their audiences
didn't fall in love with any of these plays, and history has been unkind
to the manuscripts: only one full Sophoclean script remains, along with
a few lines of the other. The Aeschylus and Euripedes have fared even
worse: neither has been preserved, even in fragment. When Edmund
Wilson surveyed the history of the Philoctetes story in *The Wound and the
Bow*, he found it left surprisingly little trace in literary history: a bungled
seventeenth-century French play by Chateaubrun, a chapter of Fénelon's
Télémaque, an analysis by Lessing, a sonnet by Wordsworth, a John Jay
Chapman adaptation, and a version by André Gide. The six decades
since Wilson's survey have added little to this short list: mentions in
Derek Walcott's *Omeros* and Seamus Heaney's *The Cure at Troy*, and a few
short poems by Michael Ondaatje, are the only distinguished examples.

This is a shame, in that the Philoctetes story seems remarkably suited
to our times. It is, after all, a story of othering, or (to steal one of

Reginald Shepherd's words) of otherhood. An archer equipped with a bow that never missed its mark, Philoctetes suffered a wound to his foot so distasteful to his fellow Greeks that they stranded him on an island en route to Troy. Ten years into their fruitless war, the Greeks learn that without the skills of the man they've wronged, they cannot win. They coax the understandably outraged Philoctetes to join them, which he does, distinguishing himself in battle. Edmund Wilson saw the story in a Romantic light, treating it as a myth of the alienated artist whose skill is somehow connected to his isolation. But we can see the story in more contemporary terms, too, as a myth of social disenfranchisement and the damage it causes. Seen this way, the real wounds aren't physical at all. They are, rather, the social and psychological burdens placed on those othered, and the losses to society caused by its failure to embrace the human potential of all of its members. It is no accident that the three poets to pick up the story after Wilson are all postcolonials.

Reginald Shepherd's poetic career mirrors the Philoctetes story in both its contemporary and Wilsonian versions. The contemporary version of the story fits in that being born gay, black, and poor in America—as Shepherd was—is to be triply othered, to be shunned and devalued for one's sexuality, race, and class. It isn't that gayness, blackness, and poverty are wounds in themselves: it is that America treats these things in a wounding way, much as the Greeks treated Philoctetes. Just as the Greeks' cause at Troy suffered because of their failure to embrace Philoctetes, America suffers from its othering of people like Shepherd. The Wilsonian version of the myth also applies to Shepherd, in that Shepherd's poetic genius is intimately connected to his otherness in American society: his work returns, again and again, to the particulars of his outsider status. Shepherd's poems also return to the same solutions to the dilemma of otherhood, seeking solace in never-quite-trusted yearnings for beauty and interracial erotic fulfillment.

Over thirteen years and five books of poems, from *Some are Drowning* (1994), and *Angel, Interrupted* (1996) through *Wrong* (1999) and *Otherhood* (2003), and on to his collection of 2007, *Fata Morgana*, Reginald Shepherd consistently explored the same issues, and tested the same forms of solace. If, as T. S. Eliot maintained, one criterion of a major poet is a career devoted to a "continuous conscious purpose" (43) then Shepherd, who died in his forties, showed tremendous promise of becoming just such a poet. Another of Eliot's criteria for the major poet is that the parts of the work add up to a whole greater than the sum of the parts, that such a poet "is one the whole of whose work we ought to read, in order to fully appreciate any part of it" (44). If this criterion is taken into account, the case for Shepherd's majority becomes even stronger. Taken as a whole, the work represents a journey through the predicament of otherness to a new way of being at home in the world.

*

Assessing Shepherd's achievement from an Eliotic point of view is particularly appropriate given how deeply Eliot influences Shepherd's poetry, especially the earlier work. *Some are Drowning* is saturated with Eliotic phrasing and imagery. A poem like "L'Enlèvenment d'Amymoné," for example, wears its influence on its sleeve, from the Eliotic French of the title to the rendition of birdsong ("Jug jug. Tereu") proudly lifted from *The Waste Land* (20). The book is also filled with despoiled landscapes familiar to readers of Eliot: Boston's Charles River appears as a close cousin of Eliot's despoiled Thames when Shepherd writes "the Charles is choked with candy wrappers, / and here a single hyacinth / surrenders to a bus's wheels" (9). Even the book's recurring images of drowning—Shepherd's symbol for the loss of self—seem to owe something to *The Waste Land*'s famous "Death by Water" section. The book's most profound affinity with Eliot, though, comes in its obsession with that most Eliotic of themes, the fear of a life not fully lived. Shepherd is no Prufrock, though, dying of a severe case of respectability. Rather, Shepherd depicts a world where lives go unfulfilled because of the wounds dealt out for reasons of otherness.

"Brotherhood" provides one of the book's most direct treatments of the way individual poverty conditions experience in affluent America. The poem begins with a slightly uneasy moment of Romantic consolation, with the poet seeking solitude in nature (a nature even here not unmarked by hints of an Eliotic despoilation):

He wonders how he should stand
at the public shore where sand and liquid salt

immerse immobile feet as if it were still summer,
as if the soothing brine weren't tainted
by the tugs plying the horizon. (13)

The lines that follow show us both how low-wage drudgery generates the need for this kind of Romantic escape to nature and solitude, and how it prevents the realization of such an escape:

He wants to know how to turn back, get on the bus
and pay the fare; how to allow the head to drift
against the window towards the scenic reverie
pavements repossess (a sheltered suburb
shaded with plane trees), and not
drift into thoughtless sleep. He'd like to steal
his life back, hour-per-hour wage, he'd like to rewrite
the working week. (13)

He yearns to take back the life that's been stolen from him by hourly-wage drudgery, but the attempt at a Romantic escape bears the imprint of his economic limitations: his trip to a "tainted" public beach can't drive away his exhaustion or his consciousness of the fare he has to pay. Everything is haunted by an economic insecurity that sets the speaker apart: the "scenic reverie" is, after all, "repossess[ed]" (13). Poetry seems like a weak tool for transcending class conditions: the poet may yearn to "rewrite / the working week," but can't. Life slips away between work and the drifting-off into "thoughtless sleep" (13). It's rare to find such frankness about class in American writing: the character's predicament here is more like that of E. M. Forster's Leonard Bast than it is like any in the American classics.

In "Tantalus in May" Shepherd examines the burden of society's barely-concealed hostility toward his sexuality. He invokes the Greek myth of a man sentenced to be forever near to the always-unattainable objects of his desire, then shows us "a frat boy who turns too sharply from my stare" with hints of violence and danger (56). Conditioned by hard experience to curb expressions of his desire, the speaker finds himself out of joint with a world blossoming out into open desire and fulfillment. "Everywhere I look," he says, "it's suddenly spring. No one asked / if I would like to open up drastically" (56). The predicament is classically Eliotic: life goes unlived, desires go unacted-upon, and there is only cruelty for the speaker in this blossoming April.

Even in environments where his sexuality is dominant, Shepherd frequently finds himself othered, ill-at-ease because of his blackness. "Three A.M. Eternal," for example, gives us "a small room full of smoke and men, / pale bodies wavering" where the speaker asks "why should it always be such pearled white skin?" He finds the men's "words / too blonde" and, in a "room so white" he tells us he'd "like to open / a door, someone, or just to breathe" (7). There's an oddness in that last phrase, in which one of the imagined forms of relief would be to open someone. But the idea of opening out a person is intended, and recurs elsewhere in the book. The image is much like the one we see in "Tantalus in May," for example, where the speaker can't open himself out. The recurrence shows us how insistently Shepherd returns to the idea of the life closed-off through the inhibitions of otherness. It also shows us how closely intertwined the poems of this book are, how they build upon shared patterns of images. The "continuous conscious purpose" Eliot found so central to the major poet is definitely at work in these pages.

Shepherd isn't content merely to log the difficulties of otherness. With tremendous candor, he writes of his yearnings to escape from the burdens America thrusts upon him. Frequently, he imagines transcendent erotic experiences with white men, moments when it seems briefly possible to pass beyond painful history, beyond social division, even beyond individual identity. In "Johnny Minotaur," for example, Shepherd describes a sleeping lover as a kind of adored blankness:

> Sullen boy, sight
> sullies you; it's made you what you are. I prefer
> to watch you sleep, your face adorned by lack,
>
> your person sacrificed to first light slatted
> through matte blinds. I'm not ready to give that up
> just yet . . . (30)

The speaker knows that the emptiness of the sleeping lover is an illusion, that no person is simply pure beauty free of subjectivity and all its complications. But Shepherd longs for such an impossibility here, as he does in "A Muse," where he looks at another beautiful man and finds himself "bewildered / by the eden of his body." The prelapsarian world seems briefly possible through eros. It is a world where physical divisions, linguistic conventions, and individual identities seem to dissolve. "He doesn't even know his name," Shepherd writes of the man, "in his body he's one with air, white as a sky / rinsed with rain" (36).

Such dreams of a paradise beyond identity and otherness may haunt Shepherd, but he never loses himself in them entirely. Often, he finds the longed-for escape from otherness and its burdens collapses into the very history it seeks to transcend. We see this in "The New World," where Shepherd begins by conflating erotic conquest with the voyages of discovery that initiated the long, sad history of slavery:

> *This is the paradise of emptiness*, I said
> and journeyed into faithless terra incognita,
> the muscles of his stomach on display
> when he wipes his face with his shirt. (6)

The connection becomes more explicit when we hear of "his stomach, peaks of nipples / briefly glimpsed before the cotton field unfolds"—the cotton of the lifted shirt becomes the cotton fields of the slave plantations. Instead of the Edenic body, we find ourselves in "the semiotic underworld / of palms and discontent" (6). The poem ends with an admission that no escape from history and its legacies of disenfranchisement is possible:

> Setting out upon the voyage of the new, one comes upon
> the well-mapped coast, Atlantic dripping in noon light
> after the flood, and orichalcum instead of gold.
> I have already misplaced his name:
> there is no new world. (6)

Just because something is impossible, of course, doesn't mean we don't desire it, even need it. Perhaps the most moving depiction of this predicament in *Some are Drowning* comes in "Paradise," where Shepherd describes the "histories of high achievement" that took place while his "great-grandparents were hidden among the cotton, / slaves." He feels bound to speak for them, but also wishes to be relieved of that burden, and speak only for himself. "Let the lost," he says, "this once, bury the lost" (10). His conflicting desires—to be true to, but also to transcend, the tragic history of the African-American experience—lead to this astonishing passage:

> Swallow, swallow, when shall I
> be like the swallow, singing the rape
> of my voice, but singing past the rape, something
> my own to sing? And not live by white men's
> myths (not to reject those too-clear eyes, but not
> to long for them, or see through their blue distances
> all colors but my own) (10)

Here, the desire to escape "white men's myths" comes couched in the form of a white man's myth: Ovid's story of Philomela, who was raped, had her tongue cut out, and was then transformed into a swallow, singing with a new voice. History and the burdens of otherness prove inescapable—even the forms in which Shepherd yearns for escape bind him to them (10). In another poem, "Wide Sargasso Sea," Shepherd gives us his most powerful image for this state of affairs, in which the sign of healing and the sign of an enduring wound become one. In the midst of a dizzying montage of suffering slaves, sugarcane plantations, and eroticized "blue-eyed / planters' sons at play," Shepherd pauses over the image of the "broken skin" of a wounded past and says "I'll be / the scar" (8).

There's more to this prodigious first collection than I've been able to describe—notably two powerful elegies for the poet's mother, which frame the book. But it is the concern with the wounds of otherness, and the ambivalence about beauty and eros as paths to healing those wounds, which connect the book to the main body of Shepherd's work.

*

The arc of Shepherd's career over his next three books of poetry is one of immersion and transformation: the Reginald Shepherd we meet in *Angel, Interrupted* has plunged more deeply than ever into desire and the attempt to transcend otherness through eros; in *Wrong* we see him coming to terms with mortality and the limits of desire; in *Otherhood*

Shepherd begins to develop a myth of death and rebirth that changes his relationship to his own dreams of desire. This journey is important, in that it shows us Shepherd developing even as he builds on his earlier work.

If *Angel, Interrupted* doesn't make Shepherd poet laureate of Chicago's Boystown, the predominantly gay neighborhood south and east of Wrigley Field, there is no justice. Should the neighborhood be destroyed, one could almost rebuild it all, from the Belmont rocks to the clubs on Halstead Street, using the descriptions in Shepherd's poems. One might expect to find Shepherd at home here, and, indeed, the place does at times seem like a paradise of male beauty to him. The opening of "The Gods at Three A.M.," for example, begins with an ecstatic (and typically classically-inflected) depiction of Boystown club life:

> The foolish gods are doing poppers while they sing along,
> they're taking off their white T-shirts and wiping the sweat
> from their foreheads with them, the gods have tattoos
> of skulls and roses on their shoulders, perhaps a pink triangle
> above the left nipple, for them there's hope. (48)

But even here (where the "gods" significantly appear as a "them," not an "us") Shepherd feels the sting of otherness. "Don't try / to say you didn't know the gods were always white," he writes. "The statues / told you that" (49).

Certainly there are times in *Angel, Interrupted* when the Dionysian world of club life seems to promise a transcendence of racial distinctions and all of its attendant baggage. Looking at the flashing dance-floor lights in "Narcissus Learning the Words to This Song," the speaker tells us how "those changing tints (blues / yellows, and reds, melding and alternating) want / to refute mere black and white" (19). But Shepherd is never at ease with the implications of a transcendence of race through the erotic. To leave race behind, even if it were possible, would in some sense be a betrayal of himself—at least this seems to be Shepherd's conclusion when, in "About the Body, Beauty" he writes: "searching for the body's hidden paradise, he / cuts off his face to spite his skin, cuts off / his black skin and calls it love" (18).

Near the end of *Angel, Interrupted* we find "A Plague for Kit Marlowe," a poem dedicated to filmmaker Derek Jarman, who had recently died of AIDS. The poem, which lists names of HIV/AIDS medications the way Renaissance lyrics listed names of flowers ("Foscarnet, Retrovir, / Zovirax, gaudy bouquets which wilt expensively" [71]), serves as a bridge to the next collection, *Wrong*, which brims with intimations of mortality. Even here, though, beauty continues to appear as an ambiguous form of redemption. "I've heard that blood will always tell," writes Shepherd in "Antibody," "tell me then, antigen, declining white blood cell count / answer, who wouldn't die for beauty / if he could?" (12–13). There's a new emotional depth to Shepherd's concern with beauty here, a new pathos.

There is also a new kind of otherness in the poems of *Wrong*, the otherness of a man denied his usual forms of solace and communion. In "About a Boy," for example, we read of a man set apart,

> Never doing the things he wants
> to the bodies he wants to do them
>
> to, Poor Eros. His arms are broken off
> at the shoulder, his eyes have worn
> shut. (36)

"Salt Point" provides what is perhaps the most poignant moment of this kind in *Wrong*. Here, we read of a kind of voyage to the kingdom of the dead. "While grieving I went down" writes Shepherd, setting sail for an underworld where he finds, if not solace, companionship: "dead men were singing / there, no longer lonely" (20).

As the title of Shepherd's next book, *Otherhood* indicates, it is a volume in which Shepherd continues to explore his characteristic concerns. It is a departure from his earlier work in several ways, though. Much of the book's geography is new. The book takes us away from urban America and into the eastern Mediterranean, meandering through Syria and Cyprus to Greece and Italy. There is a new emphasis on the natural world, too, and a new linguistic music arising from the incantation of botanical terms. The form of the poems is more often fragmented or elliptical than it had been in Shepherd's earlier collections, and in poems

like "Kingdom: An Epithalamium" Shepherd becomes interested in the
cento, or poem composed of lines gathered from other texts (in this
case, the King James Bible's version of the "Song of Solomon"). Classical Greece is still invoked as a means of expressing male beauty, but
there's a new emphasis on full-fledged mythopoeia. In a development
that returns Shepherd to his Eliotic roots, he synthesizes a number of
mythologies to create his own myth of death and rebirth.

Shepherd's most sustained effort at synthetic mythology is "In the
City of Elagabal," a longish poem composed of fragments lifted from
the Bible, Joseph Campbell's *The Masks of God*, Edward Gibbons' *Decline
and Fall of the Roman Empire*, and a number of scholarly works on Mediterranean history and mythology. The cult of Elagabal was a religion of the
sun imported into Rome from Syria by the boy-emperor Heliogabalus.
In Shepherd's version, it combines elements of the dying and reborn
god ("puissant Baal is dead / long life to puissant Baal" [21]) with a
suggestion of gender transgression (Heliogabalus flaunted the gender
strictures of Rome with his open transexuality). One element of Shepherd's richly evocative myth is the transcending of individuality: "his
personal interests melted away" reads one passage, "in the fire of the
feverish search" (18). To know one's place in a larger cycle of vitality and
mortality is to gain a distance from self-interest and the individual will.

This distancing from oneself through a consciousness of our place
in a cycle of death and rebirth finds its way into other poems from the
collection. Although it never erases Shepherd's sense of the wounds of
otherness, it does seem to allow him to experience them at a remove.
In "Polaroid," for example, Shepherd gives us these lines:

> Let empire, let rage: I said
> to worms, you are my mother
> and my sister (unearth my then),
> we are death's firstborn
> festival. (33)

There's a strong sense of letting things be, here, rather than throwing
oneself into a world of outrages and the violent history of empires. The
consciousness of mortality that opened up for Shepherd in *Wrong* has
led to a new, more distanced, way of relating to the world. It isn't that

Shepherd has ceased to speak against the injustices of the world ("Semantics at Four P.M." burns with rage against a world where a black man "is being kicked repeatedly / in the ribs by three cops" [72]). Rather, he has found a way of being both in his pains and passions and distant from them at the same time. The long meditation on otherness has brought him to this place.

*

Bin Ramke has said that *Fata Morgana* "feels like the culmination of a major project," and I can't help but agree. The book shows a strong continuity with Shepherd's earlier explorations of the otherness theme, but there's more to it than that. We also see a full blossoming of Shepherd's new consciousness of death and rebirth, and, along with it, a new sense of at-homeness in the world.

Shepherd's old sense of racial and sexual otherness is strongly present in poems like "Kinds of Camouflage." Here Shepherd reworks Edouard Manet's *"Le déjuner sur l'herbe,"* putting himself in the position of the incongruously nude female in that famous painting:

> Then I am sitting naked on damp grass
> (it rained in my yesterday)
> while two white gentlemen
> in black frock coats share lunch
> around me, passing chèvre, cold andouille,
> and baguettes, passing bon mots
> in French, in someone's nineteenth century,
> my muddled impressions of one. I can't
> understand a word. (48)

Shepherd images himself into Manet's world not through the route Manet invites us to take—through an exercise of the heterosexual male gaze—but through an identification with the objectified, othered female figure in the painting. Our sense of the speaker's otherness is only re-enforced when he says, of the white gentlemen in the painting, "they don't see me / at all" (48).

To a surprising degree, though, the poems of *Fata Morgana* dwell not on otherness, but on the final unity of all things. In "Some Kind of Osiris," for example, Shepherd invokes the Egyptian god of death and

rebirth, and presents the body's eventual union with the soil as a transcending of the black-white racial dichotomy:

> "Green" calls green into being,
> speaking my skin into color. I am free
> of song and sky and live among
> beetles and dung, my vast and trivial
>
> brown apartments: earth-like I lie with loam
> and underbrush ... (44)

Entering the larger life of nature and its cycles as the "green man" or
vegetative deity releases one from individual identity, but it doesn't mean
extinction, exactly. One remains alive as part of the whole, "awake as a
season / and oscillation, less a person / than a place..." (44).

If the price of an end to alienation is our death as individuals, we
might find ourselves thinking it is cold comfort indeed. But *Fata Morgana*
offers another path out of alienated otherness, a path we might, in
keeping with Shepherd's classicism, call agape. The penultimate poem
of the book, "One of the Lesser Epics," offers the following description
of this road:

> I am clambering
> out of the garish hells which I've domesticated,
> assorted underworlds in which I've domiciled
> my monopolies of suffering, memory's
> scares and stall tactics: love finds the way by smell
> or sound of you, touch of an index finger
> on your freckled forearm ... (100)

Coming as it does after the sometimes harrowing journey through the
pains of otherness that has been chronicled in Shepherd's poetry, the
passage is free from sentimentality. So is the declaration that comes in
the final poem of the book, "You, Therefore," (dedicated to Shepherd's
partner Robert Philen): "home is nowhere, therefore you" (101). We've
come a long way to get here, and it is a good place to arrive. At the end
of his story Philoctetes, without ever forgetting what has been done to
him, leaves the island of his wounded otherness behind to join in a
larger destiny. But that destiny is, in the final analysis, only a matter of

martial glory. By the end of *Fata Morgana* Reginald Shepherd has returned from his own exile to find something altogether finer.

Works Cited

Eliot, T. S. "What is Minor Poetry?" *On Poetry and Poets.* New York: Farrar, Straus, Giroux, 2009. 34–51. Print.

Ramke, Bin. "Untitled." University of Pittsburgh Press, n.d. Web. 9 July 2011.

Shepherd, Reginald. *Angel, Interrupted.* Pittsburgh: University of Pittsburgh Press, 1996. Print.

———. *Otherhood.* Pittsburgh: University of Pittsburgh Press, 2003. Print.

———. *Some are Drowning.* Pittsburgh: University of Pittsburgh Press, 1994. Print.

———. *Wrong.* Pittsburgh: University of Pittsburgh Press, 1999. Print.

True Wit, False Wit

Harryette Mullen in the Eighteenth Century

We live in an age of false wit in poetry, but that's not a bad thing. And "false" should not be taken to mean "bad" here, any more than "minor" should be taken to mean "insignificant" when Deleuze and Guattari use the term to describe Kafka's *oeuvre*. But if we look at the dominant mode of wit in contemporary American poetry, and describe it in terms of the classical categories of poetic wit developed in the eighteenth century, it is indeed a false wit that dominates. Of course this tells us as much about the values underlying the classical categories of wit, and the eighteenth-century England in which they were developed, as it tells us about our own poetry of wit, and the environment in which that poetry is produced and received. Both the old categories of wit, and the dominant contemporary mode of wit are, after all, products of their social and institutional contexts. Social being determines consciousness, as Marx said—and not just other people's consciousness. So when we bring classical eighteenth century categories of analysis like "wit" to bear on contemporary writing, and find contemporary wit wanting, it isn't a matter of upholding old aesthetic norms and berating contemporary poetry. Rather, it's a way of trying to understand how and why our poetry differs from the poetry valued in the past.

The word "wit" has meant many things since it tumbled out of old German into the English language, but it begins to take on something like the contemporary sense when John Locke, in his *Essay Concerning Human Understanding*, draws a distinction between judgment and wit: judgment is the capacity for discerning fine differences, whereas wit is a capacity for finding similarities, such as the similarities upon which metaphors are founded. Hence, Locke concluded, the snickering wits of London were unlikely to have much good judgment; while sage, sober men of judgment were unlikely to crack a smile at a *bon mot* (a prospect we might rightly regard with terror). But it took the eighteenth century to really codify wit, and it was Joseph Addison who popularized an elaboration of Locke's idea of wit and made it into something like a norm for poetry.

Addison first sketched out his schema of the varieties of wit in a 1711 issue of *The Spectator*. Following Locke, he defines wit as the capacity to find similarities, but he goes on to claim there's more to it than just noticing that one's mistress' eyes, being bright, are like the sun:

> [Locke's] is, I think, the best and most philosophical account that I have ever met with of wit, which generally, though not always, consists in such a resemblance and congruity of ideas as this author mentions. I shall only add to it, by way of explanation, that every resemblance of ideas is not that which we call wit, unless it be such an one that gives delight and surprise to the reader.... Thus when a poet tells us, the bosom of his mistress is as white as snow, there is no wit in the comparison; but when he adds, with a sigh, that it is as cold too, it then grows into wit. (81)

It's a decent working definition, as Addison himself isn't too shy to mention, saying it "comprehends most of the species of wit, [such] as metaphors, similitudes, allegories, enigmas . . . dramatic writings, burlesque, and all the methods of allusion . . ." (81). John Donne's famous comparison of two separated lovers as the two arms of a compass, in "A Valediction Forbidding Mourning," certainly fits the bill as a poem of wit. There, the central, unmoving arm of the compass represents the woman left behind, and the other arm represents the man who returns. The surprising resemblance is the one between the compass and a certain physiological effect of the prospect of a romantic reunion on the returning, male lover:

And though it in the center sit,
Yet when the other far doth roam,
It leans, and hearkens after it,
And grows erect, as it comes home. (52)

This isn't just wit, by Addison's definition: more precisely, it is a poem of "true wit," since wit, for Addison, can be either true or false.

True wit, in this view, involves a substantial resemblance of things in the world, or referents (the upright drawn-in compass really does have a similarity to the man's anatomy), while false wit involves only a resemblance of words. False wit, says Addison, takes many forms: "sometimes of single letters, as in anagrams, chronograms, lipograms, and acrostics; sometimes of syllables, as in echoes . . . sometimes of words, as in puns . . ." (81). Why, one wonders, does Addison hold up a wit based on the resemblance of things in the world over a wit based on verbal or phonetic cleverness without reference to the truth of the resemblance in world? Why value wit that says something about *things* rather than wit that plays with *linguistic resemblance*—the wit of puns or zeugmas or other verbal elements?

One finds the explanation in the social role of journals like *The Spectator* in eighteenth century England. More so than in any other European nation (with the possible exception of the Dutch), the English of the early eighteenth century were seeing a rise in commerce and finance, and a consequent rise of a bourgeois class without ties to the old aristocratic families. It was the Financial Revolution of the 1690s that really allowed a new elite group, based on trade and finance rather than land, to emerge—the 1690s saw the founding of the stock market, the Bank of England, and the national debt, the last of which gave unprecedented power and influence to investors in public credit. There was a new branch of the elite, a sober bunch of people who'd clawed their way up through prudence and calculation. In this, they were unlike the *bon vivant* aristocrats, inheritors of privilege and lovers of wit as a form of sophisticated play. The role of Addison's journal here was, essentially, to find a cultural ground in which these different elites could forge something like a common identity. In this context, the idea of true wit can be seen as a kind of compromise between the rational, hard-nosed, distrusting-of-mere-play viewpoint of the early commercial and financial bourgeoisie, and the more playful and aesthetic world of the hereditary landed classes.

But what about our poetry of wit, and its context? The dominant institution for American poetry in our time is the university, which Ron Silliman famously described as "the 500 pound gorilla at the party of poets" (157). The most dominant form of poetry in that institution is a broadly-conceived set of genres generally described as "linguistically innovative," "formally experimental," or "elliptical"—poetry associated with these terms is by no means the only kind found within the university, but it is the dominant kind in terms of several criteria: amount of critical discussion, prominence at prestige institutions like Brown, Harvard, Iowa, and UCLA, and so forth. Among poets associated with wit and with academe, Harryette Mullen (who teaches at UCLA) is among the best loved.

Mullen is often described as both experimental and as witty. But what would Addison think? Surely he'd look at many of her lines as examples of false wit, as based primarily on the resemblance of words or phonemes or other linguistic elements rather than on the resemblance of things in the world. The line "as silverware as it were," say, from the poem "Wipe that Simile Off Your Aphasia" gives a witty phonetic resemblance between "silverware" and "as it were," but doesn't make much of a statement about the resemblance of objects in the world (*Sleeping with the Dictionary* 80). I don't mean to judge the poem negatively, only to indicate that, by Addisonian norms, it is a poem of false wit. This tells us little or nothing about the quality of the poem, but it will, I hope, indicate something about the nature of the difference between our own aesthetic values and those of the past.

What about the verbally playful prose poems for which Mullen is known? Here's one, called "Of a girl, in white":

> Of a girl, in white, between the lines, in the spaces where nothing is written. Her starched petticoats, giving him the slip. Loose lips, a telltale spot, where she was kissed, and told. Who would believe her, lying still between the sheets. The pillow cases, the dirty laundry laundered. Pillow talk-show on a leather couch, slips in and out of dreams. Without permission, slips out the door. A name adores a Freudian slip. (*Recyclopedia* 18)

What here counts as wit? There's the pun on petticoats "giving him the slip"—where slip refers to lingerie and to a kind of escape. This is followed immediately by the reference to "loose lips," which is bound to the previous statement by the similarity in sound between "slip" and "ship" ("ship" being an absent but implied word here, as it is loose lips that sink ships). We then get another piece of verbal play in the reference to the place "where she was kissed, and told," in which we can hear a reference to the old saying "don't kiss and tell." This is reinforced by the notion of the "Pillow talk-show," a kind of portmanteau-ing of "pillow talk" and "talk show." We find much verbal resemblance between phrases in the poem and other verbal structures such as familiar platitudes. But is there anything that Addison would see as a resemblance between non-verbal things in the world? There's some sort of implied statement lurking in the poem, something about the making public of private eros, but the poem isn't really referential enough to deal in those resemblances of referents that Addison thought of as essential to true wit.

Another one of Mullen's prose poems, "Denigration," takes on weightier issues, and certainly does so with wit. But what kind of wit? Here it is:

> Did we surprise our teachers who had niggling doubts about the pica-yune brains of small black children who reminded them of clean pick-aninnies on a box of laundry soap? How muddy is the Mississippi compared to the third longest river of the darkest continent? In the land of the Ibo, the Hausa and the Yoruba, what is the price per barrel of nigrescence? (143)

The verbal resemblance between the title word "denigration," "niggling" and "nigrescence," and the most offensive of terms for "African-American" is clear enough, and there's the play on "picayune" and "picka-ninny"—so we're reminded, by analogy with the resemblance of words, of how racism manifests itself even in those places where we least expect it. The comparison of the Mississippi to the Niger River (the river near which the tribal groups Mullen mentions reside) is important in this context, in that it reminds us that there are places where Africans are identified by tribe, not by race, and are certainly not identified by the denigrating American term for their race. There is certainly a politics to the poem, but—with the exception of a comparison of a river to another river, hardly a gesture at wit—the wit of the piece is based entirely on verbal resemblances, not resemblances of objects in the world of referents (such as bright eyes and the sun, say, or a raised compass and the tumid male appendage). In Addisonian terms, we're still operating in the world of false wit. It is a judgment our time and place, where Mullen is well-reviewed and much-admired, rejects.

Indeed, Mullen is far from alone in working with forms of wit that the eighteenth century would reject. Charles Bernstein, for instance, is capable of performing with immense wit in exactly the way Addison would find false. Consider this spontaneous comic performance of Bernstein's, as reported by Daisy Fried in the *New York Times*:

> At a reading I attended in the Smith College science lecture hall a few years ago, Charles Bernstein, famous as a poet and anti-poet, pointed to the giant poster on the wall behind him and said, "I want to thank the Poetry Center for putting up my poem 'The Periodic Table of the Elements.'" He then proceeded to give a mock-dramatic rendition of the symbols, left to right, down the page. "H, He, Li, Be!" he panted, growled and spluttered. "Why!?" he complained when he got to yttrium (Y). "I!" he declared solemnly for iodine, as if toasting his own ego. He slowed down, sped up. "No!" he bellowed for nobelium, then finally whispered "Lr," the last chemical symbol. He turned to face the audience. "I've always wondered if I should have ended with 'No' rather than putting that 'Lr' on the end. I think it was a mistake. I think it would have been more emphatic with the negation." This was the funniest, most impromptu-brilliant, serious moment I've ever witnessed at a poetry reading—and very much about sound, language, expression and communication. (n.p.)

Wonderful stuff—and, in Addisonian terms, utterly false as wit. Firstly, part of the conceit here is to strip the periodic table of its reference to actual chemical elements, and to treat it as a kind of sound poem. In fact, the act of comparison is between the periodic table and a zaum-like kind of poetry based purely on sounds, such as we might find in the work of Alexei Kruchenykh. There is a verbal resemblance between the periodic table *as sound* and a kind of poetry based only on sound. It's the phonetic resemblance of the chart to a purely phonetic kind of poetry that creates the surprise and delight. Reference to things outside of language is minimal. The fact that the reading took place in academic rooms is fitting, given the historical connection between a foregrounding of language and the academic institutionalization of poetry.

To understand why the kind of wit we see in Mullen and Bernstein has become so prominent—and it is wit of this kind that we find most prominently in most branches of linguistically innovative poetry—we need to look to our own circumstances, and how they condition our sense of admirable wit, just as Addison's circumstances conditioned his. The briefest way to describe our circumstances is to say this: we live better than a century into an era of relative aesthetic autonomy in poetry. One could and should qualify this in any number of ways, but, caveats aside, to say otherwise is to misrepresent the history of Western poetry. Poetry has long-since turned against a feeling of responsibility toward the dominant logic of modernity—the logic of the market. Hollywood screenwriters and writers of genre fiction tend to write first and foremost with an eye to serving the market. At least since the days of Pater and Mallarmé, though, poets have not: they turn their backs on the market that has turned its back on them. This turning-of-backs is a feature of the bohemian environment in which poetry, like many arts, operated throughout the early twentieth century, and in which to some extent it operates in our own time. Aesthetic autonomy is also a deep, underlying principle of the institutionalization of literary study and literary creativity in university departments of English.

One of the things this century of relative aesthetic autonomy has meant is an increasing emphasis on form and medium. One might think here of Charles Bernstein's "Artifice of Absorption," with its militant rejection of poetry in which language tries to disappear to make way for its referents. Or one might think of Ron Silliman's argument in the essay "Disappearance of the Word, Appearance of the World," which argues powerfully for the foregrounding of language.

This institutionalizing of aesthetic autonomy, in both the bohemian and academic forms, is an enormous underlying force in how poets operate, a force that runs deeper than we are generally aware. Such a confluence is central to the formation of many poets, and it was central to Harryette Mullen's formation, too: she began writing in an Austin-based community of writers, artists, and musicians, and has taught at Cornell and UCLA. She's also been connected to the Black Arts movement, which adds a community-oriented dimension to her writing, along with the prominence of form. But she, like most of us, is oriented toward language itself to an extent that prior eras, such as Addison's eighteenth century, would find shocking, and false. This isn't a bad thing: it is, in fact, strong evidence that we can use in understanding where we are in the social and aesthetic history of poetry. And I think any understanding of poetry that means to get beyond the polemical expression of current norms would do well to look to this kind of historically comparative evidence. It would help us understand the poets we love, and why we love them.

Works Cited

Addison, Joseph. "Spectator 62." *The Spectator*. Vol. 1. New York: Samuel Marks, 1826. 81–83. Print.

Donne, John. *Selected Poems*. Ed. Ian Hamilton. London: Bloomsbury, 1993. Print.

Fried, Daisy. "Poet and Anti-Poet." *The New York Times*. The New York Times, 7 Apr. 2010. Web. 20 June 2011.

Mullen, Harryette. "Denigration." *Callaloo* 32:1 (Winter 2009): 143. Print.

——. *Recyclopedia*. Saint Paul: Graywolf, 2006. Print.

——. *Sleeping with the Dictionary*. Los Angeles: University of California Press, 2002. Print.

Silliman, Ron. "Canons and Institutions: New Hope for the Disappeared." *The Politics of Poetic Form*. Ed. Charles Bernstein. New York: Roof, 1990. 149–74. Print.

Emancipation of the Dissonance
The Poetry of C. S. Giscombe

The title of C. S. Giscombe's 2008 book of prose poems, *Prairie Style*, calls to mind the school of architecture that first came to life in the Midwest at the end of the nineteenth century; reached its zenith in Frank Lloyd Wright's work during the First World War; and passed out of favor after the mid–1920s. But if the title makes us try to draw an analogy between Giscombe's art and Wright's, it misleads us. A better analogy comes if we look to what the more advanced musical talents were up to while Wright was drafting blueprints in Oak Park. Consider Arnold Schoenberg's reflections, from the 1926 essay "Opinion or Insight," on the direction classical music had taken for composers of his generation. "Until our own time," wrote Schoenberg, "composers were always extremely cautious about how the succession of harmonies were arranged, at times even carrying things to the point of using only harmonies whose relationship to the tonic and their 'accessibility' to it (further underlined by convention) was easy to grasp" (259). Harmonies were always structured in relation to a dominant pitch, and the attentive, or even semi-attentive, listener could hear the coherence of the music. Over time, though, "the proportion of elements pointing to the tonic became ever smaller, as against those pointing away from it," ultimately leading to what Schoenberg called "the emancipation of the dissonance"—that is, to a kind of composition where dissonance "came to be

188

placed on an equal footing with sounds regarded as consonances"
(260–61). Giscombe's *Prairie Style* is, in some significant sense, as atonal
as the music of Schoenberg: it creates moments of coherence, but also
welcomes moments of dissonance, when the expository eloquence of
sentences and paragraphs falls apart.

Musical audiences often want to know just *why* a composer would
abandon tonality, and composers have given a number of answers, many
having to do with the hatred of cliché and the need to renew conventions. A deeper answer, though, and one more analogous to what I take
to be Giscombe's motives, comes from one of the great experimental
composers, Karlheinz Stockhausen. Stockhausen said that his refusal
to give his compositions clarity, wholeness, and accessible coherence
was in essence a reflection of his ethical stance. To take the elements of
music and "use them all with equal importance," rather than subordinating some to others, was nothing less than "a spiritual and democratic attitude toward the world" (101). Stockhausen would no more
subordinate musical parts to the whole than he would sacrifice individual lives to an abstract cause, or expropriate one person's labor for
the benefit of another. For Stockhausen, the emancipation of musical
dissonance is, at a formal level, a kind of parallel to the emancipation
of the oppressed in the world. It doesn't actually free anyone, of course,
but it exemplifies a way of thinking that has larger ethical implications.

Giscombe's emancipation of narrative dissonance has goals similar
to those of Stockhausen, and gains a great deal of weight and significance
by addressing questions of race via unconventional means. Indeed,
much of Giscombe's achievement over the course of his career, from *At
Large* in 1989, through *Here* in 1994 and *Giscome Road* in 1998, lies in how
formal dissonance becomes an instrument for understanding the sub-
tleties and complexities of several kinds of identity—personal, sexual,
familial, and racial. By the time he writes *Prairie Style,* Giscombe has come
to see the emancipation of language as a means to reflect on the aftermath
of a greater emancipation, the one brought about by Abraham Lincoln.
Few poets have found in formal dissonance a means to travel so far, and
with such subtlety, into the most profound question of American life.

*

It didn't start out this way. In addition to *At Large, Here, Giscome Road*, and *Prairie Style*, Giscombe wrote another book of poems, *Postcards*. Published a dozen years before *At Large*, it contains close to sixty short, free verse, autobiographical lyrics, written when Giscombe was in his midtwenties. The scenery is familiar to readers of Giscombe's other books: we find the campsites, the outskirts of Midwestern towns, the hiking and cycling trails, the trains and train-yards that form the primary settings of all Giscombe's writings; and we see the dreams and dreamanalyses that give Giscombe's work its surreal cast. We feel, too, the constant pull of Canada, the place that figures for Giscombe as an irresistible magnetic north throughout his entire writing life.

The animating spirit of *Postcards* is unlike that of any of Giscombe's other books. If I had to name that spirit in a single word, I'd say it was *anxiety*. The book is full of the uncanny and the eerie—dark woods, say, or bodies of the slain found in swamps, or a dinner with "next year's murderer," a time-bomb of a teenage boy ostracized by his community, whose worried sister can only keep her face "pointed down at the food she can't finish: her / brother walks funny / and she knows the other guys laugh." While the brother's eventual burst into violence has a powerful sense of inevitability, much of the anxiety in *Postcards* comes from another, opposite source: uncertainty. Often this takes the form of the speaker's inability to piece the world together into a coherent narrative. "A Brief Narrative Concerning Wall Hangings," for example, begins with the question "How could we not have seen it?" (n.p.) The "it" in question is never fully defined, but seems to have been a creature, perhaps an animal, perhaps something stranger, that passed near the speaker and has been glimpsed, but never really seen, by others. The closest thing the speaker has to evidence for the creature's existence is "the crazy photograph / the paper ran two days back" in which the creature "looked like nothing / so much as a smoking smudge pot." Haunted by the fear of that which he cannot grasp, the speaker tells us he cut the picture out, and then:

> . . . tacked it over
> my bed and at night
> when the wind comes in
> through the crack

```
I can hear it
flapping on the wall
live enough
to drown out anything
that might be happening
up there in the woods. (n.p.)
```

This is a kind of magical thinking, the hanging of a talisman against the unknown. The anxiety comes not from the fear of a particular thing, but from the inability of the mind to form a coherent narrative about the woods and what is happening there. Giscombe is far from being the poet of dissonances and narrative uncertainties, here, and not just because he's writing in a straightforward anecdotal form. It's a matter of psychological disposition: he'll have to let go of a lot of baggage about control, closure, and certitude before he can embrace a poetics of dissonance and uncertainty.

The anxious desire for certainty and closure permeates a surprising number of the poems in *Postcards*. Even when the subject matter seems benign enough—as in "Three Fishermen Watch a Shape Passing in the River"—fear of the undefined becomes the focus of the poem. Here, a large, unknown shape passes beneath the surface of a river where the men fish, after which they go home,

```
to sit awake
in their own houses
where they know the doors
and windows
and walls:
and the wall-lamp
turned off, its bulb
no longer hot or glowing
but there,
even in darkness. (n.p.)
```

Once again, Giscombe needs a talisman of sorts—here, the light-bulb that, even when switched off, holds the promise of illumination and the end of the uncertainties of the dark—to ward off a fear that there are things we will never know, things that we will never bring into consonance with our narratives about how the world works.

Giscombe's talismans of certainty in *Postcards* take many forms—at one point he refers, for example, to a gun and its "attendant box of bullets" as a kind of anchor, "the heaviest thing in the room," while elsewhere he writes of "the reassurance of diagrams" (n.p.) for anxious travelers. But the story is the same throughout the book: the world is uncertain, our mental maps of it frail and prone to failure. We yearn for some kind of whole, total, reassuring knowledge that doesn't come, and in its place we erect our little shrines where we seek solace in a world of danger and fragmentary knowledge.

What happened? Somehow, between the mid-seventies, when the young Giscombe wrote little closed-narrative poems about the anxieties of uncertainty, and the late eighties, when the formally dissonant *At Large* appeared, with all of its narrative inconclusiveness, something changed in Giscombe. One is tempted to credit his long correspondence with the Canadian poet George Bowering, which began when Giscombe was editing the journal *Epoch* as a graduate student at Cornell. Bowering, after all, came from the wing of Canadian poetry most closely associated with Black Mountain poetry, with its emphasis on open form and serial composition. One can see how Black Mountain poetry, especially the geographic writing of Charles Olson, would appeal to a poet like Giscombe, obsessed as he has always been with landscape and travel. But there's something else we should consider when we seek an explanation for Giscombe's transformation—something as unlikely as that greatest of Arabic and Persian poetic forms, the ghazal.

The ghazal has been many things to many poets, but the most significant feature of the form, for Giscombe, has clearly been the way it invites dissonance. The traditional ghazal can be a unified poem, but it can also be a collection of disparate pieces, with each couplet or *sher* working as a separate poem laid down in juxtaposition to the couplets around it. When Giscombe spoke about Agha Shahid Ali's ghazal anthology *Ravishing DisUnities* at a 2004 Modern Language Association Panel on "Poetry and the Oblique," he focused on the dissonant possibilities of the form. "The book's of interest to me," said Giscombe, because "linearity is not what's at stake" and the ghazals "are specifically about disunity, about things not holding together but diverging." This kind of disunity is "what I saw in ghazals a long time ago," continues Giscombe, it's "what attracted me to them: the big consciousness of the disunity of the world, how stuff existed in oblique relation to other stuff." How long before 2004 was that "long time ago"? One suspects something like thirty years: there is one ghazal in *Postcards*, written as a disparate collection of *sher* couplets. We might with some justification think of it as a door for Giscombe to open, one that would take him from the closed house of anxiety to the wider world of open narrative and dissonant composition.

This open world, however arrived at, is clearly the space Giscombe inhabits in *At Large*, the book that followed *Postcards* after a dozen years of relative poetic silence. Unlike *Postcards*, the book is written in the kind of dispersed-across-the-page lineation familiar to readers of Robert Duncan or Charles Olson; and, in the Black Mountain tradition, it treats the book, rather than the single poem, as the unit of composition. It also addresses notions of openness and dissonance at several levels. At, for example, the level of character and incident, *At Large* leaves behind the world of *Postcards*, with its seekers after an unattainable control and certainty and their compensatory talismans. Instead, we find characters escaping from control. The book opens with two characters (at least one of whom is African-American) refused service at a yacht club bar. They make their way back up the inlet they traveled, and find another kind of amusement on the tilted deck of a boat tricked out with Christmas lights, evading the policed space of the club for a kind of unpoliced area, beyond the mechanisms of control: exactly the kind of space that was the source of so much anxiety in *Postcards*.

At the level of metanarrative, *At Large* offers meditations on how certainty and narrative closure are often the products of our darker impulses. One section of the book, "(1978)," begins with a rehearsal of commonly accepted narratives about gender, and is Giscombe's first examination of narrative dissonance as a way of understanding gender roles:

    Women say   Men let you down
    men say   Women betray you

        so it's hard to be anything

> but inward
>
> (hopeless)
>
> :angry (in any case) (9)

Here, we see each sex's story about the other as closed, prefabricated, and ultimately expressing and offering little but hopeless anger and aggrievedness. A little later Giscombe shows himself first caught in, then escaping from, these simple and limiting narratives:

> "Men & women don't know how to talk
> to each other"
>   I was saying once
> out of nowhere in particular:
>   little acts of, for instance, refusal
> build up
>   into *something* specific to the curve,
> a sweep practically socio
> logical:
>
>   I walked out of & straight away from that house I saw
> in a dream & did not look back (9)

Giscombe finds himself, out of frustration and anger, taking up a standard-issue narrative about how men and women relate. Seeing it, though, for what it is, he walks away from the house of ordinary domestic unhappiness, leaving the old kind of story, with all its unhappy certainties and prescribed roles, behind. It's not that he has another kind of story to replace the old one: rather, in a gesture like that in the yacht club incident, he refuses the rule-defined place, leaving that closed space for an undefined outside, an existence at large.

At least that's one way to read the passage. I don't want to limit the passage to the one meaning, though. To do so would, in fact, be to impose a kind of coherence or consonance on a book that resists being read as a coherent whole. It's difficult to demonstrate the structure of the book without quoting dozens of passages, so suffice it to say that syntactic openness, combined with the repetition with variations of key phrases and images, allow the reader to find different connections between the various parts of the book, flipping back and forth and marking pages for different kinds of connections, no one set of which seems to be of central importance. The project is defined in the text itself, when Giscombe writes of how he wants to "make the story long / for its own sake" and "redundant, without / apparent point" (10).

There's an ethics to Giscombe's narrative madness: *telos*, the seeking after ends and closure, seems to Giscombe to be an ugly, instrumentalizing way of going about things—and immature, too. Consider the following passage, from a section called "(1981)":

> At 19 claiming
> not having "had" her in particular was the terms
> of death, at least
> its shape
>
> at 30 that all settings
> are exploratory at best (14)

Here, the teenage Giscombe sees the world in terms of *telos*: the point of a relationship with a woman is sexual possession, a culmination of a strategy of seduction, a using of a person as a means to an end. The story of a man and a woman is a story of pursuit, with a beginning, a middle, and an end in victory or defeat. The more mature Giscombe, though, knows the story of men and women can take many forms, and that there is no single conclusion, no simple criterion for success: everything is exploratory and provisional. The structure of *At Large* mirrors this mature conception: there is no simple narrative consonance to it, no one path to closure. In its looping narrative turns and loose connections, it remains exploratory. Here we begin to see something like Stockhausen's desire to find in disunity and dissonance the kind of non-exploitative stance that constitutes "a spiritual and democratic attitude toward the world" (101).

*

Here and *Giscome Road* make further explorations in the dissonant idiom established in *At Large*. In both books, Giscombe contrasts two different ways of avoiding coherent narrative. I have no better way of describing these than to call them *protosemy* and *polysemy*, the first of which is a neologism for which I someday hope to be forgiven. In contrast to the multiple meanings and narrative possibilities of a polysemous poem, what I'm calling the protosemous poem is one that presents us with an absence of significance. In *Here,* protosemy is a negative state, a kind of despair, while in *Giscome Road* it is enticing, a blank slate of possibilities.

Here begins with Giscombe remembering his childhood, when he traveled south from Ohio to Alabama for a family funeral. He stands dejected after the burial, unable to find meaning in his loss. "I was failing to grasp metaphorical continuity right & left," he says,

> I was in the power of silence at 11
>
> & if, in a story or description, we were "picturesque"
> along the station platform we were not a repeating shape, not even
> a vector translated into a thing of moment (11)

This is the protosemous moment: no meaning, no story is available to him, no pattern, archetype, or "repeating shape" gives meaning to the experience. His is a dejection without redeeming significance.

What saves Giscombe is, surprisingly, an encounter with one of the most defined and formally coherent of all aesthetic traditions: the pastoral. As the young Giscombe travels through a part of Birmingham where "white folks w/money still live" he observes their "big houses bespeaking the harmony of all parts" (13). These houses and their grounds, with all their classical decorum, seem to Giscombe to have been the source of his "bad attitude toward the pastoral" (14). As he thinks about the kinds of landscapes he admires, his sense of the richness of narrative possibilities and polysemous meanings returns to him. He contrasts the manicured lawns and manufactured pastoralism of rich, white Birmingham to

> the service track that runs
> through the fringe—warehouses, distributorships—
> through the lowest, most humid elevations, through the dirt
> front yards of cluster-houses hemmed by expressways and bypasses (15)

These are places of transit and intersection, not of closure (it is significant that the repeated word here is "through"). And the contemplation of these places revives Giscombe's imagination, which finally finds the metaphorical significance he could not grasp before. These places become metaphors for the structure of *Here* itself, all connections between echoing parts, without center or conclusion (an "attitude split / into vectors," as Giscombe puts it [15]). The book bursts into polysemy.

Giscome Road takes on the matter of Giscombe's journey to remote parts of British Columbia, questing after an ancestor who had explored the region and given his name to several features in the local geography. Here, protosemy is a matter of the possibilities of the virgin frontier, "something / presignified, uninhabited" (17). Enticing as the idea of the place as a *tabula rasa* may be, though, it is soon revealed as a fiction. The region is not "presignified" in the sense of existing without yet having significance: it turns out to be "presignified" in the sense of having already been inscribed with meaning. The following passage offers a good sense of the movement from the former to the latter sense of presignification:

Having wanted to drive out to the edge, right out
to the mutest edge out there,
the mutest edge, the emptiest soundstage,
out to the invisibility there, out
to all that "up" there in Canada that took place up there—
Giscome, B.C. all unincorporated now up
on the Upper Fraser Rd off desolate Rte 16 to Alberta,
off the Alberta-bound road the Yellowhead (for Pierre B—, the
    blonde
        Iroquois who'd arrived
at the mountains there at the Alberta end, the source of the road):
        miscegenation's
the longest nuance . . . (21)

The journey to a mute edge turns out to be a journey to a place already named, and bearing the marks of a history of imperial colonization, with a road named for a British explorer and a province named for Prince Albert. The presence of Yellowhead complicates things, though: a mixed-race explorer for whom one of the most important highways in Western Canada is named, he (like Giscombe's Jamaican explorer ancestor) introduces a bit of dissonance into the simple, traditional narrative of European colonizer and indigenous colonized. Giscombe introduces a similar dissonance at the level of form, collaging together different stories, maps, charts of indigenous people's belief systems, and tables of their designs and symbols. Through this kind of suggestive but non-coherent composition *Giscome Road* becomes a field in which to contemplate ancestry, family bonds, empire, exploration, race, and race-mixing.

*

If Giscombe's career from *Postcards* through *Giscome Road* can be seen as an emancipation of dissonance after an initial period of anxiety, *Prairie Style* represents the culmination of that emancipation. It is the book where Giscombe takes dissonance to an extreme as a formal principle, and at the same time it is his furthest-reaching examination of racial identity.

One of the more accessible examples of the emancipation of narrative dissonance in *Prairie Style* comes in a prose poem called "Two Directions." Here, Giscombe begins with a gesture as old as poetry itself: he offers a metaphor for love:

> To me love's an animal, not the feeling of watching one but the animal itself—blunt, active, equipped. The long body and, almost independent of that, the mobile head, the range of its movement, the obvious ambivalence. A horse in the river. (15)

So far, so good, thinks the reader uncomfortable with dissonance: love is a horse in the river. It is a kind of being-amid-things, a condition one could push forward or allow to turn back. But rather than develop or elaborate this interesting-enough metaphor for love (as a traditional composer would develop or elaborate a theme) Giscombe follows the opening metaphor with what seems to be a non sequitur, a dissonance or breach of the rules of narrative development:

> I was a sad boy in a dream on his bicycle in the marshes. Always the first question is Where? Jamaica probably along the black river itself where the boat takes one to see the crocodiles and then there's a place to eat at the end of the tour where the tour boat turns around at a low bridge. A dream of what? (16)

Of what, indeed? Certainly not love. Nor does it seem to be about being-amid-things. In fact, as we learn elsewhere, Jamaica's Black River is the place from which all of the African-American Giscombes came.

It isn't a point in the midst of a journey, it's a point of origin. The prose poem continues:

> Love's an animal to me, not working one or the expectation of one's arrival, not "love's animal." Love's full of uncorrected error, the fact of it being unseen or seen and stared at, speechless beneath a bridge, eating with its mouth instead, a croc or any animal. (16)

If we're looking for consonance, we can find a little: the idea of love seems, now, to be linked to the scene of the Black River in Jamaica. But nothing like a coherent statement emerges. If we're hoping for such a coherence in the remainder of the prose poem, we're going to be disappointed, too. Here's how it ends:

> An island, a river, a bridge. Marshes in the dream, though bird-less; and a swaying wooden bridge, and the image of a missile having gone up or come up—from where?—through it: I offered it to the boy bicycling as a kind of humorless solace for the situation, an aimless if tangential exaggeration.
>
> (But at the end was a small train station—an archetype—, just out of town, out of the marsh, and going there I got, in the dream, to long strands of passenger cars stretching out in two directions, platforms alongside.) (16)

It's tempting to read the puncturing of the bridge by the missile as an image for the puncturing of narrative coherence, though there's little in the context to elevate such an interpretation above others. And it's even more tempting to read the final image of the train station as a metaphor for the kind of journey Giscombe's been taking us on. The station, after all, isn't a final destination, any more than the poem's conclusion is a wrapping-up of all the disparate images and narrative elements Giscombe has introduced into the poem. Rather, the station is a place from which to begin journeys, which could go in either direction the track leads. When we arrive at the station, it should be clear to us that Giscombe is inviting us to begin journeys in any of the directions the lines of the prose poem leads us: into meditations on love, on origins, or on narrative disruption. Like Stockhausen, Giscombe wants to use all elements of his composition as if they were of equal importance, rather than subordinating them to a dominant principle of coherence (the love theme, say). The title of Giscombe's travel memoir, *Into and Out of Dislocation*, offers a pretty good description of what it feels like to read this kind of dissonant narrative: just as we glimpse the arrival of coherence and consonance, it slips away and something else rises into view.

How, one might wonder, could a technique of narrative dissonance like this be used to explore issues of race? After all, the most common means of addressing the painful heritage of racial identity in African-American literature hasn't been to liberate dissonance in narrative—it has been to propose a counter-narrative to the old narratives that have denigrated or marginalized African-Americans.

Back when postcolonialism and multiculturalism were first percolating through academe, the creation of counter-narratives that challenged the dominant (and often racist) narratives was called "writing back." Giscombe offers us an example of this kind of writing back in *Prairie Style* when, in the introduction to a series of prose poems called "Indianapolis, Indiana," he quotes from Hugo Prosper Leaming's idiosyncratic historical essay "The Ben Ishmael Tribe: Fugitive Nation of the Old Northwest." The Ben Ishmael Tribe was a strange, poorly documented group of renegades—poor whites, blacks, and Native Americans living together in Kentucky and Indiana in the late nineteenth century. The only contemporaneous record of the tribe is an account by one J. Frank Wright, who maintained that the tribe was "a mongrel hoard" that was "like the Indian in their habits of life," being "so lazy, so filthy, so primitive in their habits" (48). Hugo Prosper Leaming writes back against this characterization of a rare nineteenth century multiracial group, saying they were a tightly knit community of pioneers, some 10,000 strong, from whom the African-American communities of much of the Midwest sprung. They were also, in Leaming's estimate, the progenitors of Black Nationalism and the inspiration for the Black Muslim movement. After examining both Wright's and Leaming's version of the Tribe of Ishmael, Giscombe can only conclude by quoting the archivist Robert Horton, who claimed that there was little that could be trusted in either version. Old racist narratives, and the deliberate writing-back against those narratives both seem suspect to Giscombe.

The way to address a world whose narratives denigrate one's people, then, is not to fight myth with counter-myth, narrative with counter-narrative. It is to escape narrative's claims of truth and coherence altogether, to emancipate the dissonance within language.

Giscombe drives home the political nature of his disruption of narrative in "Lazy Man's Load" (a prose poem whose title brings to mind that great, self-pitying poem-manifesto of Kipling's, "The White Man's Burden"). Here, in the midst of almost but not-quite cohering meditations on landscape, race, pleasure, Indianapolis, and Leaming's Tribe of Ishmael, Giscombe pauses to tell us "I like coherence well enough but am by nature more articulate than dependable" (51). The language is here is particularly loaded, in that it conjures up two stories America tells about black people, one condescending (that it is so rare that it is worth remarking upon when an African-American is articulate) and the other overtly racist (that African-Americans are by nature undependable). Given this Hobson's choice of narratives about his racial identity, is it any wonder that Giscombe decides to eschew narrative and, as he puts it, allow "juxtaposition to do its job" of creating narrative dissonances?

Near the end of *Prairie Style*, in "A Cornet at Night," Giscombe returns to the baleful articulate/undependable dichotomy:

> Say I'm a fact of nature, a habit of life, the broad ripple. Say I'm a Usonian. Say I'm from out past the turnaround but have come in like a pack of dogs to reveal eros to you, to converse with you about the repeating shape. Say I'm teeth and crows. Say I'm voodoo-dick. Say I cleave to you or say I'm a vacant seat pulling away from the curb. Say I'm incomplete without you, sugar. Say I'm late but say how I'll come sooner or later. Say I'm doubtless. Say I'm lazy but articulate. (63)

The repetition of "say," here, is important, and not just for providing via anaphora a coherence at the level of sound that is deliberately lacking at the level of sense. "Say," in this context, can mean one of two things: it can be a statement of how the individual statements are provisional—"say" as "let's suppose." Read this way, the passage is a collection of statements about Giscombe's many potential identities (including his identity in racist discourse as "lazy but articulate"). But "say" can also be an imperative, a command to us to say various things. Read this way, we find ourselves making declarations about ourselves. The results of this way of reading the passage can be quite clever. We find ourselves declaring that we are Usonian, for example. Since "Usonian" was Frank Lloyd Wright's term for his theory of American architecture (U.S.-onian), we find ourselves declaring, near the end of *Prairie Style*, that we are fans of the prairie style. We also find ourselves declaring to Giscombe that we are incomplete without him, and calling him "sugar." But the results can be sobering, too, as when we find ourselves declaring that we are "lazy but articulate"—here, Giscombe makes us define ourselves in terms of America's racist way of seeing blackness: an act that will make us more critical than ever of America's narratives about race.

In Giscombe's hands, the emancipation of narrative dissonance becomes a means of emancipating himself—and, if we are attentive, us—from the kinds of narratives about race that perpetuate old inequities. And in using dissonance as a means of addressing race, he's bringing to his poetry an attitude long-established in African-American music: As Duke Ellington once told a journalist for whom he played some of his recordings, "That's the Negro's life . . . Hear that chord! Dissonance is our way of life in America" (153).

Works Cited

Ellington, Duke. *The Duke Ellington Reader*. Ed. Mark Tucker. New York: Oxford University Press, 1993. Print.

Giscombe, C. S. *At Large*. Rhinebeck, NY: St. Lazaire, 1989. Print.

———. *Giscome Road*. Chicago: Dalkey Archive, 1998. Print.

———. *Here*. Chicago: Dalkey Archive, 1994. Print.

———. *Postcards: Poems*. Ithaca: Ithaca House, 1975. Print.

———. *Prairie Style*. Urbana: Dalkey Archive, 2008. Print.

———. "Ravishing DisUnities." Modern Language Association Conference, Dec. 2004.

Schoenberg, Arnold. "Opinion or Insight?" *Style and Idea: Selected Writings of Arnold Schoenberg*. Ed. Leonard Stein, trans. Leo Black. Los Angeles: University of California Press, 1984. 258–63. Print.

Stockhausen, Karlheinz and Jonathan Cott. *Stockhausen: Conversations with the Composer*. New York: Simon and Schuster, 1971. Print.

In the Haze of Pondered Vision
Yvor Winters as Poet

I f you were to ask the nearest poet or critic about Yvor Winters, the response you'd most likely get would be "Ivan who?" But if your local man-or-woman of letters had in fact heard of Winters, and had not been one of Winters' own students at Stanford back in the '50s or '60s, you'd probably get a negative response to his name, something along the lines of "That reactionary!" or "Such a vicious and narrow man!" It is too easy to forget Winters, who never much cared to work the literary publicity machine, and when we do remember him, it is too easy to forget that he was many things in his time: a formalist and an experimentalist; a recluse and a public-spirited man; discerning to the point of narrowness in his conception of an enduring tradition, but adventurous in his reading and his sympathies; a traditionalist who was simultaneously an iconoclast.

Winters was a much more varied figure in his time than he is in our all-too-sketchy memory of him. As a poet, Winters presents us with an almost unique case: he is virtually the only substantial American poet in the twentieth century to have had a career that began with the avant-garde and ended with traditional formalism. Marjorie Perloff has called Winters "the great counter-critic" of his period (2), but in a century in which the master-narrative of the poet's life has been one of the break-through to new freedoms (Eliot famously modernizing himself with *The*

Waste Land, or Lowell liberating his line in *Life Studies*), Winters is also a counter-poet, whose career provides a kind of counterpoint to such stories of formal liberation. Again, one needn't accept Winters' conclusions about formal and experimental verse to find his career instructive. To read him is to see a man consciously, sincerely, and above all *seriously* struggling with alternatives that are now all too often taken up by his admirers as unquestioned dogmas.

The early, experimental Winters has not always been well-served by Wintersians, those passionate advocates of the theories Winters developed after his conversion to formalism. Most have been too quick in accepting the master's own assessment of his early, self-consciously modernist work as unhealthily solipsistic—a charge that echoes what Winters himself said in 1940 about the poems he had published in the twenties, about which he said "the earliest poems vacillate between an attitude—it was hardly more than that—of solipsism and one of mystical pantheism" (*Poems* 58).

The later Winters broke with the earlier Winters for reasons that are characteristically complex and serious: he felt that the Imagist and other experimental poetics he had been working with were not capable of engaging all of consciousness, that they privileged sensation over rationality and encouraged a dangerous solipsism. The change in Winters' poetics is evident as earlier as 1928, but it was solidified after the 1932 suicide of Winters' correspondent Hart Crane, whose dangerously self-destructive state of mind seemed to Winters to be linked, at some level, to his experimental poetics. The wrong approach to poetic language came to seem immoral to Winters, and the juxtaposition of images without a context making clear the social meaning and value of sense experience came to be distrusted. The Winters whose work had appeared alongside that of James Joyce and Gertrude Stein in such periodicals as *Broom, Pagany,* and *transition,* the Winters whom Kenneth Rexroth had called a cubist, was no more: the brooding sage of Palo Alto had taken his place.

For this new Winters, poetry was to tell, not show; poetry was to mean, not be. This approach later made Winters the most unfashionable of poets in the age of workshop poetry with its fetishizing of the simple image, but it allowed him to write some of the finest meditative poems of his generation. It also created a climate of expectations among Winters' most committed advocates in which the early work could not possibly get a fair hearing. But is the middle-aged Winters' charge of solipsism a fair assessment of the young Winters' poetry? Certainly not, if we take the word 'solipsism' in anything like its strict, metaphysical sense, as the belief that the world exists only as a content of the subject's consciousness. And not, I think, if we take it in the much looser and more vernacular sense in which it becomes a mere synonym for self-obsession. In fact Imagism, for its first practitioners, was meant as a riposte against the self-obsession of symbolism. While symbolism shunned referentiality and the external world in favor if hermetic castles of the interior, Imagism set out to place consciousness in a real, external, physical world, through acts of devout attention to that world. It is world-obsessed or other-obsessed rather than self-obsessed, and represents a philosophical position at a far pole from metaphysical solipsism.

The essential Imagist position is that we are cut off from the real by walls of discourse and dead language, and that a poetry of clear images can return us to an awareness of the world of things. Pound wrote that the Imagist poem is a record of "the precise instant when a thing outward and objective transforms itself, or darts into a thing inward and subjective" (89). It is not self-obsessed, nor is it, as the later Winters and some of his followers have implied, a loss of consciousness in a moment of pantheistic union. Rather, it is a call for a consciousness rooted in the world rather than in our habitual ways of thinking or speaking about the world, an attempt to make language and consciousness new by basing them on the immediate experience of the world. This sense of an external world that takes priority over our received thinking is at the heart of many of Winters' early poems, whether strictly Imagist or Imagist-inflected, like the remarkable "José's Country" in which the stark, hard, physical reality of "A pale horse, / mane of flowery dust" running far away across the dry New Mexico landscape presses in upon "the haze / of pondered vision." The poem aims to ground the otherwise isolated consciousness in a real world "Where a falling stone / Would raise pale earth," a world of things "beyond a child's thought" (*Selected Poems* 7). Lonely it is, and unsociable, but it is not dangerously solipsistic.

The change that strikes one most in the evolution of Winters' poetry, besides the conversion from experiment to formalism, is the growing sociability of the poems. Poems like "To William Dinsmore Briggs Conducting His Seminar," "To a Young Writer," "On the Death of Senator Thomas J. Walsh" all emerge from and speak to particular social contexts in an almost Augustan manner completely alien to Winters' early work. It is in this quasi-Augustan mode that Winters emerges as a political poet, too, one to rival the later Auden in such poems as 1942's "To a Military Rifle," which begins:

> The times come round again;
> The private life is small;
> And individual men
> Are counted not at all.
> Now life is general,
> And the bewildered Muse,
> Thinking what she has done,
> Confronts the daily news. (*Selected Poems* 99)

This has everything you'd find in one of Auden's poems from the same period: a strong sense of meter, a deep concern with the relation of the public and the private in time of war, a sense of the intersection of the muse and the news. What Auden had and Winters, to his detriment, lacked, was an ability to write an Augustan poem in the syntax and diction of our time. "I sit in one of the dives / On Fifty-second Street / Uncertain and afraid" begins Auden's own meditation on private experience in a time of public calamity (95). Nothing in it comes close to the archaism of "And individual men / Are counted not at all." One could catalog Winters' archaisms ("The evening traffic homeward burns," say, or "...there haunts me now / A wrinkled figure on a dusty road") but this would be to make too much of what is ultimately a minor flaw or mannerism for which Winters has already paid too high a price in lost reputation.

Another part of the increased sociability of Winters' poetry in his later period can be seen in his treatment of landscape. While the early work is stark and eerily depopulated, the later work increasingly gives us humanized landscapes: the Pasadena hills; the San Francisco Airport;

the highways and the vineyards outside Palo Alto. As Donald Davie observed in his introduction to the now out-of-print *Collected Poems of Yvor Winters*, there is something approaching a Virgilian *pietras* toward local places evident in such lines as these from "In Praise of California Wines":

> With pale bright leaf and shadowy stem,
> Pellucid amid nervous dust,
> By pre-Socratic stratagem,
> Yet sagging with its weight of must,
>
> The Vineyard spreads beside the road
> In repetition, point and line.
> I sing, in this dry bright abode,
> The praises of the native wine. (172)

Davie also took pains to point out that such *pietas* is one of the many treasures of Winters' poetry that we simply can't get at by reading the it too obsessively through the lens of Winters' criticism. While Winters' criticism still has much to say to us, his poetry can offer us riches undreamed of in his criticism.

Works Cited

Auden, W. H. *Selected Poems*. Ed. Edward Mendelson. New York: Random House, 2007. Print.

Perloff, Marjorie. *The Dance of the Intellect: Studies in the Poetry of the Pound Tradition*. Evanston: Northwestern University Press, 1996. Print.

Pound, Ezra. *Gaudier-Brzeska*. New York: New Directions, 1974. Print.

Winters, Yvor. *The Collected Poems of Yvor Winters*. Ed. and intro. Donald Davie. Manchester: Carcanet, 1978. Print.

———. *Poems*. Los Altos: Gyroscope, 1940. Print.

———. *The Selected Poems of Yvor Winters*. Ed. R. L. Barth. Athens, Ohio: Ohio University Press / Swallow Press, 1999. Print.

The Protestant Ethic and
the Spirit of Poetry

I n his ponderous classic of sociology, *Economy and Society*, Max Weber tells us a thing or two about the Protestants whose ethic of self-denial has formed the basis of modern capitalism:

> The person who lives as a worldly ascetic is a rationalist, not only in the sense that he rationally systematizes his own conduct, but also in his rejection of everything that is ethically irrational, aesthetic, or dependent upon his own emotional reactions to the world and its institutions. The distinctive goal always remains the alert, methodical control of one's own pattern of life and behavior. (544)

The economic payoff for those who embraced these traits was quite significant, often resulting in their rise to positions of surprising prominence given the origins of their creed in a rejection of worldliness. But as every student of sociology knows, the realm of non-popular culture is a kind of economic world turned upside down, where the ordinary rules don't always apply. In the little world of American poetry, for instance, you can't expect a whole lot of payoff for embodying such stereotypically Protestant qualities as restraint in expression, emotional reserve, a relentless self-examination of the private conscience, and an individualism tending toward isolation. While in the Weberian economic world such qualities lead to great payoffs in terms of economic capital, in the poetry world they actually impede the accumulation of cultural capital in the form of prizes, awards, and widespread critical acclaim. That, at any rate, is the conclusion to which a contemplation of the poetry of Laton Carter, Kenneth Fields, and James McMichael tends to lead us.

Carter, Fields, and McMichael all write poetry very much in what one might call a stereotypically Weberian Protestant manner of expression: tending to plain statement, gun-shy when it comes to heated emotion, obsessively self-analytic, wary of gaudy images, suspicious of the irrational, and, in some measure, tending toward individual isolation. Emotional reticence has been on the outs in poetry ever since Robert Lowell shocked his eminently WASP ancestors with *Life Studies*, and self-analytic individualism has been largely eclipsed since the rise of identity politics and its aesthetics of group affiliation. Plain statement has suffered a few blows, too, first at the hands of the deep image aesthetic, and again during the current triumph of elliptical verse.

Perhaps these shifts in taste have been behind the late emergence of Laton Carter, whose remarkable first book went unpublished for eleven years after an early draft served as his MFA thesis. Kenneth Fields and James McMichael have also received few enough of the accolades accorded to American poets: unlike their Stanford classmates, the former poets laureate Robert Hass and Robert Pinsky, Fields and McMichael have both been relatively unrecognized talents. This speaks less of the relative merits of the poets, I think, than of the shape of the American poetic field, and the kinds of poetic virtues it is most prepared to reward.

That Fields and McMichael share certain low-key poetic virtues is by no means an accident: both were students of that anachronistically Augustan poet, Yvor Winters. Winters advocated poetry of plain statement, emotional reserve, and relentless examination of the self. His abhorrence of the irrational was legendary, his defense of reason absolute. While poets like Hass and Pinsky learned from Winters and moved on, Fields and McMichael engaged with him more deeply. McMichael's doctoral dissertation is an application of Wintersian ideas to poets unexamined in Winters' critical work, and Fields was hand-picked by Winters to be his successor at Stanford—a post Fields holds to this day.

Laton Carter is too young to have been a student of Winters, but he studied under McMichael at the University of California-Irvine, and seems to have been drawn to McMichael for his more Augustan qualities. All three poets are in some meaningful sense in the tradition of Winters, without being doctrinaire followers, and all three have to some degree been kept at the margins of a poetic field that has never quite been able to appreciate the kind of work they do. This, of course, only gives us all the more reason to take the time to appreciate for their very real, and somewhat unusual, qualities.

Max Weber would certainly recognize Laton Carter's virtues as typical of the Protestant temperament. Consider the opening lines of "Counter," a poem in which an unemployed man makes a short shopping trip:

> He writes 6 a.m., 7 a.m., down to noon,
> and starts again with numbers,
> all with spaces in between for the half-hour.
> If, at six, he feeds the cats, follows the template he's
> tried to leave as open as possible,
> he can feel better about what he's doing. (8)

One imagines Weber taking out his carefully sharpened pencil and writing, in a tight hand, some marginal notes about how the man in the poem "rationally systematizes his own conduct," and how this sort of deliberate self-control embodies the notion of an "alert, methodical control of one's own pattern of life and behavior." When, a few lines later, we see that the man feels "guilty, self-reproaching" and "returns two books he bought yesterday" we can imagine Weber noting the deep suspicion of impulse, and the rejection of immediate emotional reactions to the world.

Perhaps the same concern with carefulness and deliberateness that lies behind a poem like "Counter" informs Carter's poetics of clear, direct statement. His poems often have something like a clear thesis statement, and proceed in a mixed expository and narrative manner not unlike a well-written essay. He is not a poet trying to imitate the idiosyncratic cross currents of the stream of consciousness, nor does he try to give you a sense of the mind as it tries out different avenues of thought. Instead of a drama of mental process, he wants to deliver well-

tuned products of careful meditation. Here, for example, is the beginning of "Silence," a poem that proposes a general thesis, then illustrates
and complicates that thesis:

> There is an unmeasured distance between two people that means,
> if they do not already know each other, they do not have to talk.
> The distance narrowed, the two points moving toward each other,
> causes decision: what necessary act of salutation or aloofness.
> Glass dividing this distance obviates the act.
> Behind windshield of double-pane storm window,
> a person's separation allows for closer, less regulated study of
>   the other. (18)

We're at a far pole from the ellipses of a John Ashbery here: we're
operating in a mode more like that of the Augustans, with their essayistic verse. We're also operating far outside of the norms of the old-
fashioned poetry workshop, with its emphasis on the showing of concrete
detail, on showing over telling. What could be more abstract than the
description of two people walking in opposite directions than "two points
moving toward each other"? It's spare, distant, and minimalist—it's
almost geometry.

    I don't think it's a coincidence that so many of the people in Carter's
poems seem to exist at a remove from those around them, seeking connections that never quite come into being. It seems of a piece with the
rest of Carter's sensibility that this would be the case: scrupulous self-
policing deliberateness is rarely the product of a warm and all-embrac-
ing community. Since I've already invited one German sociologist into
this analysis, I'm tempted to invite another, Ferdinand Toennies, to
explain the phenomenon. Toennies is the creator of the *gemeinschaft/ges-
selschaft* distinction, a dichotomy that distinguishes pre-modern from
modern society. In pre-modern *gemeinschaft* societies, community is
organic, interactions are face-to-face, and interactions are governed by
traditions. Modern *gesselschaft* societies have none of this warmth. Cap-
italistic and industrial, such societies are highly administered, socially
atomized, and emphasize interactions governed by rules or laws. In the
world of *gemeinschaft* you are born into a definite social position and
belong there; in the world of *gesselschaft*, you're on your own, one atom

among others. Needless to say, *gesselschaft* is the world built by Weber's Protestant ethos, with all of its self-policing deliberateness. *Gesselschaft* also seems to be the natural habitat of Laton Carter's characters, who yearn, from great distances, for the warmth of human connection. Here, for example, in lines from Carter's "Silence," we see the speaker watching an unsuspecting person's face through a window:

> The kinesics of the face, watched unmonitored from a distance,
> issues its own private speech. When the distance is at once collapsed,
> the face's eyes drawing a line to the watcher's eyes, the speech too
> collapses. (24)

The irony is palpable: in Carter's world, we come closest to really knowing each other when we catch each other unawares and give away some element of ourselves other than our public personae. When we actually encounter each other face-to-face, we withdraw behind our social roles. It's chilly in Carter's neighborhood, and not neighborly at all.

Even the titles of Carter's poems indicate reserve and isolation: the volume includes poems with names like "Unspoken," "New Distances," "Separate," "Brief Hesitation," and "Tentative" (the last of which contains the statement "A thought can be stepped back from, / watched from a close remove"—something very close to Carter's *ars poetica* [20]). Although Carter shies away from traditional rhyme and meter, many of the poems in *Leaving* follow the general form of the sonnet, containing fourteen lines and turning either between an octave and a sestet or after three quatrains. This is surely a further expression of Carter's concern with the deliberate and the controlled.

Ken Fields is also drawn to the sonnet in its looser manifestations. Almost all of the 64 poems gathered in *Classic Rough News* are sonnets of sorts: fourteen-liners, loosely rhythmic, occasionally working with rhyme, and sometimes involving the volta, or rhetorical turn, of the traditional sonnet. They are inhabited by a cast of imagined characters reminiscent of those populating the psychological territory of John Berryman's *Dream Songs*. Where Berryman had his Henry and Mr. Bones, Fields has alter egos named Billy, Billie, and Burton. As their names indicate, Billy and Billie are doubles of sorts: male and female versions of psychologically fragile violence-prone alcoholics tending toward

multiple personalities. Burton, too, manifests in many guises: he reso-
nates at some times with Robert Burton, author of *The Anatomy of Melancholy*, at other times with the explorer and erotic *littérateurs* Richard Francis
Burton, and once with the Richard Burton who played opposite Elizabeth Taylor in *Cleopatra*. In Fields' pages we meet Burton academic,
Burton erotic, Burton alcoholic, Burton cinematic, but above all we
meet Burton melancholic. Together with the various personalities of
Billy and Billie and the poet *in propria persona*, it's quite a crowd.

The core influence behind the book isn't Berryman, though: it's
Yvor Winters. The Wintersian doctrine was Augustan not only in its
embrace of clear, expository, discursive verse, but in its distrust of
impulse. For Winters, our great challenge in life was to resist our instinctive desires and impulses, and it is this element of Winters' (very Weberian) ethos that we see most prominently in *Classic Rough News*. But where
Winters liked to celebrate his hard-won victories over impulse, Fields'
book tells a tale of failed resistance, of impulse distrusted but, more
often as not, yielded to. The melancholy that pervades the book is the
melancholy of the junkie, the addict, the frequently failing policer of
instinct and desire. Sometimes it is erotic impulse that Fields distrusts.
More frequently, though, the distrusted impulse it is the lure of drugs
or alcohol. In "Right Now," for example, Fields remembers the days
when he was never without a drink in his hand, when his desire for the
artificial oblivions of drugs and alcohol drove him to the edge of death.

Now, from a position of ever-tenuous recovery, he meets others who
live as he once lived, and "talks to the ones who are not even sure / They
want to learn how to stop killing themselves" (37). The necessary resistance to the lure of oblivion was a great topic of Yvor Winters, who liked
to make much of this theme in Keats' "Ode to a Nightingale," and it is
a central theme of Fields' book as well. Like Keats and Winters, Fields
has felt the full strength of the attraction he so distrusts. In "The Hinge,"
a poem near the end of the collection, Fields begins by revisiting all of
his characters—addicts and alcoholics, his oblivion-loving Billies and
Burtons—then goes on to explore the origins of his own obsession.
Remembering a childhood moment when he underwent surgery, he
recollects how, on his recovery,

the nurse told me
"I've seen a lot of little boys dragged in here
For this business, but not a one of them
Ever said he loved the ether." (37)

None, that is, until Fields, whose dangerous impulses seem to run very deep indeed.

It isn't just the impulse toward oblivion that Fields distrusts. In his world even our nobler impulses turn out to be dangerous. "A Country Story," for example, retells an old family story from Fields' grandmother, in which a mother sends her German measles-stricken daughter away to quarantine. When the rest of the family seems to fall ill too, the mother acts on a loving impulse and brings the quarantined daughter back so the family can die together. This impulse proves fatal, though: the family had not really fallen ill, and the formerly quarantined daughter brings the disease back with her, fatally infecting her sister.

Fields does not confine himself to the examination of dubious impulse. He writes of personal humiliation, he writes poems in which he laments his own constant self-examination and self-recrimination. He only really falls flat in the poems where he vents academic spleen, complaining about dimwitted administrators, petty colleagues, and various theoretical tendencies. But the theme to which he constantly returns is that of the need to keep impulse in check, and his own failure to fulfill that need. An ever-prodigal Wintersian, a backsliding Weberian protestant, a clear-eyed chronicler of a flawed self—with *Classic Rough News* Fields has given us his confession.

James McMichael has written his share of poems about dubious emotional impulses—they form the core of his early book *Against the Falling Evil*—but a newer collection, *Capacity* is remarkable for its ability to keep the emotions at a distance. *Capacity* consists of seven poems, or perhaps I should say seven parts, since they do add up to a single, book-length whole. *Capacity* is a strangely disparate and restrained book, but no more so than his earlier long poems. Like the first of McMichael's truly ambitious long poems, "Itinerary" from 1978's *The Lover's Familiar, Capacity* takes on matters of historical importance (in "Itinerary" his matter was the expedition of Lewis and Clark; in the present volume he addresses the Irish potato famine at some length). Like *Four Good Things* (McMichael's book-length poem of 1980) *Capacity* contains many apparently disparate topics. I'm not sure which of the two books wins the prize for breadth. As Robert Hass put it in an early review, *Four Good Things* is a poem about "worry, death, taxes, planning, probability theory, insomnia, stamp collecting, cancer, domestic architecture, sex manuals, the Industrial Revolution, and real estate" (161). *Capacity* begins with a book of photographs of the English countryside, goes on to describe the wave forces working in the North Atlantic, comments on the nature of Newtonian space, describes a scene of family drama, details the process of human fertilization and gestation, outlines chilling episodes from Irish history, and works its way back to the book of photographs via World War Two and the nature of the will to live. You be the judge. Capacity also has much in common with *Each in a Place Apart*, McMichael's 1994 effort, most notably in its deep distrust of our most primal impulses, especially our sexual urges, which leads to ill-advised actions in both books. Like all of McMichael's long poems, *Capacity* is discursive, a poem almost essayistic in its drive to lay its materials out in expository fashion.

One could make a pretty good case for the Protestant ethic of McMichael's verse just on the basis of what we've covered so far: a sober, essayistic poem distrustful of the primal drives is in some meaningful sense a Weberian poem. But there's more. Capacity is notable for the strangeness of both its syntax and its diction, both of which seem designed to distance us from the immediate emotional pull of the dramatic, sometimes even melodramatic, subject matter. While most poets who invert syntax do so to add to the music and emotional punch of a statement, McMichael seems to aim at an interestingly opposite effect. These lines, for example, come from a section of the poem dealing with the urgent needs of soon-to-be-separated lovers in wartime. A man thinks of his own mind as a garden, and:

> He practices his absence
> as the stilled reflecting surface of its pool.
> With features of her person in his
> stead there,
> to what is not its

> own anymore in wanting
> the self is sent
> back by the other. (8)

Odd, isn't it? That second sentence would read more easily, and deliver its emotional weight more directly, had its clauses been ordered otherwise. But McMichael doesn't want that, he wants us to experience emotion from a greater distance.

McMichael employs all sorts of devices in pursuit of this emotional distancing, including the symmetrical A-B-B-A pattern of the chiasmus, which makes an appearance here, in lines describing the changing way of gardening in England in the nineteenth century:

> Need had been made less natural.
> Replaced was the old
> productive ideal that the useful
> good was desired.
> The desired good was
> useful in the new ideal. (7)

I suppose we shouldn't be surprised. McMichael's enduring scholarly interest is in James Joyce, who made of the chiasmus the organizing principle behind *A Portrait of the Artist as a Young Man*. You've probably already noticed the unusual nature of McMichael's diction, which even in these short passages seems remarkably abstract. He often uses terms from logic or the sciences, especially physics and biology, to describe events not normally discussed in such terms. Here, for example, is a passage on the Irish famine of the 1840s:

> Persons are
> separate in time when they are living.
> when certain maincrop tuberous parts go on being
> missed at the hearth, back as
> one again with time are persons now
> outside it for good. (28)

With "tuberous parts" the language of biology steps in for the colloquial (and, in this context, emotionally loaded) word "potato." And the business about being inside or outside of time picks up on some very abstract physics-talk from earlier in the book. It is a very accurate, but tremendously emotionally restrained, depiction of the situation. McMichael is not one to gush, or to invite his readers to shiver with emotion, at least not in any immediate way.

Perhaps the most extreme instance of this curious distancing comes in a passage in which a man and a woman who share emotionally charged secrets meet after a long absence. When they come together, the as-yet unspoken emotion strains at their fragile composure:

> His having come could pass for a family call.
> She can take it as that. So can he,
> if beyond the frugal
> greeting she tenders
> she does not speak. (31)

When she finally does speak, after a two-page buildup, we don't hear the words, nor are we told about her tone. Instead, we get an almost clinical description of the process of speech:

> . . . the next column of
> breath she issues still gives
> nothing away.
> Not so
> The column after. As it leaves,
> the lappets that she draws around it
> make it tremble so positions of the
> tongue, teeth, lips and jaw can sound it
> abroad (34)

I suppose we could interpret the tremble in her voice as emotion, but then again it could simply be a matter of the formation of a vowel-sound. What is significant here is the way McMichael chooses to depict moments of intense emotion: with restraint, and through the least-emotionally charged perspective possible. You can't get much farther from the spontaneous overflow of powerful emotion than this. It is this anti-Romanticism, this Protestant ethic, that makes McMichael a rare and important figure in contemporary poetry.

The Protestant ethos in poetry, embodied variously in Carter's careful self-analysis, Fields' self-recrimination, or McMichael's masterful acts of distancing and emotional control, will leave some readers cold. The dominant poetic tastes of our time tend toward cleverness, emotional-ism, or both, and those who have absorbed those tastes uncritically just won't know what to do with poems like these. We would do well to let this be their loss, not ours.

Works Cited

Carter, Laton. *Leaving*. Chicago: University of Chicago Press, 2004. Print.

Fields, Kenneth. *Classic Rough News*. Chicago: University of Chicago Press, 2005. Print.

Hass, Robert. *Twentieth Century Pleasures*. New York: Ecco, 2000. Print.

McMichael, James. *Capacity: Poems*. New York: Farrar, Straus, Giroux, 2006. Print.

Weber, Max. *Economy and Society: An Outline of Interpretive Sociology*. Ed. Guenther Roth and Claus Wittich. Vol. 2. Los Angeles: University of California Press, 1978. Print.

Power and the Poetics of Play

The meaning of play has been one of John Matthias' most enduring poetic concerns. But just what his poetry has to say on the issue has been a matter of some controversy even among his ablest critics. For Jeremy Hooker, Matthias' poetry is a celebration of play as a sign of human freedom. "Matthias the poet knows himself to belong to the species *homo ludens*," writes Hooker in *The Presence of the Past* (103). Hooker refers, of course, to Johann Huizinga's great study *Homo Ludens*, which puts forth the idea that play is "an activity which proceeds . . . according to rules freely accepted, and outside the sphere of necessity or material utility" (132). In Hooker's view, Matthias sets play up against the world of politics and power. Politics and power are realms of limitation and contingency, or, in Huizinga's terms, necessity and material utility, while poetry is a realm of play and freedom. "There is more of Johann Huizinga's philosophy of play . . . in Matthias' poetry, claims Hooker, "than there is Marxism" (103). A younger critic, Jere Odell, takes issue with Hooker's analysis, claiming "the terms of Hooker's dichotomy are unbalanced, stressing the playful aesthetic of Matthias' poetry at the expense of its utility" (41). In Odell's view Matthias' work doesn't so much celebrate play as it "tests play as an aesthetic—trying to see if it is ultimately useless" (43). In the end, Odell finds the opposition of the realm of play and the realm of power to be an "unsteady antithesis" in Matthias' complex and ambivalent body of work (47). Play and power cannot be separated.

Both critics are, surprisingly, correct—but only about specific periods in Matthias' career. Hooker's analysis appeared in 1987, Odell's eleven years later, and the difference is significant: by the end of the twentieth century, the center of gravity in Matthias' poetry had shifted from a position more like that described by Hooker to a position more like that described by Odell. Indeed, the trend has continued, and the unsteadiness of the antithesis between play and power has become increasingly prominent in the books of poetry Matthias has written since Odell's essay appeared. While the periodization of a body of work as dense and complex as Matthias' is, in some sense, a chump's game, I do feel fairly confident in breaking down Matthias' evolving sense of play into three distinct periods: an early period in which play exists separately from power in the manner described by Hooker; a middle period in which play is either co-opted by power or becomes a consolation for losses in the realm of power; and a later period, in which the differences between play and power blur, without one realm becoming subordinate to the other. The early period encompasses Matthias' juvenilia and his first book of poems, *Bucyrus*; the middle period aesthetic of play is at its strongest in the poems of *Turns*, and the later period comes into fullest flower in two books: *Working Progress, Working Title* and *Kedging*. The whole arc of Matthias' decades-long exploration of the meaning of play can best be summed up as the breakdown of the play/power dichotomy. Indeed, inasmuch as Matthias' early proposal of a binary is later undermined, we can say that his career offers a deconstruction of the opposition of play and power.

The earliest expression of a dichotomy of play and power in Matthias' work comes in a 1963 novella called *By Way of the Ruins*. This has never been published as a book, although parts did appear in the Stanford student literary magazine *Sequoia* and, much later, *TriQuarterly* published an extract under the title "Alto Luogo Ayasuluk." The novella follows a young American protagonist to Turkey, and much of it is relatively undistinguished work in the manner of Henry James. It is of interest in the present context, however, in that it shows the stark opposition of play and power in the young Matthias' imagination. Here, in a scene drawn from "Alto Luogo Ayasuluk," we see two characters who represent the two sides of the dichotomy:

> The Turk goes through his routine of stands, balances, twists. He's a very good acrobat. A talented acrobat, and he stares. He can juggle peaches, bananas, apples. He can do it both with his hands and with his feet, and an assistant can perch on his head while he does it. Champagne glasses are nothing, by dozens, balanced on elbows, and after a somersault, none of them breaks. A chair on each shoulder is stable, standing on only one leg, a table rests on each knee. And after all this, with tables and chairs firm and secure, he bounces beach balls with his feet and juggles six grapefruit. Through all of the acts, he keeps staring, and the Major wants me to talk. Major wants me to talk about Turkey. I should tell him about the things he'll see, things that he'll like and won't like. I should talk to my major and not stare at the acrobat. But have you ever seen such an acrobat, Major? He could spin you by the toe on his nose and you would still want to talk to me about Turkey. It's going to be law and a family, you said. How fine it must be to enjoy your work. Honest to god you're such a good major, an American major. But look at the Turk, how he stares. (91)

Matthias is a poet obsessed with names, so it is particularly significant that neither of the two characters is named here. The acrobat is defined entirely in terms of his ludic activity, and the Major is presented solely in terms of his rank—in terms, that is, of pure power. While the acrobat is a player *par excellence*, the Major is associated with law, productive work, and ideas of obligation. He occupies the territory Huizinga defined as antithetical to play: "the sphere of necessity or material utility." It matters, too, that Matthias emphasizes the officer's nationality. To be an American in Turkey in 1963 was to be a representative not only of an unquestionably preeminent global power; it was to be a representative of a country with immense influence over the Turkish government, a considerable military presence on the ground, and a vast technological superiority. It was to represent modern power in a disempowered country rich in exotic sights and ancient splendors (in portraying play as a Turkish acrobat the young Matthias certainly wasn't above a bit of orientalism). The protagonist is caught between the extremes of virtuoso play and mundane power, drawn by inclination to the former, by obligation to the latter. The division of the two realms is absolute: the representative of power could be spun by the toe on player's nose and still take no notice of him.

A similar division holds in Matthias' first book of poems, 1970's *Bucyrus*, and is seen most clearly in the prose poem "Statement," in which Matthias imagines Ezra Pound's friend, the sculptor Henri Gaudier-Brzeska, jailed by the warmongering authorities. In contrast to the masters of war and institutional power, Gaudier-Brzeska appears as the exemplar of artistic play and the freedom of the imagination:

> So then Gaudier. Gaudier choosing craft and consciousness, choosing freedom. So then Gaudier—Gaudier refusing to be enslaved by refusing to know, Gaudier refusing imprisonment. But they tried, the governments and their jailors, the governments and their jailors unconscious and therefore unfree, to jail, in the war, this conscious spirit, this Gaudier. But Gaudier loved freedom, and because he loved freedom he learned craft. Because he loved freedom learned craft so perfectly that he became a craftsman of genius. And his medium was stone. Stone were the jails of the governments and the jailors. Stone was his medium—a genius with exquisite perfectly trained controlled and controlling hands. Free hands. Free because they knew their craft. Jails, Penitentiaries, Sanatoriums, all made out of stone. Stone walls, many feet thick. Stone jails, Jail-thick stone walls where they put him, craftsman and free, they—the governments making their wars.
>
> Minutes after they threw him there in his cell, minutes after they locked him in that cage of stone, Gaudier, Pound's friend the vorticist, took, with his bare hands, an eight-foot thick wall apart and went home. (60)

Unlike the actual Henri Gaudier-Brzeska, who enlisted in the French army and died in the trenches in the First World War, the figure Matthias imagines is not subject to the power of governments or the pressures of social convention (as Michael Anania has pointed out, stone in this prose poem stands for all systems of power and social control, and is depicted as "the basic material of the confinements of family, culture, and the state" [21]). Matthias' Gaudier-Brzeska is a figure of art and play, and as such the world of power simply doesn't exist for him, or, rather, its institutions have no claim on him. When, through the free play of artistic imagination, Gaudier-Brzeska walks out of the prison, he walks out of what Huizinga called "the sphere of necessity or mate-rial utility" into a wholly separate realm.

Matthias starts to question this sense of play's autonomy from the realm of power in his next book, *Turns*, which appeared five years later. The years in which *Turns* was composed represent a turning point for Matthias, a period in which he was alternately caught up in and disil-lusioned with the radically left-wing political activism he'd been exposed to in the Bay Area of the 1960s. This context is important for under-standing his treatment of play, and we get a sense of his state of mind from the essay "A Self-Reading and a Reading of Self in the Romantic Context from Wordsworth to Parkman":

> I was not, I suppose, untypical of my generation in the 1960s by becom-ing sufficiently caught up in the machinery of protest and the language of neo-Marxist analysis to feel in the end both confused and inauthen-tic, "dragging passions, notions, shapes of faith / Like culprits to the bar," and subjecting everything, including the pleasures I took in a new marriage, in the birth of my first child, in solitude, and in the arts to a rigorous inquisition with respect to means and ends considered in the context of political activism. (*Reading Old Friends* 40)

The neo-Marxist point of view, in which aesthetic play is subordinate to structures of political and, ultimately, economic power is most clearly on view in two of the poems of *Turns*, "Double Derivation, Association, and Cliché: from The Great Tournament Roll of Westminster," and that poem's companion piece "Clarifications for Robert Jacoby."

The first of these poems takes as its source text Sidney Anglo's 1968 annotation and reproduction of the enormous illustrated scroll Henry VIII commissioned to commemorate the tournament he held on New Year's Day in 1511. The tournament, held to celebrate the presentation to Henry of a son born to his wife Catherine of Aragon, seems on the surface to be a great event in the history of play: music, sports, pag-eantry, art, and even poetry were all in abundant evidence. And there is much in the poem to indicate that play has a status equal or even superior to that of power, as it did in Matthias' early work. The much-repeated refrain "Who breaks a spear is worth a prize" (78) for example, seems to imply that the instruments of violent power are to be shattered in the new spirit of play: swords are to be turned into ploughshares, or rather, into playthings. Moreover, Matthias offers a kind of chiasmus that would seem to indicate play and power have equal status. "Out of slaughter, ceremony" (78) he writes at one point, reversing it to "out of ceremony, slaughter," at another. The worlds of ceremony and slaughter, of play and power, seem to exist in delicate counterpoint to one another. Are we in a situation like the one we found in *By Way of the Ruins*, with play and power poised in a standoff? When we consider both the historical context of Henry's tournament and the full text of the poem, I believe it's safe to say that we're not. Power, here, makes play its subordinate.

The nature of the historical tournament itself must not be overlooked. All of the ludic elements were in evidence not for themselves, but as an expression of Henry's dynastic power, and as publicity for the continued vitality of the House of Tudor. Play, here, was profoundly subordinate to power. Medieval tournaments originated as military training exercises, and the later, more elaborate renaissance versions were still expressions of power, albeit of a more sophisticated and elaborate kind. Moreover, if the tournament was a matter of a ludic expression of power, the great roll itself, a 60-foot illustration of the two-day event, was a further trumpeting of Henry's power, designed to carry the spectacle of his majestic force beyond its initial scene, outwards through space and onwards through time.

When we turn to Matthias' rendition of the tournament, we get a similar sense of the preeminence of power. Consider the opening lines:

The heralds wear their tabards correctly.
Each, in his left hand, carries a wand.
Before and after the Master of Armour
Enter his men: three of them carry the staves.
The mace bearer wears a yellow robe.
In rigth & goodly devysis of apparyl
The gentlemen ride. (78)

Firstly, there is the presence of the Master of Armour and his men. Both "Master" and "Armour" are important, for with them hierarchy enters the poem, backed by the potential for violent force in the service of hierarchy. Social class enters with the gentlemen, and around the opening lines lingers a whiff of conformity dictated by royal imperative and social convention: the heralds, one senses, had damn well better wear their tabards correctly, and if the gentlemen know what's good for them they'll keep their "devysis of apparyl" in exactly the "rigth" form. There's certainly a sense of play in this celebratory ceremony, but it's a far cry from the free play described by Huizinga (whose *Homo Ludens* Matthias references in the poem), where the rules of play are freely chosen by the players.

If shades of power surround the world of play at the start of the poem, the prospect only gets worse as we read on. When we reach the poem's second section, the economic calculation behind the tournament's extravagant playfulness becomes apparent. King Henry has made

> . . . a forest in the halls of Blackfriars
> at Ludgate whych is garneychyd wyth trees and bowes
> wyth bestes and byrds; wyth a mayden
> syttyng by a kastell makyng garlonds there;
> wyth men in woodwoos dress,
> wyth men of armes. . . .
>   Or Richard Gibson
>   busy
> with artificers and labour, portages and ships:
> busy with his sums and his accounts (78)

We begin with the spectacle of splendid play, but soon find ourselves behind the scenes with Richard Gibson (who bears the wonderful and telling title "Master of Revels and Accounts"). The grandeur of play is revealed as part of the calculation of power, and dependent on it. It is significant, too, that we move from the language of the tournament roll itself to the language of our own time when Gibson appears: we have left the world of aesthetic excess and entered the mundane world of necessity and material utility, where the language seeks merely to communicate, not to shine.

For a sense of what Henry VIII calculated on gaining by way of material utility from all of this expensive play, we need look no further than the poem's next section, where we hear of two other monarchs, Henry

VII (our Henry's predecessor) and the Holy Roman Emperor Maximilian (our Henry's great rival). We hear of "the advice of Harry VII" to
"put on elegance later" and "put off art" (79) And the effect of this
eschewal of the ludic? "No life of Harry the Seven / There in the works
of the Bard" (79). Henry VII may have saved his treasury a burden, but
he did not project his name forward in time, did not secure an aura for
the Tudor line. In contrast, Henry VIII knew the value of spectacle in
establishing legitimacy and consolidating power. Indeed, we read that
his tournament was part of a broader effort to equal Maximilian in
status, to "Rival Maximilian's mummeries, his / dances and his masques,
his / armouries and armourers the mark" (79). Mummery or armoury,
the difference matters little: each, in the eyes of power, is merely instrumental to an end.

In the middle of Matthias' poem we encounter an unlikely pair of
wanderers: two young boys (Matthias himself, it turns out, and his cousin
Robert Jacoby) in the twentieth century, playing dress-up in renaissance
costume:

> cousins in the summertime would
> ritualize their rivalries
> in sumptuous tableaux.
> Someone holds a camera. Snap.
> In proper costume, Homo Ludens wears
> Imagination on his sleeve. (80)

Here at last, it seems, is *homo ludens* proper. If Henry's play had been at
heart an exercise of power, these two at least seem to be true players,
unbeholden to exigencies of necessity or calculations of material gain.
But the tenuous and temporary nature of their free play is made all too
clear in the lines that follow, where we hear (among other things) of
"The deaths, in order and with dignity, of every child" (81). The poem
allows us to read the line in several contexts (the children could, for
example, be casualties in Henry's victory at the battle of Flodden Field);
but for present purposes the death of every child is just that: the death
of childhood resulting from the individual's growth into an adult. So
the world of pure play is proposed as something confined to childhood—and childhoods all end.

Admittedly, the point is obscurely made. That is why Matthias' companion piece to "The Great Tournament Roll"—"Clarifications for Robert Jacoby"—is in large measure an extended gloss on this passage and its implications for the status of play. The poem, in the form of a letter about "The Great Tournament Roll" to Matthias' cousin Robert Jacoby, expands on the passage about their old game of dressing up in renaissance costume:

> I wonder if you remember all those games
>   we used to play: the costumes
> All the sticks and staves, the whole complicated
>   paraphernalia accumulated to suggest
> Authentic weaponry and precise historical dates,
>   not to mention exact geographical places,
> All through August and September—the months you
>   visited. You wanted then, you said,
> To be an actor, and your father—a very practical
>   lawyer—said he found that funny, though
> I think we both intuited
>   that he was secretly alarmed.
>
> With little cause. You were destined—how obvious
>   it should have been!—to be professional,
> Respectable, and eminent. (85)

Here we see more clearly the point made in the section about the cousins in "The Great Tournament Roll": that free, autonomous play is confined to childhood, and soon surrenders to the claims of a world of power— here, the bourgeois power of law and profession, not regal spectacle.

"Clarifications for Robert Jacoby" was written at a time when Matthias was reading Wordsworth compulsively. Seeing in Wordsworth another disillusioned radical, Matthias tells us that in the early '70s he reached for Wordsworth's poetry "as one might reach for the right medicine in the medicine chest" (*Reading Old Friends* 41). It shouldn't surprise us, then, to find Matthias seeking consolation for the loss of the special world of childhood in a manner much like Wordsworth's in "Tintern Abbey." Wordsworth, of course, consoled himself for the loss of the immediacy of childhood experience by looking to his younger

sister Dorothy at the end of "Tintern Abbey" and declaring "in thy voice
I catch / The language of my former heart." He aches to see his "former
pleasures in the shooting lights / of [her] wild eyes" and longs "yet a
little while" to behold in her what he once was (39). Similarly, Matthias
in "Clarifications for Robert Jacoby" turns to a child to see, at second
hand, the survival of the world of play that seems to die with adulthood.
Near the end of the poem Matthias gives us an image of a girl playing
with a stick in a field, jumping in imitation of a nearby wren. She lives
"in the world / of her imagining, where, as the mist descends, / She is
a wren" (89). She plays for play itself, and lives in a fully autonomous
world of play. In effect, she allows Matthias a vicarious experience of
what he once was, and speaks the language of his former heart. Play
survives, only as something in memory and in acts of empathy.

Or almost. Matthias complicates this nostalgic version of Wordsworth's
poetic of loss and consolation in two ways. Firstly, he refuses to end on
this particular consoling note. "As I write this down she is leaving the
field," he says as the poem draws to a close. And what she leaves for isn't
a world of play and imagination, but a world of necessity and material
utility: she goes "to a house where her / Father and mother argue inces-
santly, where / her brother is sick." The dangers around childhood and
its innocent free play are all too real and all too near. Secondly, Matthias
reflects on his own vocation as a poet—that is, as a man who has tried to
adhere to an ethos of play even as he enters adulthood, the age in which
we are meant to assume the responsibilities of power. After depicting the
grim household to which the girl returns, he gives us these lines:

> In the house
> They are phoning a doctor. In the poem—
> because I say so,
> because I say once more
> That she enters the world of her imagining
> where, as the mist descends,
> She is a wren—
> She remains in the field. (89)

There's a kind of double vision here—perhaps that's why, earlier in the
poem Matthias confesses to Jacoby, an ophthalmologist, that he will one

day come to Jacoby "saying...frankly: cure me if you can" (85). One vision is hard and cold: Matthias knows full well that the girl has gone from the field of imaginative play to the house of material necessity. He's told us that. The other vision is happier, or wants to be: Matthias insists that in *his* poem, the girl remains in the realm of play. The important thing is the insistence, even defensiveness, with which he clings to this second aspect of his double vision. "Because I say so, / because I say once more" (89)—Matthias presents himself as willing himself to keep the second side of his vision alive, willing himself to maintain a vision of play free from material necessity. He shows us that poetry can, if we will it to, offer us a compensatory vision of free play. But he also shows us that this compensatory vision isn't the full truth: the world of power is real. It's a complex double vision fraught with sadness. Anyway, it's a far cry from the triumphant play of Gaudier-Brzeska in *Bucyrus's* "Statement."

The third period in Matthias' ongoing exploration of the fate of play begins in his 2002 book *Working Progress, Working Title*. Very early in his career Matthias presented play and power as two entirely separate spheres; later he presented play as subordinate to power, or, at best, as tenuously clung to in the face of power's encroachment. In this new phase Matthias dissolves the barriers between play and power, without making one subordinate to the other. The distinction, once a clear dichotomy, breaks down, and play and power metamorphose into one another.

"Automystifstical Plaice," the 30 page poem that begins *Working Progress, Working Title*, provides a stunningly complex example of the breakdown of the play/power dichotomy. The poem begins with an evocation of Paris in the twenties, jumbling together lines redolent of that era's playfulness with lines that remind us of the two world wars—the clashes of powers—that frame the era:

> In the beginning
> without any mother the girl was born a machine.
> In the year of erotic parades.
> The Novia poured out the oil the gears were engaged
> the études composed and the light bulb
> was Amèricaine. Voilà Picabia sweetheart of first
> occupation voilà ballet méchanique.

> We'll not eat our bread by the sweat of our brows
> in the end: Je viens pour toujours
> it is error and grief you'll be known by
> the strength of our steel
> the number of our rivets . . . (3)

We begin with a girl—in "Clarifications for Robert Jacoby" the last redoubt of play—but this one is "born a machine," and therefore somehow affiliated with the world of mechanized utility and power. Erotic parades indicate an outbreak of play in the streets of Paris, and the tremendous playfulness of the era's artistic production gets a nod. It's important that we're presented with avant-garde artists like Francis Picabia and Georges Antheil, too. After all, it is the avant-garde, with its disdain for market success or political propaganda, that represents art at its most free and playful. And the very idea of Antheil's *Ballet Méchanique* seems to imply power turned to play: it involved using airplane engines (recently developed by the wartime powers as instruments of war) as musical instruments. The optimism of the era and its artists even seems to promise a liberation from the realm of necessity and material utility: "We'll not eat our bread by the sweat of our brows" almost reverses the injunction to earn their bread by the sweat of their brows placed on Adam and Eve when they're expelled from Eden. But the signs of malevolent power are everywhere. We're reminded of Picabia's exile during the occupation of France, and we're reminded, too, of how the era *entre deux guerres* came to an end, with error and grief and the relentless wartime exercise of power by armies built of steel and rivets. The throwing together of all this indicates at the outset of the poem the blurring of the distinction between the spheres of play and power that we'll see in the pages that follow.

The poem soon unfolds a bizarre, true story that seems at first to show the subordination of play to power. We meet the starlet Hedy Lamarr in her early life in Germany, where she's an actress in pornographic movies and the mistress of Fritz Mandl, an arms merchant selling his wares to the Third Reich. "That's Mandl, Fritz, from Vienna, the armaments man, the war profiteer," we read, and with him is Hedy Lamarr, introduced as "the naked broad in the film" (3). He is a dark figure of power, while she is the thoroughly objectified woman, Mandl's plaything, and utterly subordinate to his will: he literally will not let her leave his sight. Mandl's possessiveness of Lamarr, combined with a contempt for her intellect (sadly typical of the man of power's contempt for the player) lead to a breakdown of the barrier between play and power, and to a kind of revenge of play upon the world of power.

The poem approaches this breakdown of these barriers by showing us one of the more curious scenes in the history of modernism: the riot that took place during a performance of Antheil's piano music, a performance that was being filmed for Marcel L'Herbier's movie *L'Inhumaine*. *L'Inhumaine* was intended as both a star-vehicle for the famous singer Georgette LeBlanc and as a showcase for modern art of all kinds, with figures such as Francis Picabia, Fernand Léger, and Darius Milhaud involved in the production, and luminaries such as Pablo Picasso, Man Ray, Erik Satie, Ezra Pound, and James Joyce making brief appearances. Although Antheil did not know it at the time, L'Herbier and LeBlanc were banking on the music causing a riot, as it has in earlier performances. As Antheil put it in his autobiography,

> . . . most curiously, this riot is no fake one. It is an actual riot, the same riot through which I played and lived the night of October 4, 1923. When I first viewed this movie a year later, I suddenly remembered Georgette LeBlanc walking up to my piano while the great floodlights in the balcony poured on us both simultaneously: I had thought it odd then. So I naturally asked Margaret Anderson [founder of *The Little Review* and lover of Georgette LeBlanc] about it, not without a grin of appreciation. She said yes, it been a sort of plot at that, but a plot in which she and Georgette had been sure I would greatly profit. She said that she thought I would be too nervous if I knew in advance that the house floodlights had been previously reinforced and cameras hidden in the balcony in the hope that my piano sonatas would cause the same sort of riot in Paris that they had caused in Germany. (136)

L'Herbier was correct in predicting Antheil's performance would provoke a riot, an angry expression of the power of a crowd. But this apparent trumping of play by power is by no means the end of the matter: the expression of crowd-power is harnessed by L'Herbier's cameras, and becomes a part of his own ludic artwork. Then, in a fine irony, the film itself goes on to provoke riots. As Jaque Catelain, the actor who played the scientist, wrote of it in his memoir of L'Herbier:

> *A chaque séance, les spectateurs s'insultent, il y a autant de partisans frénétiques que d'adversaires acharnés. C'est dans un véritable vacarme que passent sur l'écran, à toutes les représentations, les images multicolores et syncopées sur lesquelles se termine le film. Des femmes, le chapeau de travers, exigent d'être remboursées; des hommes, les traits convulsés, se précipitent sur le trottoir où, parfois, les pugilats continuent.* (82)

At each screening, the spectators insulted each other: there were as many frantic partisans of the film as there were crazed adversaries. The multicolored, syncopated images at the film's end were shown amid a true uproar. Women, with hats askew, demanded refunds, while men, their faces convulsed with anger, poured out onto the sidewalks, sometimes to fight.

The relation of play and power is no longer one of simple antimonies: it has become dialectic. Play becomes power becomes play, and so on.

Matthias cross-cuts his descriptions of *L'Inhumaine* and the Antheil riots with a treatment of another scandalous Antheil piece intended to accompany film, the groundbreaking *Ballet Méchanique* (which involves using airplane engines, synchronized player pianos, and modified automobile parts as instrumentation). Here, too, we see the dialectic of power and play at work:

                     a clicketyclack
      of the dactylicanapests jerking the film
      through a circle of light the soloist booed from the stage
      the piano rolls looping their loops
      in twelve pianolas electronic bells and a xylophone siren
      another Picabia made from the parts
      of a Model-T Ford (5)

This presents a strange music, a music in which the instruments of technological power and the fruits of mass production are transformed by Antheil and Picabia into the pure play of music: Picabia's constructions are a kind of *détournement* of the great symbol of modern America's industrial power. Later, the speaker asks us if we understand the mathematical principles behind Antheil's complex, automated synchronizations of his mechanical instruments: "You do comprehend these recursions are different / from those you expect" says the speaker, "the power plant cycles like no minuet?" (9). Here, our attention is drawn to the way Antheil has repurposed mathematical formulae more frequently used for the generation of power, converting them to musical play.

It's not just that these players seize the materials of power, though: power and play morph into one another throughout the poem. Consider the following passage ("Lescot" here is Claire Lescot, the leading character of *L'Inhumaine*, and an important character throughout "Auto-mystifstical Plaice"):

> So Model-T begat Picabia who as machinist made the shape that named a choreography. And then Antheil's recital drove the riot L'Herbier required for Lescot before she visits Léger's laboratory where her lover there among the angles and geometric shapes, the silver desks and rods and knobs and dials and flashing beams of light, transfigures her. (10)

Firstly, there's the business about Picabia and the Model-T: previously, we'd seen him as turning the symbol of technological power into an instrument of play. Here, though, we see things from a different angle: the kind of play Picabia and Antheil (and L'Herbier, and a host of others) are up to is enabled only by the mechanized power of Henry Ford and the powerful industrial society for which he stands. Play transforms power, but also depends on it.

It all gets more complicated, too. In drawing our attention to a scene in the Léger-designed laboratory of *L'Inhumaine*, Matthias calls up one of the central plot events of a film that is, itself, a meditation on the relation of art and play to power. In the film, the protagonist Claire Lescot is a famous singer courted by many powerful men, including the Maharaja of Nopur. She is aloof, and spurns them all, causing one of them, a scientist, to commit suicide. Her fans are appalled by her inhuman coldness, and riot during a concert she gives (this is, of course, the scene for which L'Herbier engaged the services of Antheil). Shaken by this, she goes to the tomb of the scientist and confesses her love for him. It turns out that he has only feigned his death, but no happy reunion is possible just yet: the jealous Maharaja kills Claire. Fortunately, the scientist is able to restore her to life. The events of the film involve the triumph of a singer—that is, a figure of play—over the Maharaja, a jealous figure of power. All of this is facilitated by technology.

Matthias ties the story of Hedy Lamarr and Fritz Mandl (another tale of play and power) into all this. Since Mandl wouldn't let Lamarr out of his sight—even when meeting with high-level Nazi officials and discussing new military technology—she was privy to secret information. As Matthias puts it, "she had been a silent party to analyses of radio control and interception by the politicians and engineers," and

> she'd listened first to all those conversations among guests who'd come on business with the Hertzenberger Industries. Like Krupp and Basil Zaharov, Mandl had the reputation of a man who'd start a war if that would move the goods. Goebbels kissed her hand from time to time and Göring held her chair. No one understood she could understand the technicalities. (22)

When Hedy Lamarr finally escapes from Mandl and Germany, she ends up in Los Angeles, where she meets another European émigré, George Antheil. Because he'd learned the mathematical and mechanical technicalities of signal synchronization to stage his *Ballet Méchanique*, he was able to collaborate with her on adapting Nazi war technology for new purposes. The fruits of their collaboration included what eventually became the standard remote control system for American naval torpedoes, as well as the signal technology behind cell phones and the midi technology that allows for contemporary digital music. The work of men of power is changed in the hands of figures of play, and is transformed into new forms of play and power. No longer does Matthias see play as separate from power, nor does he see it as subordinate to power. The very distinction between the realms of play and power breaks down.

Signs indicate that this blurring of the distinction between play and power isn't an aberration in Matthias' career, but a new phase in his long meditation on the relation between the two realms. In "Kedging in Time," for example, one of the most ambitious poetic sequences of Matthias' 2007 book *Kedging*, we see a similar morphing of play into power and back again. "Kedging in Time" traces the story of Matthias' wife's family, a history tied to that of the British Navy and, therefore, the British Empire. "Kedging in Time" mixes fictional and historical characters, and traces the odd, convoluted, sometimes almost too-strange-to-be-true ways certain novels and films (Anthony Hope's *The Prisoner of Zenda*, Erskine Childers' *The Riddle of the Sands*, John Buchan's *The Thirty-Nine Steps*, and Alfred Hitchcock's movie of the same name) variously predicted, reflected, and helped create key events of modern history. Of particular importance is the way Erskine Childers' seafaring novel *The Riddle of the Sands* breaks free of its function as entertainment and inspires Winston Churchill to have the Admiralty establish bases at Invergordon and Scapa Flow, bases that would play important roles when the great powers clashed in the Second World War. Play, for Matthias, continues to morph into power. The "unsteady antithesis" between play and power that Jere Odell saw in Matthias' work back in 1998 has only become more unsteady as time has gone on. One might even say that Matthias has pushed it to the point of collapse.

Works Cited

Anania, Michael. "John Matthias' *Bucyrus*." *Word Play Place: Essays on the Poetry of John Matthias*. Ed. Robert Archambeau. Athens, Ohio: Ohio University Press / Swallow Press, 1998. 20–25. Print.

Antheil, George. *Bad Boy of Music*. New York: Doubleday, 1945. Print.

Catelain, Jaque. *Jaque Catelain Présente Marcel L'Herbier*. Paris: Vautrain, 1950. Print.

Hooker, Jeremy. *The Presence of the Past: Essays on Modern British and American Poetry*. Bridgend: Poetry Wales Press, 1987. Print.

Huizinga, Johann. *Homo Ludens: A Study of the Play Element in Culture*. Boston: Beacon, 1950. Print.

Matthias, John. "Alto Luogo Ayasuluk." *TriQuarterly* 36 (Spring 1976), 88–93. Print.

———. *Bucyrus*. Chicago: Swallow, 1971. Print.

———. *Reading Old Friends: Essays, Reviews and Poems on Poetics 1975–1990*. Albany: State University of New York Press, 1992. Print.

———. *Turns*. Chicago: Swallow, 1975. Print.

———. *Working Progress, Working Title*. Cambridge: Salt, 2002. Print.

Odell, Jere. "Two Poems and the Aesthetics of Play." *Word Play Place: Essays on the Poetry of John Matthias*. Ed. Robert Archambeau. Athens, Ohio: Ohio University Press / Swallow Press, 1998. 35–49. Print.

Wordsworth, William. *The Pedlar, Tintern Abbey, The Two Part Prelude*. Ed. Jonathan Wordsworth. Cambridge: Cambridge University Press, 1985. Print.

Neruda's Earth, Heidegger's Earth

> It is good, at certain hours of the day and night, to look closely at the world of objects at rest. Wheels that have crossed long, dusty distances with their mineral and vegetable burdens, sacks from the coal bins, barrels, and baskets, handles and hafts for the carpenter's tool chest. From them flow the contacts of man with the earth, like a text for all troubled lyricists. The used surfaces of things, the wear that the hands give to things, the air, tragic at times, pathetic at others, of such things— all lend a curious attractiveness to the reality of the world that should not be underprized. (xxi)

That passage comes quote from "Towards an Impure Poetry," the editorial Pablo Neruda wrote for the first issue of the short-lived and fabulously-named Spanish journal *Caballo verde para la poesía* (*Green Horse for Poetry*) in 1935. The editorial was really an act of poetic self-defense: ever since the Chilean poet had arrived in Spain, Neruda had been under withering attack from the poet Juan Ramón Jiménez, who considered Neruda's work vulgar. Calling Neruda's imagination a sewer and a scrap heap, Jiménez objected to the world Neruda depicted. Stoked by the Mallarméan notion of *poesie pur*, with its ideal of a language as music, Jiménez wished Neruda would purge his poetry of all of the chunks of coal and shoe soles that, in his opinion, cluttered the verse with ugliness.

Neruda had been reading and translating Whitman, and had invested heavily in a very different poetic enterprise than had Jiménez. Neruda was young and provincial and felt persecuted by the older, more established Jiménez, who seemed, said Neruda, to be "publishing tortuous commentaries against me every week" (Felstiner 106). "Towards an Impure Poetry" is certainly intended as a riposte to Jiménez. But its importance goes further than its immediate occasion in the debate between the two poets: the passage offers a key to understanding Neruda's *The Heights of Macchu Picchu*, one of the most acclaimed sections of his great, sprawling *Canto General*, and a book-length poem cycle in its own right.

The Heights of Macchu Picchu was published a decade after the essay on impure poetry, and is often seen as somewhat discontinuous with his work of a decade earlier. After all, the intervening years saw the Spanish Civil War, which politicized Neruda's poetry, and his time in Mexico, when he took inspiration from Diego Rivera and the Mexican muralist tradition and turned toward broad depictions of history and society. John Felstiner claims in *Translating Neruda: The Way to Macchu Picchu* that *The Heights of Macchu Picchu* is simply "inconceivable" without the events of civil war. This is certainly true. But it's also true that there's a continuity with the project outlined in "Towards an Impure Poetry." To understand the nature of the continuity, we need to understand Neruda's essay, which has much more to it than a simple defense of the Whitmanic depiction of ordinary objects in poetry.

The most powerful idea in "Towards an Impure Poetry"—an idea Neruda acts on in the composition of *The Heights of Macchu Picchu*, is the idea of the earth. It's something very much akin to what Heidegger was articulating in his lectures on art in Zurich and Frankfurt right around the time Neruda composed his essay. These lectures would later see publication as "The Origin of the Work of Art," but not until 1950. It is not known whether Neruda knew about the lectures. It seems possible but unlikely—the main conduit bringing German philosophical ideas into Spanish intellectual life was Miguel de Unamuno, who was near the end of his life in 1935. The similarities between Neruda's essay and Heidegger's more deeply thought through exposition are probably coincidental, a matter of intellectual *zeitgeist* rather than direct influence. But the similarities of both idea and terminology are certainly very real.

When Neruda writes about the importance of looking at objects at rest, he's referring to an interestingly non-utilitarian, disinterested kind of perception, in which we become aware of the reality of things we'd been taking for granted. "Wheels that have crossed long, dusty distances with their mineral and vegetable burdens, sacks from the coal bins, barrels, and baskets, handles and hafts for the carpenter's tool chest"—these are all things that, generally, we instrumentalize, that we treat as equipment, and that we take for granted. When we're driving a vehicle, we don't think of the wheels. We depend on them, but unless they're malfunctioning as equipment, they go unnoticed even though our activities could only go on with their presence. The same goes for the handles of carpenter's tools. They're essential to our tasks, and we're very intimate with them. Often, the handles are even discolored by, or worn to, the shape of our hands. But when we're building something, we tend not to be thinking about the handle of our hammer. We're concentrating on a utilitarian action, concentrating on not hitting our thumbs while we go about our business. So whole swathes of the world go unnoticed.

For Neruda, looking at these objects the right way, when they and we are at rest, reconnects us to the world we take for granted during all our utilitarian to-and-fro-ing. From the perception of these things, says Neruda, "flow the contacts of man with the earth." When we notice them, we realize we aren't isolated, Cartesian intelligences: we're rooted in the world, surrounded at all times by things that make our lives possible. Indeed, we come to realized our interconnectedness with these, and, ultimately, with all things. It's a big idea Neruda has in his little essay. It's also uncannily similar to Heidegger's thinking.

In "The Origin of the Work of Art" Heidegger makes an important distinction between the earth and the world. When Heidegger writes about earth he isn't referring to physical stuff—not rocks, or trees, or door-latches. Instead, he's referring to the tendency of things to resist our ability to understand, or even to notice, them. There's a whole realm of the unknown and not-understood, and it surrounds and contains us, even makes up a great deal of our physical self and our psyche. In the famous passage where Heidegger writes about a Van Gogh painting depicting some old, worn-looking shoes, he says that shoes like this are generally things we don't notice—we wear them and use them as equipment, for their instrumental value, and we tend not to notice them when we do. Shoes like these, when they're actually worn, "belong to the earth" says Heidegger (159)—and they belong there not so much because they are material objects, but because they go unnoticed and un-thought-of. But we notice them in Van Gogh's painting, where they become part of something more. Here, in the painting, they are noticed or, in the standard translation of Heidegger, become "unconcealed" (172). It's the concealedness of the shoes before they get into the painting, when they're just something around us that we don't notice, that makes them belong to the earth. The earth and the things that belong to it are self-concealing, and withdrawn from our attention and understanding.

But what about the world, in Heidegger's sense? The world, for Heidegger, is the context in which and through which we apprehend, understand, or notice things—it is where things become unconcealed. History, myths, and the like give us a way of noticing things, talking about them and feeling their presence. Heidegger's world is in a way like what a later generation of thinkers would call discourse—the systems of thought and representation that let us notice things.

The work of art gives us a special kind of relation of earth and world, a dialectic. That is, in the work of art, earth and world are always involved in a struggle. If a work of art were pure world, it wouldn't be art. It would be propaganda, or ideology: a closed system of mental coordinates that never comes into contact with anything that resistant to understanding. But the artwork doesn't allow anything so easy to happen. Even as it starts to open up a whole world (or discourse, or paradigm, or way of understanding) for us, it gives us elements that resist appropriation into that world. If the work of art in question is, say, a poem, we might say that it resists paraphrase, or closure; or that parts of it remain indeterminate; or that it shoots off so many connotations that we're uneasy reducing it to a denotative meaning. Any attempt to make the artwork into mere world runs up against all kinds of elements that escape that world. The work of art has the power not only to bring elements of the earth into the world—it has an inexhaustibility in that even as it brings the earth into the world, it also conceals other elements of the world.

Neruda doesn't go into the dialectic of the earth and the world, of unconcealing and concealing, the way Heidegger does, but he certainly gives us a part of the idea: that the necessary but unnoticed things of the earth can, and should, enter into our consciousness, under the right conditions of perception. This is the kind of thinking that informs the writing of *The Heights of Macchu Picchu*. Some of the early sections of the book depict a kind the kind of modern death-in-life we're familiar with from, say, T. S. Eliot's *The Waste Land*. Here are some lines from section three:

> Being like maize grains fell
> in the inexhaustible store of lost deeds, shoddy
> occurrences, from nine to five, to six,
> and not one death but many came to each,
> each day a little death: dust, maggot, lamp,
> drenched in the mire of suburbs, a little death with fat wings
> entered into each man like a short blade
> and siege was laid to him by bread or knife:
> the drover, the son of harbors, the dark captain of plows,
> the rodent wanderer through dense streets:
>
> all of them weakened waiting for their death, their brief
> and daily death . . . (156)

This is the nightmare of the life that goes by without our noticing it. Our very being falls away from us like so many grains, and our lives consist of "lost deeds"—things we don't notice doing, and don't remember having done. This sad condition is, in the poem, the curse of modern, regimented life, the world of "nine to five," in which our instrumental, utilitarian activities, our quest for our daily bread, is a mere matter of going through the motions, a "brief and daily death." We use things and keep ourselves alive among them, but we don't notice them. The earth retreats from us into the unnoticed, the concealed.

Eliot's remedy for this sad, afflicted state involved an attempt to reconstruct the myths and religious traditions that had become discredited or obscure. But Neruda's remedy is less mythic, and more a matter of existential perception, or restoring our connection to the concealed wonder of the world in all its *dasein*, its here-and-nowness. He wants to bring the unnoticed earth back into our perceptual world.

There are three main techniques by which Neruda tries to accomplish this retrieval of the earth in *The Heights of Macchu Picchu*. First, there's an

invocation of the unnoticed earth, such as we find in some lines from
the poem's opening section:

> Someone waiting for me among the violins
> met with a world like a buried tower
> sinking its spiral below the layered leaves
> color of raucous sulfur:
> and lower yet, in a vein of gold,
> like a sword in a scabbard of meteors,
> I plunged a turbulent and tender hand
> into the most secret organs of the earth. (155)

This eroticizing of a landscape is familiar stuff in Neruda's poetry: it's
the whole charm of "Body of a Woman," the most famous poem of his
best-loved book, *Twenty Love Poems and a Song of Despair*. Here, though, the
technique is at the service of reminding us of the very nature of the
ground we stand on, showing us the gold-veined rock beneath the Andes.
Such gold is literally concealed, and literally of the earth, but it is also
concealed from our consciousness, and therefore a part of the Heideg-
gerian earth. We walk on brilliant wonders, but we're so disconnected
from them in our daily grind we need the poem to reveal them to us, to
bring them into our world. Whole sections of *The Heights of Macchu Picchu*
aim at reminding us of the forgotten wonders of the earth, often in
sweeping, incantatory fashion.

A second way Neruda tries to bring the forgotten earth to our attention is through an insistence on how, despite our inattention, we are
always already connected to it. Consider these lines from section ten:

> Stone within stone, and man, where was he?
> Air within air, and man, where was he?
> Time within time, and man, where was he?
> Were you also the shattered fragment
> of indecision, of hollow eagle
> which, through the streets of today, in the old tracks
> through the leaves of accumulated autumns,
> goes pounding at the soul into the tomb?
> Poor hand, poor foot, and poor, dear life...
> The days of unraveled light
> in you, familiar rain

> falling on feast-day banderillas,
> did they grant, petal by petal, their dark nourishment
> to such an empty mouth? (160–61)

Those first three questions are hard to answer. Things exist within themselves, independently of us. And where are we? Are we in any kind of relationship with stone, air, and time? On the one hand, the benighted nine-to-fivers Neruda described earlier don't have any kind of conscious relationship to these things. They don't stop to think of themselves in relation to air, stone, and time. On the other hand, we always have an intimate relation to these things: we stand on stone, breath air, make our way through time. Normally, though, they're like the wheels or carpenter's tools of "Towards an Impure Poetry"—we depend on them, but don't notice them. Our perceptual world, in which we think only of getting by, has shrunk away from the things of the earth. But by the end of the passage, we're reminded that things like time and light are in us, and when we're asked if the "familiar" (that is, unnoticed) rain nourishes us, the only answer is "yes." We are reminded that we aren't just the "poor life" of forlorn little isolated subjectivities, but really we are manifestations of the larger earth, connected to it in our very bodies when they take it in. We are of the earth, and the poem tries to make us notice this.

Finally, Neruda invokes the idea of ancestry to connect the reader (especially the Latin American reader with native ancestry) with ranges of time that usually lie outside of our perceptual world. "Arise to birth with me, my brother," begins section twelve (163). The brother here is one of the pre-Incan inhabitants of Macchu Picchu, a member of the civilization that built the city. "Look at me from the depths of the earth," says Neruda to this figure, before telling him to "Come quickly to my veins and to my mouth / Speak through my speech, and through my blood" (165). Neruda insists on how present-day Chileans are deeply, and intrinsically, bound to a past that they have let slip from consciousness. Their blood is, after all, the blood of the ancestors who build Macchu Picchu. They are connected to the past, even when they don't know it. Again, it is through the poem that these unthought-of things enter the world of our thought, and help save us from the forlorn death-in-life of the modern daily nine-to-five.

Of course, this think-of-your-blood business is a bit unnerving to we bourgeois liberals. And the importance the poem puts on blood ancestry raises a question about whether the coincidence between Heidegger's thinking and Neruda's goes beyond the mutual interest in bringing the unnoticed earth to our perceptual worlds in the work of art. Both Heidegger and Neruda were undeniably brilliant writers, but both were also drawn to brutal dictators (Heidegger to Hitler, Neruda to Stalin). One wonders whether there's an intrinsic connection between concerns with existential depth and attraction to ambitious, destructive absolutist rulers. Put another way, one might ask if ordinary bourgeois decency, with its aversion to the concentration of power and its general you-do-your-thing, I'll-do-mine indifference to others comes at the price of such depth. It's worth considering—the English political tradition is certainly the European tradition most powerfully immune to dictatorships, and England is also the home to the European philosophical tradition most averse to German Idealism, Existentialism, and related philosophical traditions. The challenge of reading Pablo Neruda must include, for many of us, the challenge of his philosophical and political positions. Meeting the challenge may even bring our own assumptions into unconcealment.

Works Cited

Felstiner, John. *Translating Neruda: The Way to Macchu Picchu.* Palo Alto: Stanford University Press, 1980. Print.

Heidegger, Martin. "The Origin of the Work of Art." *Heidegger: Basic Writings.* Ed. David Farrell Krell. New York: Harper and Row, 1976. 143–88. Print.

Neruda, Pablo. *The Poetry of Pablo Neruda.* Ed. Ilan Stavans. New York: Farrar Straus Giroux, 2003. Print.

———. "Towards an Impure Poetry." *Pablo Neruda: Five Decades, Poems 1925–1970.* Ed. and trans. Ben Belitt. New York: Grove, 1974. xxi–xxii. Print.

The Decadent of Moyvane

The word "decadence," in a literary context, tends to conjure up a vague whiff of Swinburne and scandal, or perhaps images of *The Yellow Book*, with its Beardsley covers and its selections of Arthur Symonds and Richard Le Gallienne. The Francophile associates the word with slogans such as *épater le bourgeois* and *l'art pour l'art*. The true connoisseur thinks of Théophile Gautier's rebellion against neoclassicism and the doctrine of art in the service of society. If the connoisseur is particularly pedantic, he may wander over to his bookshelf, pull down Gautier's *Mademoiselle de Maupin*, and, blowing the dust from its pages, refer to the once-infamous introduction, lingering over the following passage:

> There is nothing truly beautiful but that which can never be of any use whatsoever; everything useful is ugly, for it is the expression of some need, and man's needs are ignoble and disgusting like his own poor and infirm nature. The most useful place in the house is the water-closet. (xvii–xviii)

"From that," says the pedantic connoisseur, "comes all of Mallarmé." He's not wrong, really. If anything is essential to the literary movement of the late nineteenth century we've come to call the decadence, it is the rejection of the idea of art having any end other than art itself. The decadent's ideal art was autonomous, free of any ties to politics, peoples, causes, or commerce.

Despite Oscar Wilde's "Symphony in Yellow" and "Impression du Matin," we tend not to associate decadence of this sort with Irish poetry. Even Yeats, whose early work owed so much to the French *symbolistes*, doesn't really rate as a decadent: his interest in *l'art pour l'art* was always counterbalanced by the claims of national liberation. For every "Sailing to Byzantium" moment in Yeats' work there is a "Byzantium" as retraction; for every aesthete's poem like "The Cloak, the Boat and the Shoes" there's a nationalist's "Easter, 1916." Yeats is far from atypical among Irish poets in having reservations about aesthetic autonomy. Indeed, Irish poetry of the past century has overwhelmingly been written in a tradition other than the decadence's *l'art pour l'art*. From Yeats through Montague and on through Heaney and Eavan Boland, mainstream Irish poets have tended to write with a sense of the people's claim on their art. The bulk of Irish poetic achievement over the course of the twentieth century took place within a framework of heteronomous rather than autonomous aesthetics: at some level poetry served the need of a community, be it national or sectarian, for self-expression.

Declan Kiberd claims that the fundamental question posed by this heteronomous aesthetic tradition in Ireland has been "how to express life which has never yet found full expression in written literature" (118) and he argues that such a question is made most urgent in a nation striving for independence. Though we have come to think of decadence in literature as a matter of aesthetic autonomy, of art cut off from anything other than artistic concerns, Ireland's decidedly heteronomous poetic tradition makes one wonder if another kind of decadence is possible. If a heteronomous poetic tradition is born out of colonial circumstances, what happens to that tradition when those circumstances no longer apply? Could the stylistic and emotional gestures of such a tradition fall into decay, inviting a self-indulgence empty of any real vitality? Gabriel Fitzmaurice's *Boghole Boys*, gives us every indication that the answer to the question, in the Irish context, is a resounding *yes*.

Fitzmaurice introduces his book with a short essay sounding the traditional notes of the Irish poet of community. His poems, he informs us, make "the authentic sound of [the] backwater." As he describes his native village of Moyvane to us, he leans back, puts one arm around our shoulders and, gesturing widely at the "teachers and tricksters . . . priests and publicans" of the town, looks us squarely in the eyes and tells us, "I seek to give voice to these people." The locals are, he opines, an endangered group, "the forgotten people of the new Ireland" (1–2). Fitzmaurice's gesture is among the oldest in Irish literature: the defiant preservation of an all-but-extinct culture through the voice of the heroic bard. The Irish poet and critic David Wheatley once claimed that the idea "that old Ireland is dying or dead is one of our most endlessly renewable tropes," and Fitzmaurice is happy to locate himself in that tradition (82).

Fitzmaurice's place in the tradition, though, is marginal, and in a sense it is a position of decadence. He has inherited a tradition from colonial times that demands its poets speak for a threatened national community, but he lives in a nation that has become one of the youngest and most technologically and culturally advanced in all of Europe. The central bardic trope of the tradition no longer fits the circumstances of the nation, so in Fitzmaurice's iteration the trope becomes a diminished thing. Instead of protecting the threatened heart of the nation against powerful foreign oppressors, he finds himself the guardian of a relatively unremarkable village against—well, against what, exactly? Against the sneering snobbery of the newly moneyed of Dublin and Galway? It doesn't even amount to that. There's a kind of bathos to Fitzmaurice's aggrieved village patriotism when the worst image of oppression he can summon is that of a man visiting from Dublin who wants to buy him a drink in the village pub:

> They shit on us, these upstarts who return
> To the pubs in which they drank; I know their breed—
> They boast to old acquaintance as they burn
> With all the ostentation of their greed.
> Fuck off with your money as you stand
> Buying off misfortune at the bar;
> I'm a celebrant and though you shake my hand
> And act as if in friendship, this is war.
> I stand up for my people, mind them well,
> I know your kind, your money. Go to hell. (22)

One hardly needs to point out that a poem like this represents a diminution of the tradition seen in, say, Yeats' "Easter 1916" or Heaney's

"Punishment," poems born, respectively, of colonial and post-colonial struggle. The tradition born of real hardship lies, here, in utter decay.

We see more decadence in those poems where Fitzmaurice proclaims himself a celebrant of the local. The gesture is part and parcel of the tradition of Irish colonial and postcolonial poetry, but there's a curious emptiness to it in Fitzmaurice's hands. Consider "I Rhyme my Native Village with Cézanne," the book's opening poem:

> I rhyme my native village with Cézanne,
> The place I live and represent in art,
> A poet finds genius where he can,
> The picture that he paints is of his heart.
> A child, an adolescent and a man
> With a vision that the world couldn't thwart,
> And still remaining faithful to my plan,
> I write about my village, show it warts
> And all—I must. But I'm a celebrant,
> Not one whose whole ambition's to distort:
> Who would grotesque a village like Moyvane
> Is painting false, a sell-out to the smart.
> I rhyme my native village with Cézanne.
> A poet finds genius where he can. (17)

Let us leave aside the matter of cliché ("warts and all"), and the matter of straw men ("one whose whole ambition's to distort"). The real decadence here comes from the lack of any particular quality of the village that could be singled out for praise. Fitzmaurice claims to celebrate his village, but there is nothing specific here to celebrate. The localist gesture is simply generic, bland enough to adorn a Chamber of Commerce calendar. Confronted with a poem like this, one really does feel the force of those lines from Eliot's "Hollow Men": "Shape without form, shade without color, / Paralysed force, gesture without motion" (79).

Perhaps the most telling sign of the decadence of Fitzmaurice's tradition comes in "For Seamus Heaney." Here Fitzmaurice lifts a glass on the occasion of Heaney's Nobel Prize. He urges his countrymen to rejoice at a Nobel laureate named Seamus, for in the aftermath of such an honor *Punch* magazine can no longer portray the Irish as subhuman. This really is absurd. There was, certainly, a time when the Irish were depicted as subhuman, lantern-jawed simians in the cartoons of the English journal *Punch*. Indeed, the Celtic Revival was to a great extent an attempt to combat these stereotypes, to give prestige to Ireland's rich literary tradition. But the Celtic Revival's gestures of defiance were directed at real foes, present and powerful in the world at the time. No British journal would dare publish a *Punch*-like cartoon today, and if there's a popular stereotype about the Irish and literature, it isn't that they are a nation of illiterates. If anything, it's the opposite: that every Celt's a poet, through and through. The very fact that Fitzmaurice has to direct his resentment at a journal that no longer exists makes a powerful statement: the tradition that was necessary a century ago has outlived its use.

Fitzmaurice may, at some level, sense the threadbare nature of his materials. This would account for his book's frequent bouts of defensiveness. Fitzmaurice often anticipates a negative critical reception, and tries to pre-empt it by attacking the critic in advance. "At Fifty" is typical of this side of Fitzmaurice's work:

> I court the common reader, not the poet—
> The kind who browses, likes a damn good read:
> Let poets (at least the kind who think they know it
> All) ignore me. It's not for them I bleed.
> No! The ones who read me are the kind
> Who know that they can trust a fellow who
> Opens up his heart, his soul, his mind.
> Unlike words, they know that blood is true. (20)

The rhetoric here is all son-of-the-soil authenticity. Perhaps I am too much of a poet to appreciate the authenticity of verse like this, distracted as I am by the appalling, nay ghastly, rhyming of "poet" and "know it." So let me take off my poet's hat and put on another I wear, that of a teacher. Fitzmaurice, after all, includes teachers among the humble folk to whom he would give voice. Reading his poem as a teacher, I still find I can't quite praise it. The pronoun-referent problem in "Unlike words, they know that blood is true" gets in the way. It is the sort of thing I'd circle in teacherly red ink if I saw it in a student's paper, before writing "who knows that blood is true here—surely you don't mean that 'the words' know this." Or perhaps I would just write "Argh."

I don't mean to imply that Irish poetry is doomed to a long process of entropy, or that the best of Irish writing can only come from the most painful of Irish experiences. Far from it. But I do wish to argue that the particular tradition of Irish poetry born of colonial and postcolonial struggle has fallen into decline as the circumstances that gave rise to it have faded into history. Let Fitzmaurice serve as an exhibit in the making of this case. Those interested in an alternative to his faded tradition may wish to refer to the works of another cohort of Irish poets, people like Randolph Healy, Maurice Scully, Billy Mills, and Catherine Walsh. Their work—exciting, vital, and free of the clichéd gestures that so plague Fitzmaurice—takes Irish poetry into new territory, beyond that staked out by the greats of the last century. Give them a look, if you're interested in the direction of Irish poetry, and leave to the sentimental this decadent of Moyvane.

Works Cited

Eliot, T. S. *Collected Poems, 1909–1962*. New York: Harcourt, Brace, Jovanovich, 1991. Print.

Fitzmaurice, Gabriel. *The Boghole Boys*. Cork: Marino, 2005. Print.

Gautier, Théophile. *Mademoiselle de Maupin*. Paris: Société des Beaux-Arts, 1905. Print.

Kiberd, Declan. *Inventing Ireland*. Cambridge, Massachusetts: Harvard University Press, 1995. Print.

Wheatley, David. "Death and the Irish Canon." *The Dublin Review* 2 (Spring 2001): 80–89. Print.

Modernist Current
On Michael Anania

James Joyce was born in Omaha in 1939. His first book, *Dubliners*, contained the poem sequence "Stops Along the Western Bank of the Missouri River," which treated his native Nebraska with the intense realism that could only come about under conditions of voluntary exile. Nostalgia and critical distance combined to make the linked-yet-disparate pieces of the sequence so precise that the river could, if necessary, be reconstructed bend by bend from the pages of the poems. A later and much more complex work, *Ulysses*, treated the same Nebraskan territory with equal detail. Its central poetic sequence, though, the ten part "Riversongs of Arion," combined realism with a concern for myth, finding in the quotidian world echoes of a heroic past. The result was a truly modernist synthesis of past and present, the construction of an eternal now along the lines of work being produced by Joyce's modernist peers Pound, Eliot and David Jones.

Put down your copy of Richard Ellmann's Joyce biography. I know Joyce was born in Ireland. The two points I'd like to make about Michael Anania's river sequences, though, are made most clearly through an analogy with Joyce. I'd like to say that Anania, like Joyce, is fundamentally a modernist (an *unreconstructed modernist*, even); and I'd like to say that the relationship between his two major river sequences, "Stops Along the Western Bank of the Missouri River" and "The Riversongs of

Arion" is like the relationship of *Dubliners* to *Ulysses*. The works treat similar material, but the more mature work does so with greater philosophical ambition, a more profound historical sense, and a greater degree of meta-literary self-consciousness.

Omaha as Dublin, Buffalo as Trieste

> Leaving Nebraska made it clear that writing about Nebraska was like writing about Rome or Florence—it was tangible, real, nobody knew it, there were concrete things in it for poems and what was absolute familiarity for me was unknown to others.
> —Michael Anania (in Archambeau 4)

Michael Anania left Omaha in 1961, arriving in Buffalo, New York to pursue graduate studies in English. He'd been harboring literary ambitions for years, writing poems, plays and stories and editing the campus literary magazine at the University of Omaha. But he'd always had some reservations about being a writer: it didn't seem to jibe with where he came from. Growing up in an Omaha housing project, he'd attended schools where, as he put it, "standing up and saying you were a poet would be a little bit like standing up and saying you were a target" (in Archambeau 4). Literature had felt distant from his impoverished life in a provincial city that seemed antithetical to literature. Enthralled by existential philosophy and the literature of the absurd, he later described himself as "thrilled by anything complicated and remote" (4). Think of him as a Great Plains version Joyce's hero, the young Dedalus of *Portrait* who dreamed of Aquinas and Byron from the horse-piss smelling alleys of a Dublin that had yet to acquire any of its twentieth century literary glamour.

At Buffalo, Anania had hoped to study Yeats or perhaps Wallace Stevens—both complicated, and both remote—Yeats' universe of gyres and the non-places of Stevens' imaginative pagodas being equidistant from the wrong side of Omaha, Nebraska. Buffalo, though, was the repository of a huge archive of the papers and manuscripts of William Carlos Williams, the then-unfashionable patron saint of "a local pride" in American poetry. Working on Williams was one way for Anania to muster the courage to take on the matter of Nebraska. And like Joyce in Trieste, Anania found the distance between his first provincial place and his new provincial place liberating. What had been stuff to humble to tell in verse became as real and particular as Paris, London, or Paterson, New Jersey.

Nowhere in Anania's first book, 1970's *The Color of Dust*, is this more evident than in the series that constitutes one of that book's four sections, "Stops Along the Western Bank of the Missouri River." The tangible realness of Anania's descriptions here reflect his newfound local pride, his sense that Omaha had "concrete things in it for poems" and his growing sense that "what was absolute familiarity" to him could also be the matter of literature. We could just about reconstruct the neighborhood north of Omaha's Clark Street from lines like these, from "A Journey,"

> without the regimen of red brick,
> the houses, grey of old wood
> stripped of paint above
> the tilted, broken walks,
> cracked by the roots of the elms
> that hang over the walks,
> break open the retaining walls . . . (2)

A poet like Walt Whitman gets his topography from an atlas; a poet like Anania, following Williams and Joyce, gets his topography from the streets he'd walked.

Along with this sense of the minute details of the local comes a strong sense of the distance between the ideal and the real—a sense we find among a number of provincial literary prodigies, not the least being, of course, Joyce himself. In the poem we've just looked at, for example, Anania notes the ironic distance between the aspirations of a road named "Grace Street" and the actuality of that down-at-the-heels street as it meanders "past a gutted store / with a drawn coonskin / drying on the grey wall" to an old brewery and then "down to the yards, / to the open sewer that / swills into the river" (2). We see something similar in "The Square, Bum's Park," where we read these lines:

> Smells of urine,
> cheap cologne,

Tiger Rose and sour milk
hang in the staircase—
the Chicago Hotel
the elite of Omaha
overlooking beautiful
Jefferson Square. (13)

As in "The Journey," we see the distance between the ideal promised in a world of text and the real embodied in sordid actuality. It is an environment that breeds fascination with "anything complicated and remote."

The distance between language and material reality is explored somewhat differently in "Missouri Among the Rivers." Here, we read that "Bluff crests in Fontenelle are quiet, / give no emblem, figured name" (6). The place has only the weakest connection with the kind of language that can charge it with significance and make it known. It is bereft, lacking the layer of symbolic significance that makes it figuratively, as well as literally, habitable.

In this context, there is a kind of will to create significance for the place, a desire to convert the area's past into a usable and significant history. In "Arbor Lodge," for example, Anania looks at an old blockhouse and wills it to become a monument and an enduring emblem of the place's history:

Make it a monument:
where the highway
bends past the birches,
the cabin with slotted gunports,
before the shaded gate
fix a new stone marker,
an emblem freely carved. (11)

This will to find and memorialize a significant past for a place that often seems like a debased reality haunted by distant ideals is the strongest strand connecting the nine poems of the sequence. It is present from the very first poem, "A Journey," which concludes with images of the Lewis and Clark expedition. The contemplation of these images leads to a brief moment of epiphany, where ideal and real seem to become one. Addressing the Sacagawea of the expedition as well as the monuments to her, Anania's speaker bursts into the cadences of prayer. Suddenly, we see Sacagawea as the past incarnate in the present, and realize the apparently debased place as a space charged with significance:

> We move though intersections
> capable of history.
> Birdwoman, bronze lady of the river,
> figurehead of keelboats,
> steel lady of bridges,
> we pass in the dead of August. (5)

No sooner does the epiphany come than its moment passes. In the waste land of the present, history and its associations remain "Afterthoughts. First, // the city in dust" (5).

The sequence ends with a poem meditating on the ironies of provincial cultural inferiority anxieties. "The Park Above All Others Called, Riverview" begins with the image of "A bust of Schiller on a hillside" that "faces east, looking like a Medici" (15). The bust, looking out over the city of dust, is a gesture of civic fealty to a legitimated high culture located long ago and far away. By invoking the Medici, though, Anania reminds us that there was a time when Germany didn't stand for the empire of culture, but looked toward the Italian *quattrocento* as a legitimate elsewhere, a high culture that promised so much more than the seemingly debased here-and-now. The poem rehearses a brief history of such moments of cultural anxiety: "Johannes studied alchemy in Venice," writes Anania, "Monet waited to be French" (15) The poem ends by posing a question—"How does it matter, this view of the park by the river?"—and providing a kind of an answer: "it is the recurrent dream / demanding the voice that speaks through" (16). The place demands its voice, its poetry. And so the young Anania, when he'd packed his bags for Buffalo, went forth to forge in the smithy of his soul the uncreated poems of his place.

The Then that is Now

The man standing beside me is a retired stockyards drover from Sarpy County, Nebraska. The steel-guitar Western twang in his voice is real; so are the stiff curls in his cowboy boots. When he lifts his straw hat, it leaves a deep sweat-band furrow in his hair that no Sunday-morning dose of Wildroot or Brylcreem will erase. The wrinkles at the back of his neck are as sharply cut as cracks in dry soil. . . . He points across the water to a stand of cottonwoods. That's his camper, an Apache, half-shaded from the midday sun. . . . We are standing on the Overland Trail. All the pioneers, the Mormons, and the forty-niners who set off from Council Bluffs passed by here early in their long journey west, and it is impossible not to transform his camper and the others circled in the trees into covered wagons. This is the same ground, after all, the same slow, murky river . . .

—Michael Anania (*In Plain Sight* 13)

Michael Anania, introducing his prose meditation on the American west with a personal anecdote, may, in the moment, find it impossible not to see the present in terms of the legendary past. How could he not? "This is the same ground, after all," he writes, as if the coincidence in space were all it would take to make the significant past incarnate in the here-and-now. The connection between past and present that came only as a fleeting epiphany in "Stops Along the Western Bank of the Missouri River" comes effortlessly here. Such effortlessness, though, is reserved for Anania's prose. When he takes up the matter of past and present in his poetry, it is always more complicated, and the sense of incarnation comes not as an easy breeze of transcendence; it is earned by the sweat of the poet's brow.

Before Anania's next river sequence, "The Riversongs of Arion," (from his 1978 book *Riversongs*) even gets underway, it has posed its central question: what is the relationship between the here-and-now and the there-and-then? It does so in a complicated and roundabout way: through the juxtaposition of these two epigraphs, the first from the seventeenth-century English theologian Thomas Hooker, the second from the journals of Lewis and Clark:

> *The Rule is one, like itself accompanied with stability and rest; if once we go astray from that, there is neither end nor quiet in error, but restlessness and emptiness.*

> *This evening Guthrege Cought a* White Catfish . . . *tale much like that of a* Dolfin. (56)

The juxtaposition is itself interesting: we have one quote from a faraway *there*, and one quote from the newly-explored territories of the poem's western *here*. But there's more afoot here than the placing of English and American texts side by side. Each passage invokes the idea of a present reality lacking the meaning or significance that can only be supplied by appealing to something remote.

The first quote holds out two possibilities: either we find our connection with an eternal rule, a law that governs and unites all things at all times and places; or we are left with nothing but wandering, emptiness, and unquiet; a restlessness bred of a lack of meaning. That is, we either find an eternal truth that redeems time, or we wander in the wastes of error. The second quote gives us explorers who have wandered into new territory, and found new animals. They try to understand the new things by appealing to known things from the faraway world. How do we make sense of this new fish? It is like the dolphins we know from before. Both quotes, then, emphasize the appeal to an *elsewhere* to explain the present world: in the first, there is the elsewhere of eternity; in the second, the elsewhere of the eastern seaboard. Before the first poem in the sequence, then, we find that our matter will be the seeking of connections between a *there-and-then* that supplies meaning for a *here-and-now* bereft of significance. Anania had touched on these matters in "Stops Along the Western Bank of the Missouri River" (in, for example, the meditation on the bust of Schiller). Here, though, these concerns move to the fore—so much to the fore, in fact, that we see them well developed even before we've read the first poem in the sequence.

If, like me, you're the kind of reader who reads the endnotes before the main text, then you see these concerns developed even further before you turn to the first poem. In Anania's notes to the poem—which, like Eliot's notes to *The Waste Land*, are best read as a part of the poem proper—we find this explanation of the dramatic situation from which the "riversongs" are sung:

> The Arion of this sequence is a contemporary who sets off on a trip down the Missouri River from Omaha and gets stuck just south of the city. On July 22, 1804, Lewis and Clark proceeded north from the mouth of the Platte River about ten miles and pitched a five-day camp, named, for Silas Goodrich's catch of July 24, White Catfish Camp. This Arion's diversions, complaints, and plaintiff anthems while stranded opposite what he supposes is that campsite comprise the sequence. (81)

This Arion, says Anania, is a contemporary. But the Arion of Greek myth and legend—the there-and-then to this Arion's here-and-now—lurks behind him, just as the old artificer and maze-maker lurked not far behind Joyce's Dedalus. The Arion of Greek legend, like this Arion, is a sailor; and like this Arion, he is stuck while sailing. The classical Arion is captured by pirates and about to be executed, but is spared long enough to sing a final song. The song summons dolphins, which carry him away to freedom. A number of questions arise here: if the classical Arion's songs free him from distress, will our contemporary Arion's songs deliver him? If so, from what condition will he be delivered? And what are we to make of the fact that Arion only supposes he sees Lewis and Clark's camp? And why are his songs "plaintiff" rather than "plaintive" (a fact missed by the editors of Anania's *Selected Poems*, who erroneously 'correct' the poet's supposed error). What, one might also wonder, is the deal on those mythic dolphins, given the epigraph from Lewis and Clark that draws a parallel between the white catfish for which the camp was named and the dolphin whose tail resembles that of the catfish? All of these questions are answered, implicitly or explicitly, by the poems of the sequence.

The first poem suggests the nature of the condition from which the contemporary Arion wishes to be set free. The poem shows us Arion's makeshift oil-drum raft in a despoiled modern river, among "slit-bellied watermelons / and castaway chicken heads" as it is caught up "on a rusted snare of dredge cable / with the slow brown water curling / dark foam against barrel heads" (57). The material squalor of the river is reminiscent of similar scenes from a number of other poems, notably Robert Lowell's "The Mouth of the Hudson" with its "unforgivable landscape" (14) and the "Fire Sermon" section of T. S. Eliot's *The Waste Land*. The "slow brown" river, though, points to another Eliot poem, "The Dry Salvages" from *Four Quartets* as a primary allusion. "The Dry Salvages" is the poem where Eliot famously speaks of the river as a "strong brown god" (191). Anania's allusion to the poem is apposite, here, because Eliot's poem poses a problem much like that posed in Anania's epigraphs, the problem of how a bereft *now* relates to a more meaningful *then*. The first stanza of Eliot's poem gives the gist of this:

> I do not know much about gods; but I think that the river
> Is a strong brown god—sullen, untamed and intractable,
> Patient to some degree, at first recognized as a frontier;
> Useful, untrustworthy, as a conveyer of commerce;
> Then only a problem confronting the builder of bridges.
> The problem once solved, the brown god is almost forgotten
> By the dwellers in cities—ever, however, implacable,
> Keeping his seasons and rages, destroyer, reminder
> Of what men choose to forget. Unhonoured, unpropitiated
> By worshippers of the machine, but waiting, watching and waiting.
> His rhythm was present in the nursery bedroom,
> In the rank ailanthus of the April dooryard,
> In the smell of grapes on the autumn table,
> And the evening circle in the winter gaslight. (191)

Does history take us away from the eternal world of gods, through a process of modernization, to a utilitarian and ever more disenchanted world? For the Eliot of *The Four Quartets* (if not the younger Eliot of *The Waste Land*), the answer is no. The world of gods is still with us, waiting and watching. The *then* that is charged with meaning lurks within the apparently disenchanted *now*, "waiting, watching and waiting." We only need the poet to find it for us.

Anania, invoking Eliot from within the disenchanted present of his own poem, implies that an Eliotic connection between the significant past and the apparently empty present can be made. The contemporary Arion, then, is stuck not only in a literally desolate river, but in a spiritually desolate present. If the singing of the classical Arion delivers him from a literal captivity, these "riversongs" seek to deliver us from a more metaphysical captivity. Our contemporary Arion is stuck in a world without myth or legend, and his songs, if successful, will deliver him from that disenchanted world.

The second "riversong" offers us our first inkling that such deliverance is possible. Here Arion watches the odd motion of the local catfish as they swim upriver, and is reminded of an old phrase of the men who have worked on the river. "Rivermen," Arion observes, "call this / the catfish dance because / from the banks they seem // stationary" as they bob "up / and down in the dark foam" (58). This is our first hint that there is more than a squalid material world around us: there is a history of local lore. Just as the dolphins come to rescue the classical Arion, the catfish (compared by Lewis and Clark to dolphins) come to rescue the contemporary Arion. In fact, the remembered bit of riverman's lore leads Arion to think of other, more significant local lore: "Marquette," for example, "feared the thud // of their bodies against / his canoe." (58–59). The whole history of exploration and settlement opens up, giving the place significance beyond its soiled, observable surfaces. It is at this point that Arion sees the land nearby as Lewis and Clark's camp:

White Catfish Camp—that stretch

of silt, as good as any, any
song, river, now, like furrowed
loam, dendrite bluffs. They leap. (59)

The imaginative act is willed here: there is no strong evidence for Arion to believe that what he sees is the site of the explorers' camp, but it is a place "as good as any" (59) for the imagination to bloom: his willful use of limited evidence explains the endnote's description of his songs as "plaintiff" rather than "plaintive." But the willful act of imagination, with the catfish as muse, allows Arion to see his river as charged with history and significance. The complex syntax here allows the phrase "as good as any" to take on a second valence, one that reveals the liberating power of the imaginative leap. Now Arion's is a place, and a song, "as good as any." The desolate here-and-now becomes as fruitful as any mythic there-and-then.

The third poem continues the movement of re-enchantment that we've seen developing, but the fourth poem presents a complication. In the third poem of the sequence Arion remembers the Westerns that he saw in local theaters years before, and sees them as a kind of lore of the place. The fourth poem begins promisingly, with an invocation of Sacagawea as a kind of spirit of the place:

Dark-skinned with black hair
drawn tightly back, looking
northward through clay-ribbed

bluffs, she stood, I think,
ahead of the polers
in the keelboat's blunt
wet prow with a Yankee
helmsman facing her back,

and the wind, westerly—
out of my own childhood . . . (63)

She seems to unite past and present, standing in both the legendary past of Lewis and Clark's expedition, and in the wind that blows through Arion's own childhood. But the passage contains a kernel of doubt—that "I think" in the first stanza—that threatens to grow and choke the life out of the living past. Uncertainties about the veracity of his own imaginative drawing of connections between the past and the present haunt Arion, who wonders whether or not the river banks he looks on are "the same shores" seen by Lewis and Clark. "In time," he knows, "the river sidewinds its banks. / Never the same soil . . ." (63). Arion simply knows too much about rivers to believe his own fiction, that the banks he looks on were the same banks where the explorers camped. "All fancy," he laments, as his sense of Sacagawea as a governing spirit of place slips away, "She did not pass here" (64).

If he cannot believe in the literal presence of the Lewis and Clark exploration on the banks he sees, though, Arion can still believe in Sacagawea as the *spiritus locus*. Having used a bit of false history as an imaginative springboard, he can now envision the present city in her image. Instead of a squalid pile of particulars devoid of significance, the city now lives in his mind as her image:

. . . the city squats above the river,
as an Indian woman at her
day's work might squat—
oblivious to the land behind her
her hands full of the land—
red corn, dried meats, new skins. (65)

Arion may have relinquished his belief in the literal habitation of these banks by Lewis, Clark, and Sacagawea; but the afterimage of his imaginative act remains, and gives shape to what had seemed a formless and insignificant present. The city is both itself and the image of its legendary past, both *now* and *then*.

This change in the consciousness of place is subtly celebrated in the next—and most Eliotic—section of the sequence. The fifth poem is in the voice of Meriwether Lewis, who, like Arion, tries to find a form or significance in a world of material realities apparently devoid of any shape or significance ("each night I read my Journals / like a novel," says Lewis, "seeking some / inevitability of plot, a hint / of form pointing toward an end" [66–67]). His ruminations are accompanied by the sounds of "the deceptive waterthrush / imitating falling water" (66) and, later, by the actual "far-off / drip of water, thin as birdsong" (67)—an allusion to "What the Thunder Said" in Eliot's *Waste Land.* In Eliot's poem, where dryness is the symbol of a disenchanted and therefore sterile modernity, there is no water, only the deceptive sound of the "hermit thrush" that "sings in the pine trees / Drip drop drip drop drop drop drop" (67). In Anania's poem the prognosis for the here-and-now is better than in Eliot's: the "deceptive waterthrush" tells only one side of the story: the water flows, though distantly, and can be heard.

The sixth and seventh poems of the sequence take us through the topography of the region, now seen as the bearer of history. In the eighth section we read that "the present moment / trembles within other durations" (73)—a kind of affirmation of the co-existence of the present and the legendary past. The gesture here is profoundly modernist, in that it shows how—in Hugh Kenner's phrase about time in Pound's poetry—"in transparent overlay, two times have become as one" (*The Pound Era* 29). Time past and time present have, as in Pound, "folded over" letting "*now* lay flat, transparent, upon *not-now*" (30).

The Usual Suspects

Despite the proclamations of a few poets and critics that we have long since entered the post-modern period of American letters, there is little evidence that modernism is dead or even dying. The tradition of Pound, Eliot, Williams, Stevens, and their contemporaries is very much alive

and working in nearly all of the poetry being written in America today.[4]
—Michael Anania ("Afterword," *New Poetry Anthology* 108)

If Anania's transparent overlay of a mythic or legendary past and a
quotidian present is reminiscent of Kenner's Pound, it is reminiscent,
too, of other writers who we might include in the line-up of modernism's usual suspects. It is particularly reminiscent of Joyce—especially
of Joyce's *Ulysses* as explained by T. S. Eliot. Joyce's use of *The Odyssey* to
give a large, mythic significance to what he called the "ineluctable modal-
ity of the visible" (*Ulysses* 42) was, according to Eliot, unprecedented. It
had "the importance of a scientific discovery. No one else has built a
novel upon such a foundation before: it has never before been necessary" (680–81). Such an innovation was the product of a very particular
cultural convergence. As Eliot put it:

> Psychology... ethnology, and *The Golden Bough* have concurred to make
> possible what was impossible even a few years ago. Instead of a narrative
> method, we may now use a mythological method. It is, I seriously believe,
> a step toward making the modern world possible for art... (681)

Although Ezra Pound maintained that Joyce's achievement was singular—
"*Ulysses* is... as unrepeatable as *Tristram Shandy*," he wrote in *The Dial*, "I
mean you cannot duplicate it; you can't take it as a 'model'..." ("Paris
Letter," 196)—Eliot disagreed. Writing in the same magazine a few
months later, Eliot claimed that Joyce's innovation would launch a fleet
of writers along this new route to Parnassus:

> In using myth, in manipulating a continuous parallel between contem-
> poraneity and antiquity, Mr. Joyce is pursuing a method which others

---

4. Anania's afterword to the *New Poetry Anthology of 1969* is a fascinating document, not
least because what may have looked to some at the time as a rearguard defense of modernism turns out to presage, by a good thirty years, recent observations about modernism by Marjorie Perloff, Pierre Joris, and Jerome Rothenberg. Anania notes, for example,
the presence of competing versions of modernism, saying that "Most of the quarrelling
that created the poetic schools of the fifties and sixties resulted as much from variant
readings of the modern tradition as from genuine disagreements of vision and temperament" (108). He also laments the truncation of modernism during this time, which
he describes as "the long lived dominance of certain features of modernist versification"
(108). The point is much like that made in Perloff's *The New Modernisms* and the introduc-
tions to Rothenberg and Joris' *Poems for the Millennium*, in which the variety of modernism,
the mid-century truncation of its possibilities, and the currency of its poetics in our
own time, are duly noted.

must pursue after him. They will not be imitators, any more than the scientist who uses the discoveries of an Einstein in pursuing his own, independent, further investigations. It is simply a way of controlling, of ordering, of giving a shape and a significance to the immense panorama of futility and anarchy which is contemporary history. (680)

The example of Anania's "Riversongs of Arion," with its shaping of local particulars by reference to a legendary past, indicates that this round in the great boxing match of Ole Ez and the fightin' Possum of St. Louis goes to Eliot on points. What Joyce first wrought others have made anew, and Anania is among them.

Perhaps the most relevant modernist here is David Jones, who, like Anania, found the spatial coincidence of events that happened at different times significant (unlike Joyce, who made his literary echoes through coincidences of incident, character, or style). Anania himself speaks of how important Jones was for him and for his friend John Matthias when he says:

> Jones seemed like a pertinent poet to us, pertinent because he took Eliot's modernism in a different direction. For Jones, occasions of historical or mythological or religious or literary replication in space . . . aren't merely manifestations of the irony proposed by the degradation of the past in the present, as they are in Eliot. Jones is aware of the resonance of place in the significant past, but for Jones this significant past is not the source of an irony about the present: it is part of the synchronistic present. This sense of synchrony is part of Jones' Christianity, in which all time is present in the eyes of God. . . . For example, when a soldier falls in Jones, and his helmet falls down over his face, Jones associates that with the vision of the visor worn by knights at war over the same ground long ago. ("Talking John Matthias" 4)

For Jones, spatial coincidence provided what Roland Barthes would call the *puncta*, the point at which different events could be connected. In "The Riversongs of Arion," the coincidence of Lewis and Clark's expedition passing along the riverbank opens up the connection between *now* and *then* that comes to fruition in the vision of Omaha as Sacagawea.

But there is no exact spatial coincidence in "The Riversongs of Arion," only an imagined spatial coincidence. The river is too fluid, too mutable, for any actual coincidence to occur, and Arion knows it.

The riverbank is "Never the same soil," says Arion, and Sacagawea "did not pass here." If Anania is using a modernist technique, he does it with a self-consciousness, even a skepticism, that grows stronger in the sequence's final poems.

The New Science: Fictive Certainties

There are, said Ezra Pound with his characteristically hubristic confidence, three types of writers. There are, most importantly, "the inventors" who create new techniques, such as Arnaut Daniel's new methods of rhyming, or new ways of perceiving, such as those invented by Cavalcanti. There are also "the masters," who assimilate and synthesize earlier inventions; and "the diluters" who do little with existing forms other than add "some slight personal flavor" (*How to Read* 12–14). Let's put Joyce in the first category, on the ground that he gave us new ways of perceiving the modern person and the modern place through classical myth and legend. If one were feeling uncharitable, one might be tempted to class Anania among the diluters, saying that he does little more than assimilate western local color to the Joycean way of seeing. But this would be unfair, and it would involve ignoring the way that Anania deviates from Joyce. In raising doubts about the modernist process of linking past and present, Anania moves beyond modernism. He assimilates Joycean-Poundian-Jonesian modernism to the experience of his own generation, proving himself to be, in Pound's terms, one of the masters.

Anania's doubts about his own modernist project emerge most clearly in the penultimate poem of "The Riversongs of Arion." Here, the doubts about the permanence of the riverbank, and therefore about the coincidence in place between contemporary and legendary experience, come to the fore:

The sunlight on the water,
landfall shadows, treeline
edging down the slow current.

This is the land I made for you
by hand, what was touched once
then misremembered into words,

place where the soil slips out
from under its trees, where
stiff weeds fall like rapids,

It is the made emblem of time... (75–76)

Arion acknowledges that the connection in space between past and present in the coincidence of place is fictional. But this deliberate "misremembering" does not make the connection invalid. The place is still the "emblem of time," despite having been "made." The constructed is still real, and the myth of the present as the incarnation of the past lives on as what Robert Duncan would call a fictive certainty.

Daniel Guillory calls Anania's artistry "self-consciousness"(56), and one can certainly see why. In marking his epiphany of place and time as a construct, Anania distances himself from the modernist ideal of past and present "in transparent overlay," and shows himself as the product of a later generation. This is a generation for whom the affirmations of literature are made in quotation marks. This is the generation that learned from John Barth—who, in turn, learned from Borges—that the *Quixote* is still possible, but only as a quotation. As Barth says of Borges' "Pierre Menard, Author of the Quixote," Borges'

> ...artistic victory, if you like, is that he confronts an intellectual dead end and employs it against itself to accomplish new human work. If this corresponds to what mystics do—'every moment leaping into the infinite,' Kierkegaard says, "and every moment surely falling back into the finite'—it's only one more aspect of that old analogy. (Barth 69–71).

Borges, says Barth, takes an old possibility's current impossibility (being the author of the Quixote), and in the act of pointing to that impossibility both cancels and resurrects it. Similarly, Anania's "Riversongs of Arion" point to the impossibility of establishing a modernist connection of the mythic and the real in the coincidence of place—and in doing so outlines what such a connection would be like. This leaves us with a kind of afterimage of what such a connection would be like, an afterimage that endures despite our knowledge that it is a phantasm.

If Joyce was the Einstein who invented a new way of seeing the universe, Anania is no mere imitator, but a later scientist "pursuing his own, independent, further investigations." The temptation to call Anania an unreconstructed modernist, then, must be resisted. No mere diluter replicating Joyce with new local colors, Anania is a synthesizer, pouring what is most valuable in Joyce into the great postmodern delta.

Works Cited

Anania, Michael, ed. *New Poetry Anthology*. Chicago: Swallow, 1969. Print.

———. *In Plain Sight*. Mount Kisco, New York: Asphodel, 1991. Print.

———. *Selected Poems*. Wakefield, Rhode Island: Asphodel, 1994. Print.

———. "Talking John Matthias." *Samizdat* 9 (2002): 3–5. Print.

Archambeau, Robert. "Michael Anania." *Dictionary of Literary Biography*. Vol. 193. Detroit: Gale, 1998. 3–9. Print.

Barth, John. "The Literature of Exhaustion." *The Friday Book: Essays and Other Nonfiction*. New York: Putnam, 1984. 62–76. Print.

Eliot, T. S. *Collected Poems: 1909–1962*. New York: Harcourt, Brace, Jovanovich, 1991. Print.

———. "Myth and Literary Classicism." *The Modern Tradition*. Ed. Richard Ellman and Charles Feidelson, Jr. New York: Oxford University Press: 679–81. Print.

Guillory, Daniel L. "Tradition and Innovation in Twentieth-Century Illinois Poetry." *Studies in Illinois Poetry*. Ed. John E. Hallwas. Urbana, Illinois: Stormline Press, 1989. 43–60. Print.

Joyce, James. *Ulysses*. Harmondsworth: Penguin, 1969. Print.

Kenner, Hugh. *The Pound Era*. Los Angeles: University of California Press, 1971. Print.

Lowell, Robert. *Life Studies and For the Union Dead*. New York: Farrar Straus, Giroux, 2007. Print.

Pound, Ezra. *How to Read*. London: Desmond Harmsworth, 1931. Print.

———. "Paris Letter." *Pound/Joyce*. Ed. Forrest Read. New York: New Directions, 1965. 194–200. Print.

Laforgue / Bolaño
The Poet as Bohemian

ohemia, that mythical land of outsiders, rebels, malcontents,
slumming rich kids, and rent-grubbing scam artists, spreads
its porous boundaries wide in both space and time, extending
from Montparnasse to Greenwich Village to North Beach, from Thomas
DeQuincey's opium den to Barney Rosset's office at Grove Press in the
sixties, to a grimy gallery in a neighborhood too newly annexed to the
Bohemian empire for the likes of us to know about it. Bohemia is often
seen as a kind of effortless Arcadia, a patchouli-and-pot-smoke saturated world of laughter and lotus eating. But in certain works of Jules
Laforgue and Roberto Bolaño, both of whose bohemian credentials are
beyond reproach, we see something else entirely. In Laforgue's case we
see a struggle to overcome some of the habitual attitudes of the bohemian poet; and in Bolaño's, a long battle to endure the kind of alienation
that drives the bohemian away from mainstream society.

Paris, as Walter Benjamin has said, was the capital of the nineteenth
century, and it was also the capital of that great invention of the nineteenth century, literary bohemia. Though his sojourn in Paris was
brief—only five years—Jules Laforgue was in many ways the perfect Bohemian. Born in Uruguay, he was a bit of an exotic; raised in a provincial
French boarding school, he was already a veteran practitioner of the arts
of brooding alienation and scathing satire when his family took him to

Paris. He'd written biting parodies of the teachers and petty authoritarians of his school before escaping to what he hoped would be an artist's life in the city of lights. But the arrival in Paris almost coincided with the death of his mother, making the scene of liberation also a scene of loss. After a period in which he associated with Impressionists and wrote the melancholy, melodramatic poems of his abandoned manuscript *The Tears of the Earth*, he left bohemian Paris and took a position in Berlin reading to Empress Augusta of Prussia from French newspapers in the morning and French novels in the evening. A South American in France; a lonely boy in a provincial boarding school; an early sufferer of losses through death; an artistic bohemian in a great political and financial capital; a minor figure on the fringes of the Prussian court—these roles were the perfect training for a poet whose métier was deflationary observation and a self-protective ironizing of his own emotions. Perhaps his most typical work can be found in *The Imitation of Our Lady the Moon*, a series of poems celebrating sterility and irony through the images of the moon and the sad Pierrot, the cynical, alienated clown of French and Italian art and literature. By way of contrast, Laforgue's posthumously published *Last Poems*, a slim collection of a dozen linked poems, shows Laforgue at his least typical. Here, in poems written under circumstances that truly focus the mind—Laforgue was young, in love, and dying—we see the poet self-consciously struggle to overcome his own habits of reticence, to break through irony, pessimism, alienation, and cynicism, and arrive at a sincerity of expression made urgent by his situation.

The book begins, appropriately enough, with a long quote from *Hamlet*, in which we hear Ophelia speak of the prince, the archetype of all habitual bystanders trying to pull themselves out of the tangle of their own jammed-up emotions. The mystified Ophelia tells her father how Hamlet had grabbed her by the arm, stared into her face, and, with "a sigh so piteous and profound / That it did seem to shatter all his bulk" let go of her and fled. "This," replies Polonius, "is the very ecstasy of love" (17). It is a perfect introduction to the poems, giving us both the figure of the self-conscious, emotionally paralyzed protagonist, and a sense of tragedy and inevitable doom (both Laforgue and Leah Lee, the woman of whom he writes in *Last Poems*, would both soon die of tuberculosis).

The shifting of tone in *Last Poems* is incredibly rapid as the poet tries to break the "sentimental blockade" that keeps him from an open expression of love. It can be a challenge to keep up with the juxtaposition of the sublime and the disgusting, the flashes of hope, the fallings into disappointment, and the turns toward the brutal in passages like this, from the opening poem "The Winter Ahead," which shows us the sun, Laforgue's symbol for fertility and affection:

> Tonight the dying sun sprawls on a hilltop
> Turns onto his side, in the heather, in his overcoat.
> A sun as white as a barfly's phlegm
> On a litter of yellow heather,
> Yellow autumn heather.
> And the hunting horns call to him!
> Awake!
> Up and awake!
> Tally-ho! Tally-ho! View halloo!
> Oh sad refrain, you're finished!
> And in a fools game! ...
> He just lies there, like a gland torn out of someone's throat,
> Shivering, utterly alone. (19)

The tonal shifts come almost line-by-line in these poems. Often we see Laforgue almost break through into open sincerity ("If only I had fallen at your knees! / If only you had fainted at mine! / I would have been the ultimate husband") only to deflate his own sentiment with a sudden, incongruous comparison ("Just as the frou-frou of your frou-frou is the ultimate skirt") (59). At other times, he'll confess love, only to turn bitterly against the woman to whom he confesses it ("Shut up! Even your eyelids are perjuries / .... If I ever loved you, it was all a joke") (63). The overall sensation is of sincerity battering at the door of the castle of irony and self-doubt, yearning to be let in.

In the end, sincerity does gain entrance, but not in a triumphant way: this is no Beethoven's Ninth, with the stormy and troubled music driven away at last by a triumphant ode to joy. Instead, we get something in a minor key, a tentative embrace of what life can offer us in the shadow of death:

All right, then, we must love whatever stories we find
In the beautiful orphan's eye,
O Nature, give me the courage and strength
To be old enough,
Nature, life me up!
Sooner or later, we all die . . . (85)

It is the texture of Laforgue's poetry, with its *vers libre* metrical play, its enjambments, neologisms, and oddball syntax, its sudden shifts of tone, diction, and verbal surface, and its tentative affirmations, that make Laforgue a great innovator in French poetry, and a major influence on modernism. And it is the pressure of emotion in stark circumstances that fuels Laforgue's innovation.

Where Laforgue's *Last Poems* are jumpy, full of rapid changes, and attentive to the scansion of every syllable, the three parts of Roberto Bolaño's *Tres* give us a flattened, plainspoken, prosy style. The style represents a deliberate move on Bolaño's part: he follows his fellow Chilean, Nicanor Parra, in rejecting the hothouse surrealism and rhetorical grandiosity of some Latin American poets for the "antipoetry" of the colloquial. He lets the three parts of *Tres* (two sequences of linked prose poems and one long narrative poem) gain strength through large structures of parallelism, repeated themes, and narrative turns, rather than any Laforguean line-by-line linguistic flash and dazzle.

The first of the three parts, "Prose from Autumn in Gerona," is an exploded or deconstructed short story in the form of prose poems ranging in length from a couple of lines to a full page. The series begins abstractly, with an author protagonist, a stranger, and the image of a kaleidoscope. The prose poems loop around a number of themes and images: an isolated figure in a seedy apartment, a soon-to-expire visa that gives no right to work, poverty, lost love, and the disappointment of a writer whom fame has passed by (the earliest of the three pieces in *Tres*, "Prose from Autumn in Gerona" was written in 1981, long before Bolaño's astonishing launch into the international literary stratosphere). Elements of a plot slowly coalesce for us, and the kaleidoscope becomes an image for the coalescence, for the slowly changing formal arrangement of literary elements. Near the end, we find two short sections juxtaposed on a single page. One reads:

THE KALEIDOSCOPE OBSERVED. Passion is geometry. Rhombuses, cylinders, pulsing angles. Passion is geometry plunging into the abyss, observed from the depths of the abyss. (73)

In the context of the series, this reads as a statement about the formalistic satisfactions of art, about the paradox of purely aesthetic composition creating a kind of life, full of passionate geometry and pulsing angles. In juxtaposition to this we find another passage, one of the most realistic in the series:

THE STRANGER OBSERVED. Breasts pink from hot water. It's six in the morning and the man's voice offscreen is still saying he'll walk her to the train. It's not necessary, she says, her body turning its back to the camera. With precise gestures she shoves her pajamas in the bag, closes it, grabs a mirror, looks at herself (there the viewer will get a view of her face: eyes open wide, terrified), she opens her bag, puts in the mirror, closes the bag, fades out... (73)

Pink breasts, not rhombuses: we're in the realm of life itself, and living passion, rather than the abstractions of form. One wants to say the juxtaposition of the two passages poses a problem as old as Yeats' poet's conundrum: a choice between "perfection of the life or of the work" (115). But not so fast: these are the characters we've been reading about throughout "Prose from Autumn in Gerona," but now, with the woman's back turned to the camera and the man's voice coming from offscreen, we're experiencing them in one of the most popular, and most conventional, forms of narrative: the movie. What we're really being offered is a choice between the artist as formalist and the artist as the popular purveyor of romance: the bohemian's dilemma of whether to pursue *l'art pour l'art* or to bid goodbye to all that and pack his bags for Hollywood.

The second part of *Tres*, "The Neochileans" is Bolaño's pocket-sized *Childe Harold's Pilgrimage*, and, like Byron's original, depicts a pilgrimage without a destination, a setting out on the road in disillusion without hope for transformation or redemption ("in a sense," writes Bolaño, "the trip was over / when we started") (79). A Chilean rock band led by one Pancho Misterio sets out northward into the South American hinterland, eventually crossing into Peru, where the lead singer falls into a fever, and the narrator is confronted by questions about the nature of the journey:

And if we weren't
In Peru? we
Neochileans
Asked ourselves one night.
And if this immense
Space
That instructs
And limits us
Were an intergalactic ship,
An unidentified
Flying object?
And if Pancho Misterio's
Fever
Were our fuel
Or our navigational device? (99)

Here we see Bolaño at his most Romantic and bohemian: alienated to the point where he may as well be leaving the earth on a spaceship powered, and guided, by feverish dreams. Significantly, the passage's questions remain unanswered, and we switch to a scene of the impoverished, politically oppressed streets:

And after working
We went out walking
Through the streets of Peru:
With military patrols,
Peddlers and the unemployed,
Scanning
The hills
For Shining Path bonfires,
But we saw nothing. (99)

There's something of an explanation for the naïve, hopeless, objectless quest of the Neochileans here: the Latin American world they inherit is one that offers little by way of hope, and much at which to despair. Where else to go but into Byronic disillusion?

Well, perhaps into literature: at least that's the proposition made by the final section of *Tres*, "A Stroll Through Literature." In these prose poems we see a series of dreams about writers, plus snippets of imagined erotic or *noir* episodes involving figures from Mark Twain to Georges

Perec. We see literature as burden, as hope, and, in the following passage, as a dangerously volatile fuel for escape:

> I dreamt I was fifteen and was, in fact, leaving the Southern hemisphere. When I put the only book I had (*Trilce* by Vallejo) in my backpack, the pages went up in flames. It was seven p.m. and I chucked my scorched backpack out the window. (143)

Why does *Trilce* burst into flame? There's no literal explanation in the dream logic of the passage, and symbolic explanations seem ambiguous. Things become clearer when, near the end of the series, Bolaño revisits the image:

> I dreamt I went back to the streets, but this time I wasn't fifteen but over forty. All I had was a book, which I carried in my tiny backpack. At once, while I was walking, the book started to burn. It was getting light out and hardly any cars passed. When I chucked my scorched backpack into a ditch my back was stinging as if I had wings. (169)

The books we carry become the things that burn and scar us—and those marked by literature are both cursed and, just possibly, blessed. In that image of a scorched, stinging back we have the poet as a marked man, an outsider bearing his particular pain. But we have, too, the potential (perhaps illusory) of flight. The passage presents an analogy to Baudelaire's idea of the poet as a grounded albatross captured by sailors, a bird whose great wings make him ridiculous and hinder his ability to walk: hope, for the poet in an alienating and damaging world, resides in the possibility of imaginative flight. This is about as Romantic an image of the poet as one is likely to find nowadays, and it's no accident that it comes from Bolaño, who led even more of a bohemian outsider's life than did Laforgue a century earlier. One could hardly expect something as desperate, as raw, or as at risk of melodrama from that more grounded and socially embedded creature, the professor of creative writing.

Works Cited

Bolaño, Roberto. *Tres*. Trans. Laura Healy. New York: New Directions, 2011. Print.

Laforgue, Jules. *Last Verses*. Trans. Donald Revell. Richmond, California: Omnidawn, 2011. Print.

Yeats, William Butler. *The Yeats Reader*. Ed. Richard J. Finneran. New York: Scribner, 2002. Print.

Oppen / Rimbaud
The Poet as Quitter

A poet I admire once told me he was thinking of giving up poetry. The author of two well-received books, he certainly wasn't failing as a poet, but for some reason he seemed to feel that poetry was failing him. He wasn't being fired from Parnassus Industries: after establishing a successful career, he was thinking of drafting his letter of resignation. He wouldn't be alone: Matthew Arnold, for example, gave up poetry for criticism, as did Paul Valéry for a time. Basil Bunting took a long hiatus from the art, and Laura Riding Jackson left it for good to concentrate on her prose. Reasons for resignation are as numerous as poets who resign, but the abandonment of poetry by a promising poet makes one wonder what drives a poet to give up his or her art—and what, if anything, could bring that poet home to poetry?

*

Arthur Rimbaud offers perhaps the most dramatic example of the poet who resigns from poetry. Having produced some of the most startling and original poetry in the French language during his adolescence, Rimbaud gave poetry up before his twentieth birthday, embarking on a series of exotic journeys and occupations and ending up as a money-obsessed arms merchant in Ethiopia. Admirers of Rimbaud's poetry quite understandably look upon his change of careers with sorrow. André

Breton, for example, lamented the gun-running Rimbaud, calling him "*un assez lamentable polichinelle*"—"a pitiful clown" (Borer 337). How could the one-time *enfant terrible* of French verse so thoroughly break faith with his youthful self?

To frame the matter in terms of Rimbaud's betrayal of himself, though, is to beg the question. There is, after all, a meaningful sense in which Rimbaud's pursuit of poetry and his pursuit of riches in Africa weren't opposing actions, but manifestations of the same desire he'd felt from earliest childhood: the desire to rebel. It shouldn't take away from our sense of Rimbaud's accomplishments in poetry if we note that he was never, first and foremost, a poet pure and simple. The primary goal of Rimbaud's life wasn't poetry: it was rebellion, and his poetry was merely one embodiment of that rebellion. When Rimbaud lost faith in the power of poetry as a means of rebellion, he found other methods. He may well have betrayed poetry, but he never betrayed his own disposition.

Of course Rimbaud's was a special kind of rebellion, quite different from that of the more conventional social and political revolutionaries of nineteenth century Europe. Bertrand Russell, writing about another great poet-rebel, Lord Byron, draws a distinction useful for understanding Rimbaud. "The aristocratic rebel, of whom Lord Byron was in his day the exemplar, is a very different type from the leader of a peasant or proletarian revolt," writes Russell. "Those who are hungry have no need of an elaborate philosophy to stimulate or excuse discontent," since, for them, "the good is enough to eat, and the rest is talk" (747). In contrast, the rebellion of an aristocrat like Byron is an assertion of the unbending autonomy of the personality. Like Byron, Rimbaud was a rebel who gave a great shout of refusal.

In one crucial respect, though, Rimbaud was unlike Byron—but very like Joyce's Stephen Dedalus. Byron, after all, was quite literally the aristocratic rebel, whereas Rimbaud came from provincial bourgeois stock. This meant that Rimbaud was subject to a regime of social, economic, and institutional norms that Byron was free to ignore: he must escape the same kind of nets cast in the flight-path of Joyce's Dedalus when he tries to soar. In *Childe Harold's Pilgrimage* Byron attributed his rebellious spirit to having been "untaught in youth my heart to tame" (135) but Rimbaud's childhood was quite different: he was expected to tame his heart and submit to a regimented and repressive set of norms. Deferred gratification and prudent obedience to the norms of school, church, career, and family were the household gods worshipped around the Rimbaud family hearth. Rimbaud came to know these values from his parents, the glamorous but often absent Capitaine Frédéric Rimbaud, who campaigned with the French army in Algeria, and the smothering, money-conscious, all-too-present Madame Marie-Catherine-Vitalie Rimbaud, whose idea of maternal care involved punishing infractions of her rules by making the young Rimbaud memorize hundreds of lines of Latin verse. Rimbaud's rebellious self-assertion took place not in some great existential void, but in a world of firm limits and defined expectations, and the institutions that enforced them. Rebellion, in such a context, meant escape.

Among the many precocities of the young Rimbaud was the clarity with which he recognized his predicament early on. The opening lines of "Poets, Age Seven," written when Rimbaud was still 16, show Rimbaud to be wincingly aware of how thoroughly administered and planned-out his life was meant to be, and how unfit he was to follow the paths prescribed for him:

> And the Mother, closing the workbook,
> Departed satisfied and proud, without noticing
> In blue eyes beneath a pimply forehead,
> The loathing freighting her child's soul.
>
> All day he sweated obedience; clearly
> Intelligent; and yet, black rumblings, hints
> Of bitter hypocrisies, hidden, underneath.
> In shadowy corridors hung with moldy drapes
> He'd stick out his tongue, thrust his fists
> In his pockets, shut his eyes till he saw spots. (65)

Je est un autre, here, for sure. That is, we can see in this passage at least one of the meanings of Rimbaud's famous, grammar-bending formulation "I is another" (365): the little Arthur seen by Rimbaud's mother has little or nothing to do with young Arthur as he experiences himself.

If Rimbaud is going to assert himself, he's going to have to escape a whole series of middle-class expectations.

How to do it? Broadly speaking, Rimbaud follows two different paths out of the bourgeois drawing room where he "sweated obedience"—paths I like to think of as *escape from* and *escape through*. We can already see both of these at work in the passage from "Poets, Age Seven." When the poet sulks away from his mother and, through squinting his eyes, replaces the ordinary world with a world of luminous visions (here, the humble spots that appear before his bleary eyes), we see him escaping from the world of maternal expectations into his own private world of gaudy images. This strategy will serve Rimbaud well in his brief, brilliant career as poet. But there's another path of escape here, signified by the school workbook that so satisfies the mother. Imagine the context in which this workbook of a deeply unhappy child was produced: pushed to academic success by a well-intentioned but domineering mother, the child labors through the day with the hope of working his way through the paths laid out for him by the mother and emerging at the other side, free at last. Rimbaud was a tremendously talented student, but there was a ferocious edge to his studying, a kind of sublimated rebellion in his desire to master subjects so as to be done with them. The speed with which he mastered the history of French literature, for example, amazed his teachers, but in Rimbaud's poetry we see no obedience to the classical norms of poetry: having absorbed everything the tradition had to offer, Rimbaud shoves aside hexameters first for *vers libre*, then for prose poems. Rimbaud's formal waywardness has about it something of the confident, aggressive sartorial squalor of a boy who, after graduation, is finally able to ditch his school uniform.

To *escape through* was to master the regimented systems to which he was meant to submit, and emerge as a man who, having superseded his masters, was now free. We see Rimbaud make just this kind of escape through mastery when he writes to his old schoolteacher George Izambard in 1871. Rimbaud's letter, bristling with advanced literary opinions developed under Izambard's tuition, ends with a flourish of self-assertion: "you aren't my *teacher*" (365). He can't abide the idea of being intellectually subordinate. It was much the same when Rimbaud discussed the prospect of a secure career. He despised the idea of laboring away for a salary, and from an early age dreamed of escaping such drudgery by rising to the top of the economic pyramid, writing over and over, at the age of nine, "I will be a capitalist" (Rickword 4).

The twin strategies of *escape from* and *escape through* alternate and, at times, coincide throughout Rimbaud's life as a poet and as an adventurer. Consider his proposal for how to become a poet in the "*Lettre du voyant*," or "Seer's Letter." Here Rimbaud tells us that the poet should make it his business to know "every kind of love, of suffering, of madness" and become "the master criminal, the first among the damned—and the supreme Savant!" (367). On the one hand, Rimbaud is proposing an escape from all the respectable family norms. On the other hand, this is yet another bit of hard studying for the prize scholar, who will only be free to move on when he's mastered his—admittedly unorthodox—subject. Being a poet will be an act of escaping from *and* escaping through. Eventually, though, Rimbaud wearies of poetry as a means of rebellion and escape. When, in *A Season in Hell*, he writes "For some time, I'd boasted a mastery of every arena, and had found famous painters and poets ridiculous" he's on the cusp of giving up on the idea of exceeding the literary tradition as a path of rebellion and self-assertion (208). After all, he says, despite all of his skill poetry had led him to a point where he'd "settled into run-of-the-mill hallucinations," escapes from reality no more real or lasting than the spots of light the child of "Poets, Age Seven" saw when he squinted his eyes (210). Lasting escape via poetry seemed, in the end, impossible.

It's tempting to see Rimbaud's acquisitive participation in the economic colonization of Africa as something inexplicable and entirely alien to the young man who'd written such extraordinary poetry. But to look at it this way is to fail to see how the same patterns that motivated the poet motivated the man who dealt in arms and, according to some disputed accounts, in slaves. After all, when Rimbaud ran off to Ethiopia, he was engaging in his two oldest habits. He was, of course, escaping from the mores of his parents, the strictures of middle-class morality, and the values of European civilization. But there's something else at work in Rimbaud's African adventures: he was also escaping the pressure to submit to the ideals of his parents by mastering the things his parents most valued—on his own terms. After all, profitable gun running at the edge of known civilization satisfied both the macho, military ethos of his father and the financial acquisitiveness of his mother. If Rimbaud's career in poetry had been an act of both escaping through and escaping from, his career in Africa was, in effect, much the same thing. He had geographically escaped from the world of bourgeois restrictions, and at the same time he saw in the accumulation of wealth an escape through that most bourgeois of things, wealth: he was on his way to becoming the capitalist he'd hoped to be. He may have betrayed the art of poetry, but he never betrayed his true calling, that of the escape artist. Poetry, for him, had been only the opening act.

*

The story of George Oppen's abandonment of poetry is a similar tale, in that it too, involves a man leaving poetry because he remains true to his own disposition. It's a sunnier tale than Rimbaud's story, of course, and not just because of the refreshing absence of morally questionable business dealings: Oppen finds a way to return to poetry while remaining true to the very ideals that had driven him from it.

While the great motivating forces in Rimbaud's life and work were rebellion and escape, the forces animating Oppen were sincerity and solidarity. In his early life Oppen had something of the poor little rich boy about him: a son of economic privilege, he suffered the early death of his mother, had a difficult and possibly abusive relationship with his stepmother, and at the age of 11 was packed off to a military school from which he would eventually be expelled. Like so many people from unstable backgrounds, he yearned for the kind of firmness and certainty that he'd lacked growing up. In many respects, his background made him just the sort of young man young man who'd be driven into the arms of one or another of the extremist ideologies on offer during the Depression. While his strong sense of social justice did lead him into Communism in the 1930s, Oppen was never a party-liner. He shied away from ideological abstractions, and came to poetry, especially Imagist (and, later, Objectivist) poetry, because he felt it offered a way of saying only those things of which he could be sure, only those things he could base on direct observation. If Rimbaud sought hallucinogenic escape from the world, Oppen looked for a poetry that would make possible fidelity to the world as it was. He wanted a language that would be simple, honest, and rooted in the things around him. He was, he said, attracted to Imagism "as a position of honesty": the concreteness of the Imagist and Objectivist poem kept him from slipping into empty rhetoric, and served as "a test of truth," mooring the poem in experience (interview with Dembo 160, 161). Imagism and Objectivism also offered ways to show solidarity with the common man by dwelling on the humble objects of the observed world. Hence William Carlos Williams became more of a guide for the young Oppen than did a figure like T. S. Eliot: the small-town doctor moving among the people of his town, writing of the importance of everyday things, was more appealing than the distant sage of culture. One could feel confident in one's statement about the importance of a red wheelbarrow in a way one couldn't about the shored fragments of a broken mythology.

Discrete Series, Oppen's first collection of poems, is very much an example of his poetics of sincerity. The title comes from mathematics where, in Oppen's words, "a discrete series is a series of terms each of which is empirically derived, each one of which is empirically true" (interview with Dembo 161). The poems are each tested against reality, not derived from one another in a chain of increasing abstraction. The Oppen of *Discrete Series* is the farthest thing from a system-builder like Yeats, whose towers and winding stairs are less real objects than tokens in a game of symbols. And unlike Yeats (or, for that matter, Rimbaud), Oppen writes a poetry of conspicuously common things. The images Oppen chooses for *Discrete Series*—a soda jerk at work among the shiny surfaces of a malt shop, a man in overalls working a steam shovel—are implicit statements of the poet's solidarity with the ordinary people around him. But already there are signs of worry about the possibilities of poetry, signs that the man who looks clearly on the world, who refuses its platitudes and common sense in favor of the few things he can sincerely say with certainty, is an isolated man cut off from those with whom he would feel connection. In "Party on Shipboard," for example, we find Oppen looking back to the shore, "from this distance thinking toward you" but "not encountering you" (10).

After *Discrete Series* came out in 1934, Oppen gave up writing poetry. As the economic and political crisis of the 1930s ground on, Oppen simply couldn't sincerely convince himself that poetry was an effective way to help others, nor could he convince himself that it was more important than the immediate needs of his fellow man. "There are situations that cannot honorably be met by art," said Oppen, "and surely no one need fiddle precisely at the moment that the house next door is burning" (*Selected Letters* 65). So he set it aside for political activism, organizing labor and coordinating a Farmer's Union strike in Utica. Later, as economic crises gave way to war against Fascism, Oppen stepped up to do his part there, as well, landing with the 103rd antitank division in Marseilles. He simply couldn't

> believe in the honesty of a man saying, 'Well, I'm a poet and I will make my contribution to the cause by writing poems about it.'. . . . If you do something politically, you do something that has political efficacy. And if you decide to write poetry, then you write poetry, not something that you hope, or deceive yourself into believing, can save people who are suffering . . . (interview with Denbo 175)

He wouldn't be deceived: poetry, for Oppen, had become impossible.

It may at first seem puzzling that Oppen stayed away from poetry after the Depression and the war had passed. Having fled McCarthyism, Oppen spent the better part of the fifties in Mexico, removed from his old activist associations. But there was a new kind of concern for solidarity that came to occupy Oppen, one that filled the space that poetry had once taken in his life: family. He and his wife Mary had a daughter, and the man whose own childhood had been so fraught with troubles made his priorities clear: he set up a household and a carpentry business and turned to private life. "We devoted ourselves," he later said, "to creating happiness for the three of us" (*Selected Prose* 109). For those years his focus was—in the apt, blunt phrase of critic James Longenbach— "being a good dad."

Oppen began to return to poetry when his daughter left home for Sarah Lawrence College in 1958, and the bonds of parental responsibility loosened. But the prodigal Oppen's true return to poetry, and the great flourishing of his work, comes after he moves back to the United States in 1960. The return to poetry wasn't untroubled, though. For Oppen to be able to function as a poet he needed to find some kind of solution to the old problem of sincerity and solidarity. In the thirties, he couldn't commit to poetry because he felt it kept him from solidarity with people in need. When he returned from Mexico, the old problem had to be confronted again.

Oppen wanted to be a poet again, but he was afraid it would separate him from others. It was a strange fear: although writing is a solitary activity, must it really set one apart from one's community? For Oppen, the answer was yes, and it was an answer that troubled him deeply. We get a sense of this from his comments about a letter sent to him by a young student at Columbia in the '60s, Rachel Blau (later the poet Rachel Blau DuPlessis). The letter asked about Oppen's poetry of careful observation, then asked "whether, as the intensity of seeing increases, one's distance from them, the people, does not also increase?" The question ate at Oppen, and he later brought it up in an interview, saying that intense observation could, indeed "lead to the growing isolation of the poet" (interview with Denbo 173).

Perhaps surprisingly, given their antithetical personalities, it is Nietzsche who can help get at Oppen's conundrum. In *The Birth of Tragedy* Nietzsche makes his famous distinction between the Dionysian and Apollonian dispositions. The Dionysian spirit involves a loss of self in the churning crowd, a surrender of individuality in favor of being absorbed into something greater than oneself. We lose our bearings and our powers of judgment in the Dionysian experience, but we gain something, too: a sense of the primordial unity of all people. Music, for Nietzsche, is the great Dionysian art, because music tends to unite a crowd, the members of which find themselves swaying and bobbing their heads in unison. In contrast, the Apollonian spirit is one of self-possession and observation. Visual art is the most Apollonian art form, for Nietzsche, since when we look at something we are in possession of ourselves: we stand apart from the thing we see. We describe and assess it, rather than find ourselves caught up in it, as we do with music. Oppen's poetry is an art of observa-

tion, and it involves a kind of separation of the self from the world. To
be a poet, and at the same time to yearn for solidarity with the people one
met, is a core problem for Oppen, an Apollonian with Dionysian desires.

What to do, when faced with such a problem? After 1960, Oppen
knew just what to do with the conundrum: he made poetry out of it.
That is, he chose to thematize the problem in his poetry itself. Consider these lines from the opening section of "Blood from the Stone,"
a poem from *The Materials,* Oppen's first book since *Discrete Series:*

In the door,
Long legged, tall,
A weight of bone and flesh to her—
        Her eyes catch—
Carrying bundles. O!
Everything I am is
Us. Come home. (31)

The poem relies on visual observation, but it strives for a sense of shared
identity. There's an "us" in the poem, something beyond the mutual
isolation of the me-here and the you-there. But Oppen doesn't even
know the woman's name, and the sentence "Come home" indicates that
the community Oppen desires is a yet-to-be-achieved state. Oppen isn't
in community, he's alone, looking at the world—but he's aiming at community, and making poetry out of the effort.

It's in 1968's *Of Being Numerous* that Oppen makes his most profound
exploration of the question of poetry and community. Images of a shipwreck and an isolated Crusoe figure haunt the 39-section poem from
which the book draws its name. But no matter how deep Oppen's fears
of isolation run, he remains committed to solidarity with others:
"Obsessed, bewildered / By the shipwreck / Of the singular," he writes,
"We have chosen the meaning / Of being numerous" (151). Again, we
see the desire to come together. But the urge for community is coun-
terpoised to a skepticism about public platitudes: committed to concrete
observation, Oppen cannot fathom those who, with such ease and
abstraction, "talk / Distantly of 'The People'" (157).

The series ends with a quotation from Walt Whitman's *Specimen Days,*
in which he looks on the capitol building rebuilt after the Civil War:

> The capitol grows upon one in time, especially as they have got the great figure on top of it now, and you can see it very well. It is a great bronze figure, the Genius of Liberty I suppose. It looks wonderful toward sundown. I love to go and look at it. The sun when it is nearly down shines on the headpiece and it dazzles and glistens like a big star: it looks quite
>
> curious . . . (179)

The choice of Whitman, the great American Everyman, is significant: his presence signals an interest in a poetry of national community. But the break mid-sentence, together with the lineation, put a great deal of stress on that final word, "curious." What is Oppen's take on the idea of national community? Is he skeptical? Intrigued? He certainly can't bring himself to yawp with a full-throated Whitmanesque enthusiasm. The question of whether solidarity can be reconciled with poetry isn't so much answered as it is left hanging there in front of us. The poem becomes a way to meditate on the difficulty of writing the poem.

In the end, Oppen did something that Rimbaud didn't do, something that any poet who feels that he or she can't go on as a poet should consider: when poetry became impossible, he wrote the impossibility.

Works Cited

Borer, Alain. *Rimbaud en Abyssine*. Paris: Seuil, 1984. Print.

Byron, George Gordon. *The Works of Lord Byron: Childe Harold's Pilgrimage*. Ed. Thomas Moore. Boston: Niccolls, 1900. Print.

Longenbach, James. "A Test of Poetry." *The Nation*. The Nation, 11 Feb. 2008. Web. 10 July 2011.

Oppen, George. *Collected Poems*. New York: New Directions, 1975. Print.

———. *The Selected Letters of George Oppen*. Ed. Rachel Blau DuPlessis. Durham: Duke University Press, 1990. Print.

———. *Selected Prose, Daybooks, and Papers*. Ed. Stephen Cope. Los Angeles: University of California Press, 2007. Print.

———. "Untitled Interview with L. S. Dembo." *Contemporary Literature* 10.2 (1969): 159–77. Print.

Rickword, Edgell. *Rimbaud: The Boy and the Poet*. Essex: Daimon, 1963. Print.

Rimbaud, Arthur. *Rimbaud Complete*. Ed. and trans. Wyatt Mason. New York: Modern Library, 2003. Print.

Russell, Bertrand. *A History of Western Philosophy*. New York: Simon and Schuster, 1945. Print.

Remembering Robert Kroetsch

Robert Kroetsch, who died in a car accident at the age of 84, was one of the most important Canadian writers of his generation. I had the privilege of knowing him a little when I was an undergraduate. Though I never took a course with him, he was a presence on the local literary scene, and a few times I found myself having a drink with him. He was a novelist, and something of a critic, and one of the founders of the journal *boundary 2*, but for me he'll always be two things: a poet, and a benign godfather of a movement in Canadian literature that suffers the fate of all movements in Canadian literature: utter invisibility in the non-Canadian world. But it was a real movement, with its own journals and presses and contretemps and aspirations, and it made a difference where it wanted to make a difference, in the prairie provinces of Manitoba, Saskatchewan, and Alberta.

As a poet, Kroetsch was many things. Sometimes he was a proceduralist, foregrounding the artificiality of writing, and the agility of the poet, by adopting an arbitrary restriction, Oulipo-style, and forcing himself to work within its constraints. In *The Sad Phoenician*, for example, Kroetsch writes a long meditation in which new lines of poetry begin, alternately, with "and" and "but," making for an ode-like snaking-through of strophe and antistrophe. At other times Kroetsch was a master of found texts, writing through his family's account books in *The*

Ledger and through a ubiquitous document of the Canadian prairies in *Seed Catalog*. In both cases, he was concerned with the way written documents were the binding agents of a collective, of family and of region. The best way I can describe the effect of reading these poems is to say that it's like encountering a secularized version of scribal commentary on religious texts. What a poet like Norman Finkelstein does with the Jewish textual tradition in a book like *Scribe*, Kroetsch did with the ordinary found texts that bound together his family and the rural communities of the Canadian prairies.

Kroetsch was also a serialist poet, who kept a long project called *Field Notes* simmering for years, adding and inserting sections in the manner of Olson's *Maximus Poems* or Duncan's *Passages*. There was none of the history and grandeur of Olson, and none of the mysticism of Duncan, though. Instead, there was a kind of constant, amused intellectual probing of the everyday. And Kroetsch was always ready to surprise his long-time readers. After developing a theory of the ever-incomplete, constantly-ongoing poem, and inspiring a host of other Canadian poets to begin ambitious serial projects, he suddenly called his poem to a halt, issuing his *Completed Field Notes* in 1989. I remember the arguments in the student pub about whether that word, "completed," represented a transcendence or a betrayal of Kroetsch's project: I left in a huff, consoled by a young woman who wore even more eyeliner than I did back then. She gave me a peck on the cheek and one of her earrings before ditching me over a midnight cappuccino.

Kroetsch was also a postmodernist. For me, he'll always belong to that generation of poet-professors whose natural habitat was the brutalist concrete campus office lined with books by Robert Scholes and Jonathan Culler. I picture him now as he appeared on the cover of a 1987 issue of *Border Crossings* magazine: tweed jacket, beard, Remington typewriter on the desk in front of him, ready for a fresh sheet of paper and a new page of poetry composed by field in the manner of the Olsonite wing of Black Mountain poetry.

One reason to think of Kroetsch as a postmodernist was what I can only call his loving suspicion of language and of the apparent coherence of narrative truth. Jean-François Lyotard's distinction between the *grand récit* and the *petit récit*, in *The Postmodern Condition: A Report on Knowledge*, gets at the kind of thinking that informed Kroetsch's writing. For Lyotard, the *grand récit* was a kind of authoritative story that purported to offer a comprehensive explanation of the world. For example, certain hard-core vulgar Marxists might think of Marxism as a *grand récit*, and the overconfident Victorian bourgeoisie took "progress" as their *grand récit*. In postmodern conditions, Lyotard claims, such comprehensive stories become unsustainable, and instead we have a proliferation of smaller, more fragmentary, localized, tentative explanatory stories. In postmodernism, one lets a thousand *petit récits* bloom.

Kroetsch was very much a man of the *petit récit*. He would write paratactic, self-reflective works like those collected in his *Field Notes*, bend the conventions of narrative in his fiction, or hesitate at the brink of narrative, as in his first book of poetry, *The Stone Hammer Poems*. Here, he begins with an artifact, a stone hammer found on the prairies. The poem starts this way:

> This stone
> becomes a hammer
> of stone
>
> . . . .
>
> The rawhide loops
> are gone, the
> hand is gone, the buffalo's skull
> is gone;
>
> the stone is
> shaped like the skull
> of a child. (3)

We begin with the sense that the explanation of the artifact is a matter of framing: the stone, when literally framed with an apparatus of wood and rawhide, becomes a hammer. It has since been many things, entering other narrative frames. But the literal history of the stone, speculative and ultimately unknowable, isn't the only frame. As the last stanza above indicates, the stone can also enter a metaphorical frame: its shape and size allows it to become a metaphor for a child's skull, for birth and for death.

The poem goes on, trying to locate the stone in a narrative, and failing to find much authoritative purchase on the truth of things. A few sections later in the poem, for example, we find this:

Grey, two-headed
the pemmican maul

fell from the travois or
a boy playing   lost it in
the prairie wool or
a woman   left it in
the brain of a buffalo or

it is a million years older than
the hand that
chipped stone or
raised slough
water (or blood) or (4)

The section ends there, with "or," a gesture much like Olson's opening of a parenthesis that never closes: it's a sign of indetermination, of the impossibility of *grand récit*. The poem goes on to trace the losing and finding of the stone in many histories, some speculative—Kroetsch imagines it moved in the last ice age by "the retreating ice," then moved much later by "the retreating buffalo" and later still by "the retreating Indians" (5)—some grounded in family stories of how this same stone was lost by his grandfather and found again by his father plowing in a field.

There's another reason to think of Kroetsch as a postmodern poet, rather than a modern one, a reason having to do with tone. While the generalization I'm about to make has the flaw of all generalizations (i.e., that it is full of holes and therefore untrue), I'm still making it: modernism is more serious and less funny than postmodernism. I grant all your objections regarding specific texts, and yet I return to the generalization. Wry as he can be, T. S. Eliot is more grave and less funny than Frank O'Hara. While he's not above jokes, Ezra Pound is more often dead serious than is John Ashbery. And when Robert Kroetsch is meditating on the perspectival nature of truth, he's less sublime, and funnier, than Wallace Stevens when Stevens does something similar. I'm sure the model for Kroetsch's "Sketches of a Lemon" is Stevens' "Thirteen Ways of Looking at a Blackbird," but the tone is entirely different. Here's Stevens' opening stanza:

> Among twenty snowy mountains,
> The only moving thing
> Is the eye of a blackbird. (58)

This is straight-up Kantian sublimity: the little living eye comprehends the huge, rugged world that so exceeds it in scale and in grandeur that it renders the bird's eye insignificant—except for the fact that the little eye comprehends the vastness. Here, by contrast, is the opening of Kroetsch's series of lemon sketches:

> A lemon is almost round.
> Some lemons are almost round.
> A lemon is not round.
>
> So much for that. (76)

There's a skepticism about our ability to intellectually frame the world here—it's *The Stone Hammer Poems* again, or *The Postmodern Condition: A Report on Knowledge*—but there's also a kind of philosophical pratfall. The poem is full of this sort of thing: it's a self-deflating comic text that also has something serious to say about how intellectual frames fail, or about how narratives and descriptions end up mutating into something other than what they were initially meant to be. Something like that happens in the following passage ("Smaro" is the name of the poet's wife):

> Sketches, I reminded myself,
> not of a pear,
> nor of an apple,
> nor of a peach,
> nor of a banana
> (though the colour
> raises questions)
> nor of a nectarine,
> nor, for that matter,

of a pomegranate,
nor of three cherries,
their stems joined,
nor of a plum,
nor of an apricot,
nor of the usual
bunch of grapes,
fresh from the vine,
just harvested,
glistening with dew—

Smaro, I called,
I'm hungry. (76)

What began as a kind of attempt at negative definition, doomed to a seemingly infinite series of specifications, suddenly warps, and we see that all along, without our knowledge, the list or catalog had been functioning in ways we hadn't suspected, inciting the appetites rather than providing definition. A hidden subordinate function unexpectedly becomes the dominant function of the list, and the sentence lurches jarringly in a new direction. I remember reading this poem to the woman who would become my wife, and how much she liked it. But it wasn't her favorite section of the poem. This was:

poem for a child who has just bit into
a halved lemon that has just been squeezed

see, what did I tell you, see,
what did I tell you, see, what
did I tell you, see, what did
I tell you, see, what did I
tell you, see, what did I tell
you, see, what did I tell you,
see, what did I tell you, see,
what did I tell you, see, what
did I tell you, see, what did
I tell you, see, what did I
tell you, see, what did I tell
you, see, what did I tell you

One could, of course, go on. (80)

If straight-up sublimity lies a bit beyond Kroetsch's range, something like this lies a bit beyond Wallace Stevens, and I think the difference is generational, the modern vs. the postmodern poet.

It's poems like "Sketches of a Lemon" that first attracted me to Kroetsch's work, but I knew of him in his capacity as the godfather of a literary movement before I'd read him. He was a kind of benevolent, presiding presence for whole generations of aspiring writers in the Canadian west, and a great intellectual sponsor for a regionalist / post-modernist movement in the poetry produced on the Canadian prairies. The point of the movement, I think, was a kind of mild intellectual and literary decolonization. The western provinces have, in the minds of many of their inhabitants and more of their intellectuals, always been the resentful pseudo-colonies of the bankers and politicians of Toronto and Ottawa. Ignored by a Canadian cultural establishment that was itself marginal and barely visible in the wider world, many of the writers of the west needed a good, strong dose of William Carlos Williams-style local pride, and Kroetsch, by writing out of western experience, pro-vided exactly that. And he was one of a group of writers and academics who built a regional literary infrastructure where none had been. The journal *Prairie Fire*, Turnstone Press, *Grain*, *Open Letter*, a number of critical books, a bunch of reading venues: Kroetsch was one of the leaders in building something outside of the established literary networks. I remember, in particular, one moment of Kroetschian direct action in the establishing of local literary institutions: a group of student poets were trying to launch a magazine called *Ca(n)non* (it was the eighties, and journal titles were filled with parentheses, backslashes, and other signs that the language was plural and unstable and self-deconstructing). They approached Kroetsch as he was heading for the elevator outside his office, and asked if he could help them out. He opened his wallet, hauled out a wad of bills, including a couple of the old red Canadian fifties with their Mounties on horseback, and handed it over. "Wait," he said, taking back a ten, "I need this for lunch." Not a lot of professors would have been so unhesitating with a crowd of scruffy and callow young poets. It's an image that's stayed with me, and the image I'd like to remember him by.

Works Cited

Kroetsch, Robert. *Completed Field Notes: The Long Poems of Robert Kroetsch.* Edmonton: University of Alberta Press, 2000. Print.

Stevens, Wallace. *Selected Poems.* Ed. John N. Serio. New York: Random House, 2009. Print.

Myself I Sing

Nothing in this Life

A pair of young poets once approached me and asked if I'd like to contribute to an anthology they were editing. I write prose quickly, but I'm a slow poet, and don't keep much ready-to-publish material on hand, so I was a bit wary. "What's the theme?" I asked, as a series of possibilities for an anthology in which I might belong flickered through my head. Rapidly graying poets? White guys who could lose some pounds? The last generation of poets to get on the tenure track before the general derailment of academe? It turned out to be none of the above: the young poets wanted to put together an anthology of poetry inspired by Nick Cave.

When I mentioned the project to the Scottish poet Roddy Lumsden, he didn't miss a beat. Nick Cave? Lumsden had written a poem for Nick Cave and, through a series of events too complex and unlikely to present here, he'd heard from an octogenarian friend who'd lunched with Cave that the great man himself had pored over the little chapbook in which the poem appeared—pored repeatedly, apparently fascinated, but inscrutable. There seems to be some special connection between Cave and the poets, and I think I know what it is.

*

It was in December of 1983—right around the time Cave's early band The Birthday Party was breaking up—that I first put my hands on a scuffed-up bootleg cassette of "Prayers on Fire," an album the band had cut in Melbourne a couple of years earlier. I remember clamping the headphones of my Walkman on—that's the verb that seems most right for the kind of willful, teenaged, cutting oneself off from the world that those headphones represented—hitting play, and hearing the familiar tape-hiss (oh sound of my generation!). But how to describe what happened after that? I think Emily Dickinson's words may be the only way to get at it: "If I feel physically as if the top of my head were taken off," said Dickinson, "I know *that* is poetry. These are the only way I know it. Is there any other way?" (474). Somehow, during that cold night on the Canadian prairies, the top of my head was indeed taken right the fuck off. We can actually calculate how long it hovered there: between the 2:38 of "Zoo Music Girl" and the 2:03 of "Just You and Me," my scalp, with its lamentable gel-tipped spikes of hair, took some 29 and a half minutes to reattach to the rest of my thunderstruck self. I've been able to count on a similar effect from Cave's music—at least from a track or two from every album—ever since.

I think at least part of the connection I felt, and still feel, to Cave's music, comes from the one—and, really, only one—fundamental similarity between us. We're both the progeny of provincial culturati—which puts us into the same metaphorical shoes, even though his literal shoes are savagely cool black cowboy boots and mine are, more often than not, dopey looking sandals or grubby sneakers.

Cave was born in Warracknabeal, Australia—a boondock town of some 2,000 souls midway between the glittering metropolises of Wycheproof and Dimboola, a place known mainly for its statistically improbable abundance of highly freckled redheads. His parents, though, were great lovers of literature—his father was an English teacher, and his mother a librarian. Later, the family moved to Wangaratta, another small town, one best known for being near the site of the outlaw Ned Kelly's last stand. As the son of an art professor in western Canada, I like to think I know a little bit about what this means. It means a certain division of loyalties, even a kind of dislocation. On the one hand, you love the place you're from with the kind of intensity that only the provinces can inspire. The love of a great metropolis like New York is dif-

ferent, more sophisticated and perverse, and tends to take the form of
a kind of hatred—would any real Manhattanite be caught dead in an
un-ironic "I heart New York" tee shirt? The love of the provinces is a
simpler thing. On the other hand, you feel connected to a set of high
cultural traditions that have their deepest roots somewhere else. It's not
that there aren't serious readers in Warracknabeal, or art lovers in Winnipeg—it's just that, if that's your thing, you know you're a little at odds
with the dominant local culture. A colleague of my father's once com-
plained that there could never be much of an art scene in Winnipeg
because there was no money to support it. "There's enough money," my
dad replied, "but it doesn't get spent on art—it goes to fishing boats,
cabins in the woods, and hockey tickets." Nothing wrong with that—but
it can leave a young aesthete feeling vaguely dislocated.

And this brings us to the Romantic poets—the first great laureates
of artistic dislocation. Much ink has been spilled trying to define the
nature of Romanticism. Carl Schmitt argued that Romanticism was all
about the individual's "subjective occasionalism," (161) a kind of fetishizing of the moment of individual spontaneity—one might think of Jack
Kerouac, hopped up on Benzedrine, and clattering away on his scroll-
fed typewriter, or shouting "Go, man, go!" at Ginsberg's Six Gallery
reading of *Howl* as the late-blooming apotheosis of this sort of Romanticism. *The Encyclopédie Larousse* assures us that it's really all a matter of
form, of artists who "freed themselves from the classical rules of composition and style" (6:30)—one thinks of Paganini cutting loose with
defiantly flashy and unruly solos. M. H. Abrams said it's all a matter of
emphasizing the visionary imagination, with the mind seen as a light-
casting lamp, not a mirror reflecting the world as it is. Morse Peckham
said it was all a matter of self-assertion, and so did Bertrand Russell.
Irving Babbitt went a step further, saying Romanticism was an "anarchy
of the imagination," such as you might find in Rimbaud (378). But Karl
Mannheim went the other way, saying Romanticism was fundamentally conservative; dead-set in opposition to the ever-rising "bourgeois-
capitalist mode of experiencing things" (90)—if you've had a look at
Wordsworth's depiction of Bartholomew Fair in *The Prelude* as a Dantean
circle of hell, you've seen this kind of Romanticism.

Since Romanticism can appear in so many aspects, it's no wonder, really, that Arthur O. Lovejoy shook his head in despair and said we should give the term the chuck. I was almost willing to join him, until the great Franco-Brazilian sociologist Michael Löwy set me straight. What holds all these loose strands together, for Löwy, is their opposition to modernity, their sense of not fitting at a comfortable angle vis-à-vis industrialism, the quantification and rationalization of all things, technocracy, and the general disenchantment of the world. Anarchists? Backward-looking reactionaries? Imaginative visionaries? Stylistic malcontents? Individualist outsiders? Come on in, people—Löwy's bigtop is a commodious place. But its inhabitants all have one thing in common: the modern world has left them homeless—sometimes literally, in the form of the *poète maudit* kicked out of his garret by a greedy landlord—but usually in a more metaphorical way. It makes sense. Think about the state of things when the first generations of Romantic writers came of age: the arts, long the handmaidens of church and state, had lost that affiliation in the breakdown of the old social order, and had yet to find a new one in the gaudy commercial world that would take its place. Displaced from their old social roles, Romantic writers would leap into invented worlds, like Blake did. Or they'd dream of a transformed future world, of revolution and Utopia, like P. B. Shelley. Or they'd look to what they imagined as a lost, better world: like childhood, or village life deep in the provinces—Wordsworth's great themes. Sometimes they yearned for the fuller, more organic social life in the middle ages, the period of the romances that gave the Romantic movement its name. If they were particularly bright and observant, like the nineteen year old Mary Shelley, holed up in Switzerland with her husband Percy, Lord Byron, and their egos, they might dream of monstrous outsiders whose great minds and open hearts meant nothing to the torch-and-pitchfork bearing peasants who drove them to endless wanderings. The world did not fit, felt these dislocated artists and intellectuals, and wherever they looked, it was to turn away from the modern bourgeois world of getting and spending that seemed to have no place for them. Perhaps Baudelaire got at the situation best, when he called for a voyage going "anywhere out of the world" (51).

Of course all this mattered for the kind of art these writers produced. Earlier poets, sitting comfortably on the knee of aristocratic patronage, knew their audiences, and how to write for them. When Lord Godolphin asked Joseph Addison for a poem commemorating the battle of Blenheim, Addison knew the political point of view, the formal norms, and the level of readability his patron expected, and for which he would pay. Even when the market began to make its first inroads into the old patronage system, the world of paying readers was small enough that Alexander Pope knew exactly what they'd want—commonly shared views elegantly expressed in digestible couplets; or, as Pope put it, "what oft was thought but ne'er so well expressed" (61). But how to write in conditions when no patron, no institution, and no real market exists for the poet's work? What to do, that is, in the Romantics' position? Well, if there's nothing left to lose by way of worldly reward, there is, at least, a compensating freedom—a freedom for art to get as freaky as it wants to be. And so with the Romantics we enter the world of cryptic symbols (what *does* Coleridge's pleasure dome stand for?); we launch off into the deep space of visionary dreams (have a look at Blake's *Book of Urizen*, but only after you strap yourself in for a long, strange trip); and instead of the clear, crisp pronouncements of Pope, get ready for Keats' negative capability, with its refusal to settle down into a clear statement of fact. From here to Surrealism is just short ride on the Metro.

*

If we ride that same train a few more stops, we arrive at the early concerts given by Nick Cave and The Birthday Party. I was too rusticated in the provinces to see them, and too young to get in even if I'd been in the right places. But Duane Davis, the great bearded guru of rock history and presiding spirit of Wax Trax Records in Denver, Colorado, was kind enough to clue me in about those shows. Here's what he said about them in *Waste Paper* #30 some 20 years ago, in prose he has since come to see as a bit hot-house ("I was deep in the grip of Bataille and Baudrillard," he told me, when he sent his article my way):

> The intensities of experience, the desire to act out a daily suicide in the face of an uncertain and questionable re-birth, the compulsion to burn

away all the wicker of the socially woven masks our families and communities demand we wear, the immersions in pain and pleasure that
take brute feeling past all points of endurance and the arrogance of
total marginalization, the refusal of a Utility that measures the individual only to determine his/her productive capacities: somehow Cave
has survived all this—and more: is still searching for a performance that
is a language at once private, personal and interior that can be understood by the audience, the Other, that haunts his darkest, most solipsistic, nightmares.

That's the Romantic stuff: implacably opposed to the modern, utilitarian world, and acting out its alienation in intense, dark ways. "Everything
that was him is mere charcoal and waste;" says Davis, "what is left standing is monstrous and alien." This is Cave as Childe Harold, as Fran-
kenstein's monster, as Baudelaire's disheveled nighttime-wanderer in
the city streets.

Unlike a lot of rock Romantics, Cave never really left that alienation
behind. Instead, he made it the bedrock of his career. Consider the
lyrics to "There She Goes, My Beautiful World," from Nick Cave and
the Bad Seeds' 2004 double album *Abattoir Blues / The Lyre of Orpheus,* a song
I've chosen more or less at random (it came on my iPod Shuffle when
last I hit the treadmill). The song makes all the big Romantic gestures.
Here's the opening:

> The wintergreen, the juniper,
> the cornflower and the chicory,
> all the words you said to me
> still vibrating in the air.
> The elm, the ash and the linden tree,
> the dark and deep, enchanted sea
> the trembling moon and the stars unfurled
> there she goes, my beautiful world,
>
> There she goes, my beautiful world,
> There she goes, my beautiful world,
> There she goes, my beautiful world,
> There she goes again. (n.p.)

Well, it's certainly cryptic—the opening imagery is a bit hard to parse,
but I do think there's a unifying theme to it. Cornflowers were tradi-

tionally worn by young men pining for love, the idea being that their hopes would wither with the flowers. Chicory was used in times of deprivation to substitute for coffee, and wintergreen was similarly used as a substitute for tea. And the juniper? Well, it was in a juniper tree that the prophet Elijah found shelter. So we're dealing with a time of deprivation, a time when we need shelter and sustenance to get by. The notion of the prophet in hard times is important, too: as we'll see in lines to come, the thing that Cave is missing here is his muse, so he's presenting himself as a kind of Romantic poet-prophet deprived of inspiration, which had been the only thing that made the world a beautiful, bearable place. And, like a true Romantic, Cave sees the best world as something in the process of disappearing.

Things become a bit clearer as the song goes on, introducing a catalog of outsider writers producing their work in a world that doesn't care for it, or for them:

> John Wilmot penned his poetry
> riddled with the pox;
> Nabokov wrote on index cards,
> at a lectern, in his socks;
> St. John of the Cross did his best stuff
> imprisoned in a box;
> and Johnny Thunders was half alive
> when he wrote "Chinese Rocks" (n.p.)

John Wilmot, better known as the Earl of Rochester, the man Lord Byron wished he could be; Nabokov, the amoral émigré aesthete; San Juan de la Cruz, mystic and martyr; Johnny Thunders, prototypical rocker junkie—Cave's given us a roll-call of alienated creative visionaries. It's sort of perfect, and only an odious, ink-stained pedant would point out that it was Dee Dee Ramone and Richard Hell, not Johnny Thunders, who wrote "Chinese Rocks."

Let's send the pedant away, then, and get on with the song. The next bit is where we see that it is of the muse Cave sings:

> Well, me, I'm lying here, with nothing in my ears.
> Me, I'm lying here, with nothing in my ears.
> Me, I'm lying here, for what seems years.

I'm just lying on my bed with nothing in my head.

Send that stuff on down to me,
Send that stuff on down to me,
Send that stuff on down to me,
Send that stuff on down to me. (n.p.)

The world offers nothing: only inspiration from on high matters. We hear this, and then we hear about more alienated visionaries enduring, or failing to endure, in an uncaring world:

Karl Marx squeezed his carbuncles
while writing *Das Kapital*.
And Gauguin, he buggered off, man,
and went all tropical.
While Philip Larkin stuck it out
in a library in Hull.
And Dylan Thomas died drunk in
St. Vincent's hospital. (n.p.)

At home or abroad, these are exiles, displaced, working without hope of worldly reward, and sustained only by a kind of autotelos, a commitment to one's private muse. The fate of the artist deprived of this one sustaining thing is made starkly clear with the invocation of Dylan Thomas' inglorious end.

The next verse shows with absolute clarity the Romantic bargain: utterly alienated from this mundane world, the disciple of the muse receives something eternal instead:

I will kneel at your feet
I will lie at your door
I will rock you to sleep
I will roll on the floor
And I'll ask for nothing
Nothing in this life
I'll ask for nothing
Give me ever-lasting life (n.p.)

"Weave a circle round him thrice, and close your eyes in holy dread," say the townsfolk, when they see the poet-visionary at the end of Coleridge's "Kubla Khan," "for he on honeydew hath fed / And drunk the milk of paradise" (71). Cave offers the other perspective, that of the visionary who's turned his back on the quotidian. He'll ask for "nothing in this life," but that's not because he's unambitious, it's because, to paraphrase Lord Byron, he aspires beyond the fitting medium of ordinary desire, and aims at the eternal.

With this vast ambition comes the dream—perhaps the delusion—of the outcast visionary or Romantic prophet:

I just want to move the world,
I just want to move the world,
I just want to move the world,
I just want to move. (n.p.)

In the first three lines, we're not just out to free ourselves from an uncaring, mundane world: we're out to transfigure it with the power of the muse. I've always thought there should be a band called the "Unacknowledged Legislators," since there's such a powerful strain of mystical world-changing desire in rock music, just as there was in Shelley's dream of a world secretly remade by poetry. Greil Marcus wrote, in *Lipstick Traces*, about the strange feeling one gets at a great rock show, the sense that something powerful is happening, that the disenchanted world outside the club doors is somehow about to be transformed forever. He knew what he was talking about. But Cave does him one better, with the change we see in the last line of the verse. It's a confession of sorts, an acknowledgement that the world won't be remade by the song. But the singer might be, and the deliriously dancing audience in front of him—at least as long as the spell lasts.

As we move toward the end of the song, there's a further acknowledgment of limitations, along with a kind of affirmation:

So if you got a trumpet, get on your feet,
brother, and blow it.
If you've got a field, that don't yield,
well get up and hoe it.
I look at you and you look at me and
deep in our hearts know it—
that you weren't much of a muse,
but then I weren't much of a poet. (n.p.)

The muse, it turns out, wasn't some celestial goddess, but merely a real person. The song wasn't earth-shattering prophecy. But that doesn't mean we should give up in resignation. It just means we'll have to carry on, doing the best we can with whatever means of creation we have available in this otherwise fruitless world. It's important, as Cave makes clear in the closing lyrics, still addressed to the muse despite his understanding that she is, to some extent, the creation of his own imagination, a projection onto the real person at whom he's looking:

> I will be your slave,
> I will peel you grapes,
> up on your pedestal,
> with your ivory and apes
> with your book of ideas,
> with your alchemy.
> Oh come on,
> send that stuff on down to me,
>
> send that stuff on down to me,
> send that stuff on down to me,
> send that stuff on down to me,
> send that stuff on down to me,
> send it all around the world.
> 'Cause here she comes, my beautiful girl.
>
> There she goes, my beautiful world ... (n.p.)

The double movement at the end's the thing, isn't it? The muse arrives—but at just that moment the vision slips away again. That's the real Romantic state, burning with passionate intensity that can never slip into complacency, because the better world for which one wishes is always in the process of vanishing, and the merely mundane world from which one feels alienated—the world of Coleridge's farmer from Porlock—is always ready to intrude on the evanescent realm of the visionary.

So. When I think about all the poets I know who love Cave's work, and all the poets I don't know, whose poems on Cave will soon fill an anthology, I think I understand the connection. Poets, more than novelists or playwrights or memoirists, are out on the fringes of the utilitarian world we live in. "Give up verse, my boy, there's nothing in it," said Mr. Nixon, the successful novelist in Ezra Pound's "Hugh Selwyn Mauberley" (68). That was 1920, and the world hasn't become less commercial since. If you're plugging away as a poet nowadays, odds are you're in some sense a Romantic. And I bet when you hit the treadmill (since only the most Romantic of Romantics aims at an early death), you've got Nick Cave on your iPod.

Works Cited

Babbitt, Irving. *Rousseau and Romanticism*. Boston: Houghton Mifflin, 1919. Print.

Baudelaire, Charles. *Baudelaire: His Prose and Poetry*. Ed. T. R. Smith. New York: Boni and Liveright, 1919. Print.

Cave, Nick, and the Bad Seeds. *Abattoir Blues / The Lyre of Orpheus*. London: Mute Records, 2004. Print.

Coleridge, Samuel Taylor. *The Poems of Coleridge*. New York: Dutton, 1905. Print.

Davis, Duane. "Nick Cave: On Mongrel Wings." Wax Trax! Records, n.d. Web. 15 July 2011.

Dickinson, Emily. *The Letters of Emily Dickinson*. Ed. Thomas Herbert Johnson and Theodora van Wagenen Ward. Cambridge, Massachusetts: Harvard University Press, 1986. Print.

Larousse de XXe siècle. Paris: Librarie Larousse, 1933. Print.

Mannheim, Karl. *Conservatism: A Contribution to the Sociology of Knowledge*. Trans. David Kettler and Volker Meja. London: Routledge and Kegan Paul, 1986. Print.

Pope, Alexander. *An Essay on Criticism*. Ed. Alfred S. West. Cambridge: Cambridge University Press, 1908. Print.

Pound, Ezra. *Selected Poems*. New York: New Directions, 1957. Print.

Schmitt, Carl. *Political Romanticism*. Trans. Guy Oakes. Cambridge, Massachusetts: MIT Press, 1986. Print.

My Laureates

I t was a summer day in 2010 when it hit me: it was Coleridge now, and had probably been for a year or more. The 'it' in question is something I suppose I'd call my personal laureate: the poet with whom I feel the strongest connection, but also something more than that. My laureate is also the poet who serves as a kind of private patron saint. It's not a lifetime appointment like the British laureateship—nor does it, like that storied office, come with a butt of sack. The term of service is variable, but generally longer than the single-year renewable appointment of the American laureate, whose demeaning position, with its low pay, uncertain possibility of coming back, and its chorus of constant subtle derision from one's peers, seems to mirror that of the American adjunct instructor. I can count half a dozen personal laureates since I was 18, plus two contenders of equal influence and merit whom I must disqualify for different reasons. On average the term seems to be about four years.

I remember exactly the moment when Walt Whitman became my first personal laureate, because I discovered two dubious pleasures right around the same time: hero-worship and reading while smoking marijuana. I'd encountered both Whitman and the herb earlier, of course, but it was only toward the end of my first undergraduate year that I put them together. My dad was a professor at an enormous, provincial university, and I'd long had the run of the place, particularly enjoying it in

the summer, when I'd go there to spelunk in the underground tunnels
connecting the buildings, to hang out in the big, brutalist student center,
to shoplift those little Loeb Classical Library editions from the campus
bookstore and—best of all—to sneak, by secret paths, up onto the roofs
of the buildings, where I could feel like the only person in the world. It
was on the roof of one of the science buildings that I pulled my brick-
thick Norton Critical Editions copy of *Leaves of Grass* out of one compart-
ment of my backpack, and a pair of tightly-rolled joints out of another,
and spent a good four hours poring over the pages. I remember being
impressed by "The Ox-Tamer," and especially by "The Last Invocation,"
and feeling very clever for thinking that "What Place is Besieged" must
be a poetic reply to John Donne's "Batter My Heart, Three-Person'd
God" (I'm sure, now, I was wrong). I suppose what really got to me,
though, what made Whitman my hero and my laureate, was his mysticism, or perhaps I should say the callower side of Whitman's mysticism.

There's profundity in Whitman, of course, but what I took from
him, up on the roof on that clear-skied prairie day in 1987, wasn't the
profundity. It was almost a kind of innocent's mysticism, something I'd
recognize some fifteen years later when I read William James' comments
on Whitman in *The Varieties of Religious Experience*. In a chapter called "The
Religion of Healthy-Mindedness" James says Whitman has a powerful
sense of the goodness and unity of existence, that he rejects the "old
hell-fire theology" of America's Puritan past for a sense that "evil is
simply a lie, and any one who mentions it a liar" (107). There's a kind
of Dr. Pangloss quality to the Whitman I loved back then. James gets it
exactly when he says:

> Whitman is often spoken of as a 'pagan.' The word nowadays means
> sometimes the mere natural animal man without a sense of sin; some-
> times it means a Greek or Roman with his own peculiar religious
> consciousness. In neither of these senses does it fitly define this poet.
> He is more than your mere animal man who has not tasted of the tree
> of good and evil. He is aware enough of sin for a swagger to be present
> in his indifference towards it, a conscious pride in his freedom from
> flexions and contractions, which your genuine pagan in the first sense
> of the word would never show. (85–86)

James then quotes from and comments on Whitman's "Song of Myself":

> I could turn and live with animals, they are so placid and
>   self-contained,
> I stand and look at them long and long;
> They do not sweat and whine about their condition.
> They do not lie awake in the dark and weep for their sins.
> Not one is dissatisfied, not one is demented with the mania of
>   owning things,
> Not one kneels to another, nor to his kind that lived thousands of
>   years ago
> Not one is respectable or unhappy over the whole earth.

> No natural pagan could have written these well-known lines. But on
> the other hand Whitman is less than a Greek or Roman; for their con-
> sciousness, even in Homeric times, was full to the brim of the sad
> mortality of this sunlit world, and such a consciousness Walt Whitman
> resolutely refuses to adopt. (86)

When I first read Whitman with some intensity it was that swagger in
the face of the first intimations of mortality that caught my eye from
across the gulf of time. I suppose, in my hazy way, I thought I'd discovered the Great Secret—that despite our individual deaths, we live on as
part of the whole. The lines "I bequeath myself to the dirt to grow from
the grass I love, / If you want me again look for me under your boot-
soles" (93) were, of course, particularly appealing to me. Cocky stuff,
aiming at profundity, and failing, in the final analysis, to address the
tragic side of our condition. When I think of who I was, then, I think
of words from another poet, one (perhaps not coincidentally) working
in the Whitmanic tradition: Carl Sandburg. His personification of
Chicago as a brawling man "laughing as a young man laughs, / Laughing
even as an ignorant fighter laughs who has never lost a battle" seems
about right as a description of who I was, then—at least in this one respect
of having a cocksure, arrogant affirmativeness that was predicated on
little more than a lack of experience (4).

Whitman's term as my personal laureate didn't last long—less than a
year and a half. It wasn't that I encountered any terrible tragedy that
stripped me of my relative innocence. Rather, it was that I was seduced

by some of the less legitimate qualities of another poet, Ezra Pound. It wasn't Pound's *least* legitimate qualities that seduced me—his politics and his anti-Semitism were never things I cared for, though perhaps I was too blithe about separating those things from the things I did admire in his work. Unlike Whitman, Pound was a poet I initially encountered in the classroom, in a class on modern American poetry taught by a kindly, indulgent old professor doing what I later learned was his last lap around the teaching pool before retirement. We were reading the slim, austerely black-and-white covered New Directions edition of the *Selected Poems*, which became, for me, a springboard to the extracurricular pleasures of Pound's *Literary Essays*, *Guide to Kulchur*, and *ABC of Reading*, and to his edition of Fenollosa's *Chinese Written Character as a Medium for Poetry*. Looking back, I see now that what attracted me to Pound's cranky, often naïve essays was the fact that they seemed to offer shortcuts: shortcuts to erudition, to a knowledge of the shape and import of literary tradition, and shortcuts to a set of aesthetic principles.

There were reasons such shortcuts appealed to me. I had always cared for history, especially European history. Some of my most vivid early memories are of sitting on the floor of my family's weekend place in the Canadian wilderness, oblivious to the shimmering lake in the front yard and the huge forests all around us, utterly absorbed in reading about Leonidas at Thermopylae, or the destruction of the Athenian fleet by Syracuse on the ill-starred Sicilian expedition during the Peloponnesian wars. But now, at university, I was encountering literary history in detail, and where I'd once felt a kind of supreme confidence (no kid at Acadia Junior High knew, or cared to know, as much as I did about the Babylonians), I now felt a kind of lack. There was so much I didn't know, and, my teenaged self-esteem hanging in the balance, I wanted to know *now*. Real knowledge, whatever that may be, takes time. I've been studying literary history for decades now, and make a living teaching it, and every year I find myself thinking that I'm still just getting started. These days I consider this a blissful state of affairs—not many people get to feel an ongoing excitement of discovery in their work, still fewer get to sense of an inexhaustible richness in the materials they spend time with. But back then I wanted to fill the gap as quickly as possible. The young Ezra

Pound had been the same way, except he conducted his education in public, coming up with a slightly harebrained scheme of cultural history on his own and publishing it as he went along.

Europe, or the idea of Europe, was another reason I found Pound so appealing. I never quite understood this until 1997, when I sat down in the poet Michael Anania's office up in a skyscraper just west of Chicago's loop to interview him for the article I was writing on his work for the *Dictionary of Literary Biography*. Anania told me about his childhood in Omaha, and how as a student he was initially "thrilled by anything complicated and remote," and how he became immersed in modernism and European literary history. Like Pound, and like me, Anania was a provincial, and he wanted to know about Europe—not about Sussex or the Dordogne or the Veneto, but *the whole damn thing*, all of it, from way back then to just this minute.

As if all this weren't enough, Pound offered what seemed like a formidable set of aesthetic principles, ready-made for deployment in creative writing classes and arguments with my fellow honors students in the little coffee shop that occupied a strange, cave-like space just off one of the university's building-to-building tunnels. "Go in fear of abstractions," said Pound, and so said I, when called upon to comment on another students work. "Pay no attention to the criticism of men who have never themselves written a notable work," said the mighty impresario of American modernism—words I'd parrot over my fourth jittery cup of java when one of my friends quoted the opinion of a professor who had the sad misfortune to be a scholar of medieval literature—a creature (I'd proclaim) who, no matter his distinction, must always be outranked by an actual poet, such as I then believed myself to be (5, 4).

Looking back, I notice that Pound's poems rarely entered into my thinking about him, except in the abstract. There were exceptions: I remember liking the windblown sentimentality of *Cathay*, and thinking, with a combination of great self-importance and insensitivity, that "Portrait d'une Femme" was pretty much right on about the girl with whom I'd split up. But for the most part the poems were less important to me that the crank scholarship, the hip-shooting aesthetic pronouncements, and the idea of the great literary *enfant terrible*. *The Cantos* stood in hard-covered splendor on my shelf, an object of veneration, largely unread for many months to come.

Eventually I did read Pound's *Cantos*, and it was through a combination of Poundianism and a growing interest in the poetry of place that I ended up going off to graduate school to work with the first poet whose candidacy for personal laureate is strong, but ultimately invalidated: John Matthias. (Matthias is disqualified through no defect of his own, but by the simple fact that no living man can be a patron saint). I'd discovered John's work while trolling through the library stacks, pulling down random books of poetry. This, like my attraction to Pound's prose, was a manifestation of my sense of lack, of a void in knowledge that I wanted to fill. There were so many poets we didn't get on the syllabus, and I wanted to know about all of them. So, when I'd had enough of studying whatever I was studying in the library, I'd get up, walk over to the PR, PS, or PN sections, pull down a couple of slim volumes, and read for a bit, leaning back against the stacks. Once in a great while I'd shuffle over to the Slavic Languages collection, in a corner of the library where mortal feet rarely trod, and where ventilation conditions allowed me to read stealthily in the manner in which I'd read Walt Whitman, but for the most part I read tanked up on coffee and No-Doze.

What I liked about Matthias was how he seemed to square a certain circle for me. As attracted as I was by the arcane, the remote, the European, and the Poundian, I was also reading a lot of the poetry and polemics of the local campus poet-professors (Dennis Cooley, Robert Kroetsch, David Arnason) and their peers elsewhere in western Canada. They were militantly against everything I liked about Pound. Postmodern-loopy rather than Modernist-serious, and locally proud in the William Carlos Williams manner, they were part of a movement to decolonize the local mind. They were from the provinces and committed to the provinces, and wanted to write out of a sense of place, a sense of the history and geography around them, claiming it as important and literary. Their world, after all, wasn't part of the world they saw on television or the movies or read about in novels from commercial publishers, so they would have to make it part of the imagined community by putting it in words themselves. They knew they were never going to be much noticed by people in Toronto, much less New York or London. They didn't see this as a problem, though, so much as an opportunity, and set about making their own scene, with presses, journals, readings, conferences, and seminars. They had a very real local effect: you could count on any decent Winnipeg bookstore having a shelf dedicated to local writing, something I rarely see in an American city.

How, I often wondered in some semi-inchoate way in the back of my mind, could one reconcile all of this son-of-the-local-soil, poet-of-place business with Pound? Standing in the library stacks with John Matthias' poem "An East-Anglian Diptych" on the page in front of me, I saw an answer. Here was a poet who was deeply concerned with the history and geography of out-of-the-way places, but who came to those places from elsewhere, and saw in them the Big Story of European Civilization. Here was a Poundian of sorts, but also someone writing his own, expatriate version of Williams' *Paterson*. Later, once I'd discovered Basil Bunting's poetry, I saw Matthias' long poems less as *Paterson* and more as *Briggflatts*, a comparison since made in a much more specific and insightful manner by Mark Scroggins, writing on Matthias in *Parnassus*. If I was going to understand more about these things, the only thing for it was to go off to grad school and study with Matthias, which I did, chucking the letters of acceptance from the schools foolish enough not to employ Matthias into the trash.

So I found myself in South Bend, writing poems about the Canadian west (only one of which, a little effort about barbed wire, would eventually make it into my book *Home and Variations*), arguing critical theory in the coffee joint in Notre Dame's O'Shaughnessy Hall, and—in order to get at the roots of the poetry of place—reading Wordsworth. Wordsworth stuck, though South Bend didn't, and I soon found myself reading Wordsworth in the tiny apartment in Chicago's Lakeview neighborhood I shared with my new wife, Valerie. I'd take the South Shore train out to Notre Dame every now and then to teach a freshman lit class, meet with my thesis committee, and spend the evening with friends at a local oyster bar before crashing dizzily on someone's couch for the night. What kept me reading Wordsworth—and what elevated him to the level of personal laureate, displacing Pound, wasn't really the regionalism. It was the organic conception of personal and cultural identity, the side of Wordsworth that comes out of Burke's view of history as something that grows, rather than something that is made, and as something whole, from which nothing is truly separable.

In its way, Wordsworth's vision was as mystical as Whitman's, but without the Panglossic quality you sometimes find in Whitman: Wordsworth's mystic unity is one that retains a strong sense of loss and tragedy. The sense of loss comes in many ways: in "Ode: Intimations of Immortality" we begin to lose the visionary gleam, the sense of the oneness of all things, almost immediately upon birth. We come into the world "trailing clouds of glory," but soon enough we find that "shades of the prisonhouse surround the boy"—loss comes in the form of our alienation from the world, our sense of a difference between self and other, our sense of the world as something different, hostile, confining (588). The "Blest the Infant Babe" passage of *The Prelude* shows us Wordsworth at his most grateful for never having fully lost the sense of the world as a benevolent, enveloping force to which he was linked. I used to return to those lines again and again, underlining parts of it and never quite knowing what to write next to them in the margins.

I remember being particularly struck by "The Ruined Cottage" because of how, on the one hand, it showed the organic unity of nature and history, and yet, on the other hand, it remained sensitive to the reality of loss, sorrow, and destruction. The image of a ruined cottage and a mourning woman, whose world had fallen apart since her husband was shipped off on one of England's seemingly endless wars, is set against the slow return of the cottage to nature, as the vines and forest-growth reclaim it. Whitman's easier mysticism appealed to me when I went around like an arrogant young man, "laughing even as an ignorant fighter laughs who has never lost a battle." But this poem appealed to an ever-so-slowly maturing version of myself. By this point in my life I'd had just enough of a view of the world—especially poor, run-down South Bend—to think that any representation of it that didn't make one feel the pathos of our condition wasn't going to adequate. I think really caring for someone had something to do with it, too: thinking how devastated I'd be if I lost my wife, or how she'd feel if something were to happen to me, made the Whitmanic embrace of death as just one more phase we go through, on the journey in which our identities as individuals are a very brief station-stop, seem like a half-truth. I suppose some of these thoughts lie behind "Wordsworth at the Cuyahoga's Mouth," a poem of mine where I imagine an American Wordsworth, and wonder if he'd have become more like Whitman had he lived in this country. That poem and its companion piece "Marinetti at Union Station, Chicago" are also attempts to square the circle of local pride vs. Poundian Europhilia. And they're full of industrial imagery, coming from the view out the South Shore Line windows as that train chugged through Gary and Hammond on the way to South Bend and back. I was certainly thinking better in those poems than I was in my doctoral dissertation on Wordsworth's influence on modern poets.

Wordsworth had a good, long tenure as my personal laureate—seven years, I think: all through my studies for my MA, MFA, and doctorate, and into my first year as an assistant professor, when I directed a student's thesis contrasting Wordsworth's populism with that of Whitman, still one of the best theses I've had the privilege to direct. I'm sure the student who wrote it would have made a good English professor, but he opted for a more adventurous life, moving to Thailand, starting a punk band, and scoring a #1 hit in Southeast Asia.

Sometime late in 1997 Wordsworth's star began to set for me, though, and Byron's began to rise. Byron's tenure as my personal laureate really consists of two consecutive terms, the first based on the defiant strength of *Childe Harold's Pilgrimage*, the second on the irony of *Don Juan*. I imagine Byron's first term as my laureate came about because his earlier poetry offers so much to anyone who feels alienated, and the experience of being a young assistant professor on the tenure trail is a bit alienating. I shouldn't complain: the whole experience for me was easier than it seems to be for most people, and I actually think Byron had something to do with that.

By this point in my life I've listened—as peer, as old friend, and now as Senior Guy Who's Been Through It All; in faculty lounge, in office, at back-yard barbecue, on barstool, by Skype—to a lot of junior faculty *angst* from people at many different institutions, and the people who suffer the most seem to be those who look on the whole process as a set of hoops one is commanded to jump through. They treat everything as a means to the end of tenure, trying to get on the right committees to get noticed, trying all kinds of tricks to change their teaching (and sometimes their grading) habits so as to get higher evaluation numbers, and they try to write the sort of thing that will get published in the kind of journal they think will impress the powers-that-be. I understand: the job is, after all, on the line. But there's a way in which all this is to get things backwards. The idea, after all, is to do one's job and then stand back while others assess it, not to try to do one's job by what one imagines will be the criteria of assessment. To go about it otherwise is to alienate yourself from the work that you love, and to end up like one of those embittered kvetches one sees writing so often in the advice pages of *The Chronicle of Higher Education*. Of course stepping back and just doing what you do—writing things that come out of who you are, allowing yourself to grow unselfconsciously into teaching better—doesn't come easily. You've got to find some way to be inner-directed, rather than governed by the norms of those around you.

And that's where Byron—or, rather, the Byron of *Childe Harold's Pilgrimage*—comes in. I was lucky to be teaching that poem often in my early days of professoring. The book sprang from Byron's sense of being an alienated outsider: club-footed, wrong-accented, bisexual, taunted at school, attracted to his half-sister, and sexually abused as a child, he had good reasons to feel this way. But Byron turns that alienation into pure glamour and self-assertion. He selected as his heroes Napoleon and Rousseau, and loved them for their ungovernableness. Childe Harold, the Slim Shady to Byron's Marshall Mathers, the Ziggy Stardust to his David Bowie, tells us that he cannot "herd with man" (137)—those unalienated conformists who are little better than cattle. He may be wounded and fraught with discontent, the powers of respectable authority may judge and despise him, but Childe Harold does not give a fuck. He stands above them on his melodramatic mountaintop, rejects their reality, and substitutes his own. He will be who he is, in all his defiant majesty, and he, not the square community, will be the first and last judge of all things. There's a passage from Bertrand Russell's essay on

Byron I used to show my students that gets at the gist of these things
better than I can:

> The aristocratic rebel, of whom Byron was in his day the exemplar, is
> a very different type from the leader of a peasant or proletarian revolt.
> Those who are hungry have no need of an elaborate philosophy to
> stimulate or excuse discontent, and anything of the kind appears to
> them merely an amusement of the idle rich. . . . No hungry man thinks
> otherwise. The aristocratic rebel, since he has enough to eat, must have
> other causes for discontent. . . . It may be that love of power is the
> underground source of their discontent, but in their conscious thought
> there is criticism of the government of the world, which, when it goes
> deep enough, takes the form of Titanic cosmic self-assertion, or, in
> those who retain some superstition, of Satanism. Both are to be found
> in Byron. (747)

That's Satanism of a kind like the Romantic version of Milton's *Paradise
Lost* Russell's referring to—self-assertion, *non serviam*, and all that, not
Aleister Crowley and the black mass. And all that Titanic cosmic self-
assertion, all that inner-direction, can serve you well on the road to
tenure. It can convince you that you're above the whole process, and let
you get on with your life and your work. At least that's how I felt, as I
stood under the patronage of Saint Byron. But if a self-image as aristocratic rebel will get you through the tenure trail, at some point the gulf
between the rebel aristocrat and the comfortable, portly, bookish college
professor becomes apparent—even to a thick-headed narcissist such as I
was. Even Byron caught on to the fact that he wasn't really *Byron*, that he
couldn't ever be the man he'd convinced half of swooning Europe he was.

　This is how he came to write *Don Juan*, the poem for which the term
"Romantic irony" was invented, and the poem that won Byron a second
term as my personal laureate. The poem's eponymous hero is, of course,
meant to be the dashing, brooding, devil-may-care lover extraordinaire
of legend—but in Byron's telling of Juan's adventures, that figure is
constantly inflated and deflated. We see him built up, we see him knocked
down. He is alternately the man you'd hope him to be and a hapless
schmuck. In fact, the poem alternates between moments of high sentiment, even sincere pathos, and moments when the very things for which
we'd been feeling such strong sentiment become ridiculous. This isn't

a bad attitude for a recovering narcissist to take. Narcissists, as I've learned through long experience, are never "recovered"—like addicts or alcoholics, they're always only in remission, always about to slip. But self-irony that doesn't blot out other sensations, including the occasional belief in one's own (soon to be ironized) awesomeness, is a good thing. Or so I thought for a number of years. I don't think it's a coincidence that it was during these years that a former student with whom I'd had a few too many drinks down at the bar in Chicago's Heartland Cafe leaned laughing over the table as she told me, not without some affection, I hope, "You're an asshole, Archambeau, but you know you're an asshole, which helps a little"—it's a comment I've heard in one version or another from several quarters, though (I write this with a sigh) rather less frequently over the years.

It was in this period—the final years of the last century, and the opening years of the present one—that my second disqualified candidate for personal laureate hove into view. This was Samuel Johnson, whom I hadn't read since my student days. But then I found myself teaching a seminar on the intellectual history of the 18th Century with a friend from the history department. We'd divvied up the various Enlightenment and Augustan figures before the semester started, and I'd taken Johnson, not because I knew much about his work, but because my colleague wanted both Voltaire and Rousseau, and I needed to shoulder a little more of the curricular weight. When the time came to teach "The Vanity of Human Wishes," I found myself a bit flummoxed about how to do it. It certainly didn't seem like the kind of thing that would appeal to a group of people in their early twenties. When I talked to John Matthias about it, he told me of a poet friend of his who once wrote to him about the poem, proclaiming "I hope I am never old enough to like this." What to do? In the end, I played a little game of compare and contrast with the people in the seminar, showing them Johnson side by side with some passages from *Childe Harold's Pilgrimage*. I don't know if it was instructive for them, but it was for me. I'd shown them Byron's passages on Napoleon, where the poet praises the deposed emperor for his self-assertion, his refusal to acknowledge authority or limit, saying that in Napoleon and men like him:

>   ...there is a fire
> And motion of the soul, which will not dwell
> In its own narrow being, but aspire
> Beyond the fitting medium of desire;
> And, but once kindled, quenchless evermore,
> Preys upon high adventure, nor can tire
> Of aught but rest; a fever at the core (150)

Byron adds, almost as an aside, that this fever of endless desire is "Fatal to him who bears, to all who ever bore," it, but that's the merest quibble (150). All the glamour lies with Napoleon and with aspiration "beyond the fitting medium of desire."

After this, I pointed to Johnson's poem, particularly a passage where he talks about the fate of Cardinal Wolsey, who'd risen from obscurity to great power, and dreamed (oh quenchless was his fever) of ever more:

> In full-blown Dignity, see *Wolsey* stand,
> Law in his Voice, and Fortune in his Hand:
> To him the Church, the Realm, their Pow'rs consign,
> Thro' him the Rays of regal Bounty shine,
> Turn'd by his Nod the Stream of Honour flows,
> His Smile alone Security bestows:
> Still to new Heights his restless Wishes tow'r,
> Claim leads to Claim, and Pow'r advances Pow'r;
> Till Conquest unresisted ceas'd to please,
> And Rights submitted, left him none to seize.
> At length his Sov'reign frowns—the Train of State
> Mark the keen Glance, and watch the Sign to hate.
> Where-e'er he turns he meets a Stranger's Eye,
> His Suppliants scorn him, and his Followers fly;
> Now drops at once the Pride of aweful State,
> The golden Canopy, the glitt'ring Plate,
> The regal Palace, the luxurious Board,
> The liv'ried Army, and the menial Lord.
> With Age, with Care, with Maladies oppress'd,
> He seeks the Refuge of Monastic Rest.
> Grief aids Disease, remember'd Folly stings,
> And his last Sighs reproach the Faith of Kings.

Speak thou, whose Thoughts at humble Peace repine,
Shall *Wolsey's* Wealth, with *Wolsey's* End be thine?
Or liv'st thou now, with safer Pride content,
The wisest Justice on the banks of Trent? (121)

Maybe the passage made such an impression on me because I'd started reading Kant's aesthetics, and was thinking a lot about disinterest as an ethos, a way to try to live. Or maybe it was the perspective I'd gained from watching people I know angle for the various gewgaws on offer in the American professional classes—promotions, prestige jobs, McMansions, what passes in the literary sphere for fame, prizes of various sorts—and making themselves miserable in the process (or, worse, becoming toadies of one sort or another). Or maybe it was the even sadder spectacle of seeing people for whom I had the utmost respect—poets and critics with real achievements to their names—lament, in their later years, the loss of the spotlight. Or maybe it was catching myself scheming, a couple of times, about how I could begin a campaign to end up Somewhere Grand in my career, and not liking that kind of calculating mind in myself, a mind that could conceive of instrumentalizing people and using them as means to my own ends. One way or another, conditions were right for me to hear what Johnson had to say, and I started tearing through his works, his *Idler* and *Rambler* essays, his fiction, his poems. He's a good antidote for much in American culture, and he became the foundation for my way of feeling about academe, about the poetry business, and about status of all kinds. I suppose I should mention that I live and work in towns populated by some of the richest people in America—watching those people jostle for status with one another must surely have played into the appeal Johnson had for me.

In some ways, Johnson's not a truly great writer, not in the way my other laureates have been. I remember the critic Gerald Bruns once telling me that "compared to *Candide*, Johnson's *Rasselas* is trivial; compared to Pope's *Essay on Man*, 'The Vanity of Human Wishes' is trivial—but I see why people keep coming back to him." I suppose I feel that way, too, and would gladly have awarded Johnson my laureateship, but for one thing: I'm sure he'd have turned the honor down, as a vanity unbecoming for a man to covet.

Instead, it was William Blake who became my next laureate. I never thought he would. I'd been reading him since I was a teenager, and liking him, but somehow I'd always had a bit of not-quite-conscious snobbery about him. Being such a creature of academe myself, at some level I condescended to Blake's autodidacticism. I had no conscious idea of it at the time, but looking back on myself, I'd say my attitude to Blake was something along the lines of "You've got to love the poems, but isn't he, after all, a bit of an intellectual hick? Hadn't he woven together his personal mythology out of Evangelical tracts and the dubious theology of Emanuel Swedenborg? Come on!" I was reading Kant and Fichte and Hegel and Schiller and Marx and Adorno and Bourdieu and Deleuze, and I wasn't about to be intellectually impressed by a guy who was home-schooled by religious freaks. Was I poetically impressed? Sure. But I had too much at stake in my own sophisticated intellectual grandeur to think of Blake as a serious intellect. Until, of course, I decided to really dig into the long, strange, prophetic works. Then (neither for the first time nor the last) I came to a realization: I'd been an idiot.

It was *The Book of Urizen* that broke things open for me, and took me back to poems I thought I knew well, like "The Mental Traveler" and *The Marriage of Heaven and Hell*. What I saw in Blake was, in fact, something very like what I'd been getting at by reading all those philosophers from the German Idealist tradition, and all those critical theorists from the Marxian and post-structuralist traditions: a dialectical vision of truth, in which forces create, and in some sense require, their own opposites. It's not easy to make a decent verbal artifact out of dialectics. My own record is quite poor in this regard: I once tried to explain dialectics to a skeptical colleague by using the image of a water-heater whose release-valve had become clogged. It builds and builds and builds pressure, until it suddenly releases it in an explosion—that's a negation of the first force (constraint), but it is also a kind of continuation, and couldn't exist without the first force. He didn't like the analogy, so I tried again, saying that an instrumentalist view of trees, as potential lumber, could create an environment where we'd cut down all the trees, and consequently we'd develop an opposite view, a kind of "Earth First!" idea of ecological preservation—once again, the thesis creates its antithesis. He didn't like that either, so I swirled the cheap white wine in my plastic cup, shuffled over to a cluster of people at the other side of the room, and concluded that I wasn't any good at explaining dialectics. Of course Hegel's explanations, while more profound than mine, are utterly turgid. But Blake can make these kinds of things into music, and image, and set them dancing in front of you. In *The Marriage of Heaven and Hell* he's even funny while doing it. And for him it isn't merely a set of empty ideas: it's a truth about how the universe, and human consciousness, is structured. It's an apprehension, a mystical vision, of the essence of our being, and the necessarily contradictory nature of any kind of understanding or representation of things.

Coleridge, of course, is no slouch when it comes to thinking about metaphysics and the nature of consciousness, and it's through his concern with these things that he's won the coveted laurels. What Coleridge has got, and Blake hasn't, is a strong sense of the historical nature of truth, how the way it manifests depends on where we stand in the temporal scheme of things. Since I'd been reading a lot of Raymond Williams and much of the British cultural studies tradition, and seeing ideas as embodied in their moment, this had real appeal for me.

Consider "The Rime of the Ancient Mariner," where we have a kind of model of the evolution of the way our understanding of truth evolves over time. At the core are the experiences of the Mariner, events that actually happened to him, and for which he seeks meaning. Then we have the story the Mariner tells, which includes his attempt at understanding the significance of those events. He sees everything as a morality tale about the oneness of all being, about how we should respect all things as we would respect ourselves, the division of self and other being essentially fictional. But this grand vision doesn't quite add up: the events of the story don't all fit the moral the Mariner draws. We could say that the Mariner's message is holistic—a statement about the unity of all things and the falseness of any sense that any part can be separated from the ultimate unity. It's a kind of version of Hegel's "the true is the whole" (11). But the failure of the moral to account for all the contradictory details of the narrative points in the opposite direction, to Adorno's dictum that "the whole is the false" (50)—that is, that any attempt to represent the whole of things, and say this representation is true, is bound to fail, since the only truly adequate explanation of the thing is the thing itself. And the poem gets more interesting when we look at the marginal notes Coleridge added. They're meant to be the notes of some scribe who has found the manuscript of the poem, and written his interpretation in the margins. He's sophisticated and learned, this scribe, and represents a later historical stage than the Mariner, whose tale we're meant to see as having been found many years after its composition. But he's wrong, too, imposing too much of Christianity on the tale, and having too much pride about his erudition. And then there's the level of where we, the readers, stand: still trying to make a full, total interpretation out of the weird, apparently contradictory world before us. This is Coleridge telling us about the evolution of insights, from experiences to moral injunctions to scholarly concepts—an ongoing process of increasing sophistication that remains, in the end, based on a world that is ultimately enigmatic.

One might say that Coleridge is like Blake, but more of a historicist. He's also less imagistic and more concept-driven. You can look at this in one of two ways: as either a great leap forward in clarity and specific- ity, or a terrible falling backward, from the vivid and moving to the deathly-dull and ink-stained. Indeed, you may, should you so desire, look at my own trajectory, from mostly-poet poet-critic, to mostly- critic poet-critic, in the same two ways—and I'm fairly sure my realiza- tion that Coleridge had been my laureate for more than a year was the product of my own shifting emphasis toward the spirit of criticism.

I suppose what continues to attract me to Coleridge is the way he takes a kind of insight into the unity of things, and shows us what the mind does with it, slowly, over time, in each phase taking on the colors of local conditions. He manages to be both a mystic and a historicizer of mysticism, which is no small feat. It's particularly impressive to someone whose own journey has been a matter of adding layers of self- reflexivity to a fundamentally mystical apprehension of experience.

Works Cited

Adorno, Theodor. *Minima Moralia: Reflections on a Damaged Life*. Trans. E. F. M. Jephcott. London: Verso, 2005. Print.

Byron, George Gordon. *The Works of Lord Byron: Childe Harold's Pilgrimage*. Ed. Thomas Moore. Boston: Niccolls, 1900. Print.

Hegel, G. W. F. *The Phenomenology of Spirit*. Trans. A. V. Miller. Delhi: Motilal, 1998. Print.

James, Henry. *The Varieties of Religious Experience*. Cambridge, Massachusetts: Riverside, 1902. Print.

Johnson, Samuel. *The Works of Samuel Johnson*. Troy, New York: Pafraets, 1903. Print.

Pound, Ezra. *Literary Essays of Ezra Pound*. New York: New Directions, 1968. Print.

Russell, Bertrand. *A History of Western Philosophy*. New York: Simon and Schuster, 1945. Print.

Sandburg, Carl. *Chicago Poems*. New York: Henry Holt, 1916. Print.

Whitman, Walt. *Leaves of Grass*. Philadelphia: David McKay, 1901. Print.

Wordsworth, William. *Collected Poems*. Ware: Wordsworth Editions, 1994. Print.